⚖ NOLO The Trusted Name
(but don't take our word for it)

"In Nolo you can trust."
THE NEW YORK TIMES

"Nolo is always there in a jam as the nation's premier publisher of do-it-yourself legal books."
NEWSWEEK

"Nolo publications…guide people simply through the how, when, where and why of the law."
THE WASHINGTON POST

"[Nolo's]…material is developed by experienced attorneys who have a knack for making complicated material accessible."
LIBRARY JOURNAL

"When it comes to self-help legal stuff, nobody does a better job than Nolo…"
USA TODAY

"The most prominent U.S. publisher of self-help legal aids."
TIME MAGAZINE

"Nolo is a pioneer in both consumer and business self-help books and software."
LOS ANGELES TIMES

15th Edition

Make Your Own
Living Trust

Attorney Denis Clifford

FIFTEENTH EDITION	MARCH 2021
Editor	BETSY SIMMONS HANNIBAL
Cover Design	SUSAN PUTNEY
Book Design	SUSAN PUTNEY
Proofreading	JOCELYN TRUITT
Index	UNGER INDEXING
Printing	BANG PRINTING

ISSN: 2329-4256 (print)

ISSN: 2329-4264 (online)

ISBN: 978-1-4133-2840-0 (pbk)

ISBN: 978-1-4133-2841-7 (ebook)

Please note

We know that accurate, plain-English legal information can help you solve many of your own legal problems. But this text is not a substitute for personalized advice from a knowledgeable lawyer. If you want the help of a trained professional—and we'll always point out situations in which we think that's a good idea—consult an attorney licensed to practice in your state.

Dedication

Once again, to Naomi.

Acknowledgments

My thanks to all those friends who helped me with this book, both putting it together and over the years:

First, to friends at Nolo, without whose aid this book would never have remained in print: Betsy Simmons Hannibal, my editor extraordinaire, and a pleasure to work with; my former editors, Mary Randolph and Shae Irving; Stephanie Harolde, who prepared so many drafts of the book so well and did much fine editing, too; and Ella Hirst, for her fine research.

Second, to Mark Peery, of Greenbrae, California, a superb estate planning lawyer (and great friend).

Third, to Toni Ihara, a spirit forever joyous—thanks again for getting me into all this.

Fourth, to Attorney Magdalen Gaynor, of White Plains and New York City, New York, an excellent estate planning lawyer who gave me information generously and cheerfully.

Fifth, to other friends who helped me with this book: Linda Moody, of Mill Valley, California, a law school friend who's become another superb estate planning lawyer; Ken Fisher, of Pleasant Hill, California; and the many, many other people who helped with this book and, over the years, with earlier materials I've written about living trusts.

And finally, my heartfelt thanks to my clients from past years, from whom I learned so much reality I could never have learned in books or school (sure never did in law school), and also to the many readers of earlier editions of this book who wrote me with suggestions, comments, corrections, and other thoughts that contributed greatly to this edition.

About the Author

Denis Clifford practices estate planning law in Berkeley, California. He is the author of several Nolo books, including *Plan Your Estate* and the *Quick & Legal Will Book*. A graduate of Columbia Law School, where he was an editor of the *Law Review,* he has practiced law in various ways, and has become convinced that people can do much of their own legal work.

Table of Contents

Your Legal Companion for Making Your Own Living Trust

Would you like your property to avoid probate after your death? Would you like to learn what a living trust is and how it avoids probate? Have you thought about creating a living trust but been put off by the prospect of high legal fees? If you answered "yes" to any of these questions, you've come to the right place. With this book, you can understand living trusts and create one yourself, without a lawyer. If you make a trust using this book, after your death, your property can be transferred to your beneficiaries without probate courts or attorneys.

Many so-called authorities on living trusts assert that it is foolish to try to make your own living trust. They maintain that you must hire a lawyer or even a team of experts—lawyer, accountant, financial planner. (This "team" will do their best to consume much of your estate with their fees.) Some even argue that doing your own living trust is like trying to do your own brain surgery. This is ridiculous. Preparing a simple living trust that will avoid probate and transfer property after death is not brain surgery or anything close to it. For many people, there's no reason to hire a lawyer to accomplish these goals.

The trust forms in this book have been carefully prepared to be both clear and legally acceptable. Anyone who asserts that trusts must be written in "legalese" (language that is peculiar to the legal profession) is flat-out wrong. A living trust functions just fine if it covers the basics, such as what property is in the trust, who gets it, and who manages the trust after you die. And although no legalese is mandated, it is prudent to have a trust form that, like the ones in this book, is sufficiently traditional so it looks familiar to institutions that may see it—such as banks, title companies, stockbrokerage companies, or other financial institutions.

Although many people can make a living trust without the help of an expert, there are some situations that require professional help. This book is clear about which situations warrant seeking the advice of a professional. If you do decide to get an expert's help to prepare your living trust, this book will help you make the most of hiring a professional. It even offers information about how to find a good lawyer who will charge a reasonable fee.

Make Your Own Living Trust is a workbook. Its purpose is to help you understand and prepare your own living trust. While reading this book, take notes, record information about your own situation, use the worksheets to the extent you find them helpful, and decide how you want your trust to work. Then, draft your own living trust using one of the trust forms in Appendix B or downloaded from Nolo.com. Before you actually start to prepare a living trust, read through the book once. You need to know how a living trust really works and how it fits in with your overall estate plan. You'll also need to resolve basic personal issues, such as what property to transfer to your trust and who will inherit what. You can do it yourself, but you must do it right, which means educating yourself about your options so you can make well-informed decisions.

Congratulations on starting your estate planning —it's a wonderful thing to do for your family. We at Nolo know from long experience that putting a sound estate plan into place can bring peace and satisfaction to those who take the time to do it.

> **CAUTION**
> **Louisiana residents cannot make a trust with this book.** This book is designed for residents of all states except Louisiana, which has a legal system based on the Napoleonic Code, different from all other states.

Overview of Living Trusts

iving trusts are an efficient and effective way to transfer property at your death to the family members, other relatives, friends, or charities you've chosen. Essentially, a living trust performs the same function as a will, with the crucial difference that property left by a will must go through the probate court process. In probate, a deceased person's will is proved valid in court, the person's debts are paid, and, usually after about a year, the remaining property is finally distributed to the beneficiaries. In the vast majority of instances, these probate court proceedings waste time and money.

By contrast, property left by a living trust can go promptly and directly to your inheritors. They don't have to bother with a probate court proceeding. That means they won't have to spend any of your hard-earned money to pay for court and lawyer fees.

TIP

You don't need to maintain separate tax records for your living trust. While you live, all transactions that are technically made by your living trust are simply reported on your personal income tax return. Indeed, while some paperwork is necessary to establish a probate-avoidance living trust and transfer property to it, there are no serious drawbacks or risks involved in creating or maintaining the trust.

These trusts are called "living" or sometimes "inter vivos" (Latin for "among the living") because they're created while you're alive. They're called "revocable" because you can revoke or change them at any time, for any reason, before you die.

While you live, you effectively keep ownership of all property that you've technically transferred to your living trust. You can do whatever you want to with any trust property, including selling it, spending it, or giving it away. A revocable living trust becomes operational at your death. At that point, it allows your trust property to be transferred, privately and outside of probate, to the people or organizations you have named as beneficiaries of the trust.

Living Trusts Explained

A trust can seem like a mysterious creature, dreamed up by lawyers and wrapped in legal jargon. But don't let the word "trust" scare you, even though it might initially sound impressive or even slightly ominous. True, trusts were an invention of medieval England, used by aristocrats to evade restrictions on ownership and inheritance of land. Also true, complex trusts have traditionally been used by rich American families to preserve their wealth over generations. But happily, the types of living trusts this book covers are not complicated or beyond the reach of regular folks. Here are the basics.

The Concept of a Trust

A trust is an intangible legal entity ("legal fiction" might be a more accurate term). Beyond a few pieces of paper, you can't see a trust, or touch it, but it does exist. The first step in creating a working trust is to prepare and sign a document called a "Declaration of Trust."

Once you create and sign the Declaration of Trust, the trust exists. There must, however, be a flesh-and-blood person actually in charge of this property; that person is called the "trustee." With traditional trusts, the trustee manages the property on behalf of someone else, called the "beneficiary." However, with a living trust, until you die, you are the trustee of the trust you create and also, in effect, the beneficiary. Only after your death do the trust beneficiaries you've named in the Declaration of Trust have any rights to your trust property.

Creating a Living Trust

When you create a living trust document with this book, you must identify:

- Yourself, as the "grantor"—or for a couple, the grantors. The grantor is the person who creates the trust.
- The "trustee," who manages the trust property. You are also the trustee, as long as you (or your spouse or partner, if you make a trust together) are alive.

- The "successor trustee," who takes over after you (or you and your spouse or partner) die. This successor trustee turns the trust property over to the trust beneficiaries and performs any other task required by the trust.
- The "trust beneficiary" or "beneficiaries," those who are entitled to receive the trust property at your death.
- The "property" that is subject to the trust.

A Declaration of Trust also includes other basic terms, such as the authority of the grantor to amend or revoke the document at any time, and the authority of the trustee.

How a Living Trust Works

The key to establishing a living trust to avoid probate is that the grantor—remember, that's you, the person who sets up the trust—isn't locked into anything. You can revise, amend, or revoke the trust for any (or no) reason, any time before your death, as long as you're legally competent. And because you appoint yourself as the initial trustee, you can control and use the property as you see fit while you live.

What Is Competence?

"Competent" means having the mental capacity to make and understand decisions regarding your property. A person can become legally "incompetent" if declared so in a court proceeding, such as a custodianship or guardianship proceeding. If a person tries to make, revoke, or amend a living trust and someone challenges that person's mental capacity, or competence, the matter can end up in a nasty court battle. Fortunately, such court disputes are quite rare. However, if you suspect that someone in your life might question your capacity (and the validity of your estate plan), see a lawyer to help guard against a legal challenge to your estate.

And now for the legal magic of the living trust device. Although a living trust is only a legal fiction during your life, it assumes a very real presence for a brief period after your death. When you die, the living trust can no longer be revoked or altered. It is then irrevocable.

A Miniglossary of Living Trust Terms

Here are a few key words about living trusts that you'll want to know as you read this chapter. You'll find a full glossary of trust-related terms in the back of the book, and Nolo provides a complete legal dictionary at www.nolo.com. Some basic terms:

- The person who sets up the living trust (that's you, or you and your spouse or partner) is called a **grantor, trustor,** or **settlor.** These terms mean the same thing and are used interchangeably.
- All the property you own at death, whether in your living trust or owned in some other form, is your **estate.**
- The market value of your property at your death, less all debts and liabilities on that property, is your net or **taxable estate.** The IRS allows your successor trustee to choose market value at your death or six months later.
- The property you transfer to the trust is called, collectively, the **trust property, trust principal,** or **trust estate.** (And, of course, there's a Latin version: the trust corpus.)
- The person who has power over the trust property is called the **trustee.**
- The person the grantor names to take over as trustee after the grantor's death (or, with a trust made jointly by a couple, after the death of both spouses) is called the **successor trustee.**
- The people or organizations who get the trust property when the grantor dies are called the **beneficiaries** of the trust. (While the grantors are alive, technically they themselves are the beneficiaries of the trust.)

With a trust for a single person, after you die, the person you named in your trust document to be successor trustee takes over. That person is in charge of transferring the trust property to the family, friends, or charities you named as your trust beneficiaries.

With a trust for a couple, the surviving spouse or partner manages the trust. A successor trustee takes over after both spouses or partners die.

There is no court or governmental supervision to ensure that your successor trustee complies with the terms of your living trust. *That means that a vital element of an effective living trust is naming someone you fully trust as your successor trustee.* If there is no person you trust sufficiently to name as successor trustee, a living trust probably isn't for you. You could name a bank, a trust company, or another financial institution as successor trustee, but doing so has serious drawbacks.

After the trust grantor dies, some paperwork is necessary to transfer the trust property to the beneficiaries, such as preparing new ownership documents. But because no probate is necessary for property that was transferred to the living trust, the whole thing can usually be handled within a few weeks. The successor trustee may need to hire an attorney to prepare some of the required documents. See Chapter 13.

No court proceedings are required to terminate the trust. After the job of getting the property to the beneficiaries is accomplished, the trust just evaporates, by its own terms. See "Trust Administration After Death of a Grantor" in Chapter 13.

In some cases, a living trust can continue some time after the trust maker dies—for example, a "child's trust." The trust forms in this book allow you to create a child's trust if you wish, to leave trust property to one or more minors or young adult beneficiaries. These trusts are managed by your successor trustee and can last until the young beneficiary reaches the age you specified in your Declaration of Trust. Then the beneficiary receives the trust property, and the trust ends.

Probate and Why You Want to Avoid It

Given that you're reading this book, you probably already know that you want to avoid probate. If you still need any persuasion that avoiding probate is desirable, here's a brief look at how the process actually works.

Probate is the legal process that includes:

- filing the deceased person's will with the local probate court (called "surrogate" or "chancery" court in some places)
- taking inventory of the deceased person's property
- having that property appraised
- paying legal debts, including death taxes
- proving the will valid in court, and
- eventually distributing what's left as the will directs.

If the deceased person didn't leave a valid will, or a trust that distributes all of the deceased person's property, the estate must still undergo probate. The process is called an "intestacy" proceeding, and the property is distributed to the closest relatives as state law dictates.

In some cases, the court oversight that probate brings can prevent fraud in transferring a deceased person's property. It can also protect inheritors by resolving claims creditors have against a deceased person's property. However, when the estate is simple and its property is transferred within a close circle of family and friends, very few estates have problems with fraud or creditors' claims. Therefore, most estates have no need of the benefits of probate, and probate ends up being a waste of time and money.

The actual probate functions are essentially clerical and administrative. In the vast majority of probate cases, there's no conflict, no contesting parties— none of the normal reasons for court proceedings or lawyers' adversarial skills. Likewise, probate doesn't usually call for legal research or lawyers' drafting abilities. Instead, in the normal, uneventful probate proceeding, the family or other heirs of the deceased person provide a copy of the will and other financial information. The attorney's secretary then fills in a small mound of forms and keeps track of filing deadlines and other procedural technicalities. Some lawyers hire probate form preparation companies to do all the real work. In most instances, the existence of these freelance paralegal companies is not disclosed to clients, who assume that lawyers' offices at least do the routine paperwork they are paid so well for. In some states, the attorney makes a couple of routine court appearances; in others, normally the whole procedure is handled by mail.

Because of the complicated paperwork and waiting periods imposed by law, a typical probate takes up to a year or more, often much more. (I once worked in a law office that was profitably entering its seventh year of handling a probate estate—and a very wealthy estate it was.) During probate, the beneficiaries generally get nothing unless the judge allows the immediate family to receive a small "family allowance."

RESOURCE

Read more about probate online. To learn more about avoiding probate and estate planning, go to Nolo's "Wills, Trusts & Probate" section at www.nolo.com/legal-encyclopedia/wills-trusts-estates.

Most states now allow simplified probate for certain types of estates. While simplified probate can speed up the process and result in lower attorneys' fees, even simplified probate can be a waste for most people.

Probate usually requires both an "executor" (called a "personal representative" in some states) and someone familiar with probate procedures, normally a probate attorney. The executor is a person appointed in the will who is responsible for supervising the estate, which means making sure that the will is followed. If the person died without a will, the court appoints an "administrator" (whose main qualification may be having a close relationship with the judge) to

serve the same function. The executor, who is usually the spouse, partner, child, relative, or friend of the deceased, hires a probate lawyer to do the paperwork. The executor often hires the deceased person's lawyer (who may even have possession of the will), but this is not required. Then the executor does little more than sign where the lawyer directs, wondering why the whole business is taking so long. For these services, the lawyer and the executor are each entitled to a hefty fee from the probate estate. Some lawyers even persuade clients into naming them as executors, enabling the lawyers to hire themselves as probate attorneys and collect two fees—one as executor, one as probate attorney. By contrast, most relatives and friends who serve as executors do not take the fee, especially if the person who serves is a substantial inheritor.

Extreme Probate Fees

Marilyn Monroe died in debt in 1962, but over the next 18 years, her estate received income, mostly from movie royalties, in excess of $1.6 million. When her estate was settled in 1980, her executor announced that debts of $372,136 had been paid, and $101,229 was left for inheritors. More than $1 million of Monroe's estate was consumed by probate fees.

Then there's the 1997 U.S. Tax Court case upholding an attorney's probate fee of $1,600 per hour for a total of $368,100. The court declared the fee was "reasonable under New York law."

While probate can evoke images of greedy lawyers consuming most of an estate in fees, lawyers' fees rarely actually devour the entire estate. In many states, the fees are what a court approves as "reasonable." In a few states, the fees are based on a percentage of the estate subject to probate. Either way, probate attorneys' fees for a routine estate with a gross value of $700,000 (these days, in many urban areas, this may be little more than a modest home, some savings, and a car) can amount to $15,000, or more. Fees based on the "gross" probate estate means that debts on property are not deducted to determine value. For example, if a house has a market value of $800,000 with a mortgage balance of $500,000 (net equity of $300,000), the gross value of the house, $800,000, is used to calculate attorneys' fees.

> **EXAMPLE:** In California, lawyers' probate fees are set by statute. (§ 10810, Cal. Prob. Code.) The fee for probate of a house is based on the gross value of that house. Given the prices of California real estate, this can result in a lot of money wasted on attorneys' fees. For example, a house purchased for $150,000 years ago may now be worth $900,000. The probate fee for transferring this house will be $21,000. That fee will be charged no matter how little equity the owners have in the house.

In addition to the probate lawyer's fees, there are executor's fees, court costs, appraiser's fees, and other possible expenses. Moreover, if the basic fee is set by statute and there are any "extraordinary" services performed for the estate, the attorney or executor can ask the court for additional fees.

Other Ways to Avoid Probate

The most flexible and complete probate-avoidance method is, undoubtedly, the living trust. However, there are a number of other effective methods, some of which are quite easy and inexpensive to use.

Informal Probate Avoidance

While I'm a fan of living trusts, I don't believe they are always the best probate-avoidance device for all property of all people in all situations. It's up to you to determine whether a living trust is the best way for you to avoid probate for all your property, or whether you want to use other methods.

Besides the living trust, these are the most popular probate-avoidance methods:

- joint tenancy or tenancy by the entirety
- pay-on-death financial accounts
- transfer-on-death registrations
- transfer-on-death real estate deeds
- retirement accounts
- life insurance
- state laws that exempt certain (small) amounts of property left by will from probate, and
- gifts made while you are alive.

These methods are discussed briefly in Chapter 14.

You may wonder why surviving relatives and friends can't just divide up your property as your will directs (or as you said you wanted, if you never got around to writing a will), and ignore the laws requiring probate. Some small estates are undoubtedly disposed of this way.

For example, say an older man lives his last few years in a nursing home. After his death, his children meet and divide the personal items their father had kept over the years. What little savings he has have long since been put into a joint account with the children anyway, so there's no need for formalities there.

For this type of informal procedure to work, the family must be able to gain possession of all of the deceased's property, agree on how to distribute it, and pay all the creditors. Gaining possession of property isn't difficult when the only property left is personal effects and household items. However, if real estate, securities, bank accounts, cars, boats, or other property bearing legal title papers are involved, informal family property distribution can't work.

Further, whenever outsiders are involved with a deceased's property, do-it-yourself division by inheritors is not feasible. For instance, creditors can be an obstacle; a creditor concerned about being paid can usually file a court action to compel a probate proceeding.

Finally, for an informal family property disposition to work, all family members must agree on how to divide the deceased's possessions. Any inheritor who is unhappy with the result can, like creditors, file for a formal probate.

In sum, informal probate avoidance, even for a small estate, isn't something you can count on. Realistically, you must plan ahead to avoid probate.

RESOURCE

More on avoiding probate. These and other probate-avoidance techniques are discussed in detail in *Plan Your Estate*, by Denis Clifford (Nolo), and *8 Ways to Avoid Probate*, by Mary Randolph (Nolo).

Living Trusts and Estate Taxes

Probate-avoidance living trusts, like those you can make with this book, do not eliminate or reduce estate or inheritance taxes. However, very few people need to worry about federal estate taxes. Current federal law exempts more than $11 million per person from estate tax, so no tax will be assessed against the estates of most readers of this book. In a few states, state inheritance taxes or state estate taxes with lower exemptions could affect more modest estates, but there is not much you can do to avoid them. Chapter 14 provides details about federal estate taxes, as well as state inheritance and estate taxes.

Other Advantages of a Living Trust

As you know, the main reason for setting up a revocable living trust is to save your family time and money by avoiding probate. But there are also other advantages. Here is a brief rundown of the other major benefits of a living trust.

Out-of-State Real Estate Doesn't Have to Be Probated in That State

The only thing worse than regular probate is out-of-state probate. Usually, an estate is probated in the probate court of the county where the decedent was living before the decedent died. But if the decedent owned real estate in more than one state, it's usually necessary to have a whole separate probate proceeding in each one. That means the surviving relatives must find and hire a lawyer in each state, and pay for multiple probate proceedings.

With a living trust, out-of-state property can normally be transferred to the beneficiaries without probate in that state.

You Can Avoid the Need for a Conservatorship

A living trust can be useful if the person who created it (the grantor) becomes incapacitated, because of physical or mental illness, and can no longer take care of financial affairs. In that situation, the person named in the living trust document to take over as trustee at the grantor's death (the successor trustee) can also take over management of the trust. (See Chapter 6.) When a couple sets up a trust, if one person becomes incapacitated, the other takes sole responsibility. If both members of the couple are incapacitated, their successor trustee takes over. The person who takes over has authority to manage all property in the trust, and to use it for the benefit of the grantor or grantors.

> **EXAMPLE:** Wei creates a revocable living trust, appointing herself as trustee. The trust document states that if she becomes incapacitated, her daughter Li-Shan will replace her as trustee and manage the trust property for Wei's benefit.

If there is no living trust and no other arrangements have been made for someone to take over property management if you become incapacitated, someone must get legal authority from a court to take over. Typically, the spouse, partner, or adult child of the person seeks this authority and is called a conservator or guardian. Conservatorship proceedings are intrusive and often expensive, and they get a court involved in your personal finances on a continuing basis.

Financial Durable Power of Attorney

You should also give your successor trustee (or spouse) the authority to manage property that has not been transferred to the trust if you become incapacitated. The best way to do that is to prepare and sign a document called a "Durable Power of Attorney for Finances." (See Chapter 14.)

Your successor trustee has no power to make health care decisions for you if you become incapacitated. If you have any end-of-life preferences—like to die without the unauthorized use of a life support system—you'll want to prepare and sign health care directives. (This is discussed in Chapter 14.)

Your Estate Plan Remains Confidential

When your will is filed with the probate court after you die, it becomes a matter of public record. A living trust, on the other hand, is a private document. Because the living trust document is never filed with a court or another government entity, what you leave, and to whom, generally remains private. There are just a couple of exceptions. First, records of real estate transfers are always public, so if your successor trustee transfers real estate to a beneficiary after your death, there will be a public record of it. Second, some states require the successor trustee to disclose information about your living trust to trust beneficiaries. These requirements are explained in Chapter 13.

A few states require that you register your living trust with the local court, but there are no legal consequences or penalties if you don't. (Registration is explained in Chapter 11.) Also, registration of a living trust normally requires that you just file a paper stating the existence of the trust and the main players; you don't file the document itself, so the terms aren't part of the public record.

In most cases, the only way the terms of a living trust might become public is if—and this is very unlikely—after your death, someone files a lawsuit to challenge the trust or collect a court judgment you owe them.

You Can Change Your Mind at Any Time

You have complete control over your revocable living trust and all the property you transfer to it. You can:
- sell, mortgage, or give away property in the trust
- put ownership of trust property back in your own name

- add property to the trust
- change the beneficiaries
- name a different successor trustee (the person who distributes trust property after your death), or
- revoke the trust completely.

If you and your spouse or partner create the trust together, both of you must consent to changes, although either of you can revoke the trust entirely. (See Chapter 12.)

No Trust Record Keeping Is Required While You Are Alive

Even after you create a valid trust that will avoid probate after your death, you do not have to maintain separate trust records. This means you do not have to keep a separate trust bank account, maintain trust financial records, or spend any time on trust paperwork.

As long as you remain the trustee of your trust, the IRS does not require that a separate trust income tax return be filed. (IRS Reg. § 1.671-4.) You do not have to obtain a trust taxpayer ID number. You report all trust transactions on your regular income tax returns. In sum, for tax purposes, living trusts don't exist while you live.

You Can Name Someone to Manage Trust Property for Young Beneficiaries

If there's a possibility that any of your beneficiaries will inherit trust property while still young (not yet 35), you may want to arrange to have someone manage that property for them until they're older. If they might inherit before they're legally adults (age 18), you should definitely arrange for management. Minors are not allowed to legally control significant amounts of property, and if you haven't provided someone to do it, a court will have to appoint a property guardian.

When you create a living trust with this book, you can arrange for someone to manage property for a young beneficiary. In most states, you have two options:
- Have your successor trustee (or your spouse, if you created a shared living trust) manage the property in a child's trust until the child reaches an age you designate.

- In every state except South Carolina, you can appoint an adult as a "custodian" to manage the property until the child reaches an age specified by your state's Uniform Transfers to Minors Act (18 in a few states, 21 in most, but up to 25 or 30 in a few).

Both methods are explained in Chapter 8.

No Lawyer Is Necessary to Distribute Your Property

With a living trust, the person you named as your successor trustee has total control over how the property is transferred to the beneficiaries you named in the trust document. With a will, the executor is technically in charge of the property that passes under the terms of the will, but the probate lawyer usually runs the show. This can include the personal show as well as the silly court show. I've heard of a lawyer calling a family in for a reading of the deceased's will immediately after the funeral service, which some family members found highly insensitive. There's much less chance of this type of crassness if only close personal relations are involved in the transfer of the property.

Possible Drawbacks of a Living Trust

A basic living trust can have some drawbacks. They aren't significant to most people, but you should be aware of them before you create a living trust.

Initial Paperwork

Setting up a living trust requires some paperwork. The first step is to create a trust document, which you must sign in front of a notary public. So far, this is the same amount of work as is required to write a will.

There is, however, one more essential step to make your living trust effective. *You must make sure that ownership of all the property you listed in the trust document is legally transferred to the living trust.* (Chapter 10 explains this process in detail.) Transferring property into your trust is simply a

matter of doing the paperwork correctly. What you have to do depends on the kind of property you're putting in the trust:

- If an item of property doesn't have a title (ownership) document, then in most states, listing it in the trust document is enough to transfer it. So, for example, no additional paperwork is legally required for most books, furniture, electronics, jewelry, appliances, musical instruments, paintings, and many other kinds of property.
- If an item has a title document—real estate, stocks, mutual funds, bonds, money market accounts, or vehicles, for example—you must change the title document to show that the property is owned by the trustee of the trust. For example, if you want to put your house into your living trust, you must prepare and sign a new deed, transferring ownership from you to your living trust.

After the trust is created, you must keep written records sufficient to identify what's in and out of the trust whenever you transfer property to or from the trust. This isn't burdensome unless you're frequently transferring property in and out, which is rare.

> **EXAMPLE:** Misha and David Feldman put their house in a living trust to avoid probate, but later decide to sell it. In the real estate contract and deed transferring ownership to the new owners, Misha and David sign their names "as trustees of the Misha and David Feldman Revocable Living Trust, dated March 18, 20xx."

Transfer Taxes

Transfers of real estate to revocable living trusts are almost always exempt from transfer taxes usually imposed on real estate transfers.

If you're the cautious type, you can check with your county tax assessor to learn if there will be any transfer tax imposed on the transfer of your real estate to your trust. Your county land records office (county recorder's office or registry of deeds) may also be able to provide this information. As I've said, you're very likely to learn that no tax is imposed. If there is a tax but it is minor, it may impose no serious burden on creating your trust. If the tax is substantial, you may decide it's too costly to place your real estate in a trust.

Difficulty Refinancing Trust Real Estate

Because legal title to trust real estate is held in the name of the trustee of the living trust—not your name—some banks, and especially title companies, may balk if you want to refinance it. They should be sufficiently reassured if you show them a copy of your trust document, which specifically gives you, as trustee, the power to borrow against trust property.

In the unlikely event you can't convince an uncooperative lender to deal with you in your capacity as trustee, you'll have to find another lender (which shouldn't be hard) or simply transfer the property out of the trust and back into your name. Later, after you refinance, you can transfer it back into the living trust. It's a silly process, but one that does work.

No Cutoff of Creditors' Claims

Most people don't have to worry that after their death creditors will try to collect large debts from property in their estate. In most situations, there are no massive debts. Those that exist, such as outstanding bills, taxes, and last illness and funeral expenses, can be readily paid from the deceased's property. But if you are concerned about the possibility of large claims,

you may want to let your property go through probate instead of a living trust.

If your property goes through probate, creditors have only a set amount of time to file claims against your estate. A creditor who was properly notified of the probate court proceeding cannot file a claim after the period—about six months, in most states—expires.

> **EXAMPLE:** Elaine is a real estate investor with a good-sized portfolio of property. She has many creditors and is involved in a couple of lawsuits. It's sensible for her to have her estate transferred by a probate court procedure, which allows creditors to present claims, resolves conflicts, and cuts off the claims of creditors who are notified of the probate proceeding but don't present timely claims.

On the other hand, when property isn't probated, creditors still have the right to be paid (if the debt is valid) from that property. In most states, there is no formal claim procedure. (California has enacted a statutory scheme for creditors to get at property transferred by living trust.) The creditor may not know who inherited the deceased debtor's property, and once the property is found, the creditor may have to file a lawsuit, which may not be worth the time and expense.

If you want to take advantage of probate's creditor cutoff, you must let all your property pass through probate. If you don't, there's a good chance the creditor could still sue (even after the probate claim cutoff) and try to collect from the property that didn't go through probate and passed instead through your living trust.

Human Realities and Living Trusts

Before plunging deeper into the mechanics of creating your own living trust, I want to switch gears and acknowledge the underlying realities we're talking about here: death, and the transfer of your property after death. Although property concerns can be minor indeed in the face of the overwhelming force and mystery of death, these deep imponderables are beyond the scope of this book and are appropriately left to poets, philosophers, clergy, and—ultimately—to you.

Planning for the transfer of property on your death can raise deep emotional concerns, problems, or potential conflicts. No matter how well you deal with the legal technicalities of making your living trust, it won't achieve what you want unless you take human concerns into account.

For many people—probably most—no serious personal problems arise when preparing a living trust. They know to whom they want to give their property. They have no difficulty deciding whom to name as successor trustee. They do not foresee conflict among their beneficiaries or threat of a lawsuit by someone angry at not being named a beneficiary. These people can, happily, focus on the satisfactions they expect their gifts to bring.

However, not everyone's situation is so clear and straightforward. Some people must deal with more difficult human dynamics, such as possible family conflicts, dividing property unequally between children, providing care for minor children, or handling complexities arising from second or subsequent marriages.

Before beginning the work of preparing your living trust, it's vital that you assess your personal circumstances and resolve any potential human problems regarding distribution of your property. If you're sure you don't face any such problems, wonderful. If, however, you think you might face complications—or if you're not sure what kinds of problems can come up—try to identify and resolve those problems now, or as you go along. After all, you surely don't want the distribution of your property to result in bitterness, family feuds, or fights between former friends.

A self-evident truth about a living trust is that it transfers property—money or things that can be converted into money. Money, as most of us have learned, is strange stuff indeed. It has power to do good in a number of material ways, and can alleviate anxiety and provide security. Unfortunately, however, human flaws and fears can be unleashed when substantial sums of money are involved; meanness, greed, and dishonesty have certainly been known to surface. Naturally, in making your gifts, you don't want to unnecessarily stir up negative feelings or emotions.

Sadly, bitterness, strife, and lawsuits are far from unheard of upon distribution of property after one's death. This chapter discusses a number of personal concerns, based on examples drawn from my living trust legal practice.

Leaving Unequal Amounts of Property to Children

Most parents feel it's very important to treat their children equally regarding the distribution of property, to avoid giving the impression that they value one child more than another. However, in some situations, parents sensibly conclude that the abstract goal of equal division of property isn't the fairest or wisest solution for their children. The most important issue here, I suggest, is to explain your reasoning to your children.

> EXAMPLE 1: A single mother with three grown children feels that one, a struggling pianist, needs far more financial support than her other two, who have more conventional and well-paying jobs. She wants to give the pianist the bulk of her money, but worries this might cause problems among her children. So she writes a letter explaining that she loves all three children equally and that her decision to give the pianist more is a reflection of need, not preference. She attaches the letter to her living trust. She also leaves most family heirlooms, which are emotionally but not monetarily valuable, to the other two children to emphasize how much she cares for them.

EXAMPLE 2: An elderly couple owns a much-loved summer home in the Poconos. Only one of their four children, Skip, cares about the home as much as they do, and they plan to give it to him. But they question whether they should reduce his portion of the rest of their estate by the value of the home, or divide the rest of their estate equally among their four children, and on top of this, give the summer home to Skip.

As the family is a close one, they discuss the problem with the kids. One of them doesn't think their last alternative is fair. Skip doesn't think so either. The parents decide to give Skip less than one-fourth of the rest of their estate, but not to reduce his share by the full value of the summer home. They explain their decision to the others on the basis that Skip helped maintain the summer home for many years, and that his work should be recognized. It is, and the plan is accepted in good grace by all.

Second or Subsequent Marriages

People who marry more than once may face problems reconciling their desires for their present spouse (and family) with their wishes for children from prior marriages. Individual situations vary greatly here, and you must work carefully through your needs and desires. How much of one spouse's property might a surviving spouse need? How much property does each spouse want to leave to his or her own children? Sometimes, spouses can readily resolve such concerns and use a Nolo living trust to leave their property.

EXAMPLE: Ben and Estelle met in the 1970s, as teachers in an alternative school. They fell in love, ran away to Oregon to live in a commune, and had two daughters. What a long, strange trip it was; they wound up, to their considerable surprise, owning a prosperous business in San Francisco. Now that it is time to draw up their living trust, Ben and Estelle are in complete accord about how to distribute their property, with one exception—Ben's daughter, Susan (now age 47), from his first marriage. Ben wants to leave her a substantial part of his estate; he

suggests 20%. Estelle thinks that is outrageous, since his daughter has treated him terribly for decades, and is a wastrel with money besides. Estelle says it's too late to try to buy her love. Ben insists he feels a duty to his child no matter how she treats him.

Fortunately, both Ben and Estelle recognize signs of trouble and understand they're talking about a lot more than property here. What, if anything, does Ben owe his child? Will his ex-wife get involved if his daughter inherits money? If so, so what? Ben and Estelle discuss these problems themselves and with a therapist they see from time to time.

Eventually, they reach a compromise. Ben will leave some property to Susan, but not a percentage of his total estate. He and Estelle agree on a figure of $40,000.

You may, however, want more control than a Nolo living trust offers. Many couples in subsequent marriages with substantial assets create a trust leaving property to the surviving spouse for life, with specific, limiting controls over how that property can be spent for that spouse. Then, when that spouse dies, the trust property goes to children from the other spouse's prior marriage(s). These types of "life estate" trusts are briefly discussed in Chapter 14. (They are discussed in more depth in Nolo's *Plan Your Estate*.) You need a lawyer to draft this kind of trust.

Couples in subsequent marriages have additional estate planning concerns. First, spouses need to make legal provisions for what is to be done medically if one spouse becomes incapacitated—that is, if he or she can no longer make decisions for himself or herself. Family members have been known to disagree about appropriate medical care needed. Fortunately, there are standard legal documents you can prepare to make your wishes for medical care clear and mandatory. (See "Planning for Incapacity" in Chapter 14.)

Another concern can be characterization of assets: What's hers, what's his, and what's theirs? You'll want to be sure that property is properly classified, so there can be no confusion about who owns what. (See Chapter 5.)

EXAMPLE: Ellen and Alex, a married couple, each have children from prior marriages. Both spouses want to eventually leave their property to their own children, but both also want to protect the interest of the survivor. They own a house in equal shares. If the first spouse to die leaves half directly to his or her children, they may want to sell it or use it before the other spouse dies. At best, the surviving spouse will be insecure and, at worst, may be thrown out of the house. Neither spouse wants to risk that.

They decide to each leave the other what's called a "life estate" in their one-half of the house, specifying that the surviving spouse cannot sell the house. For instance, if Alex dies first, Ellen can live in the house during her lifetime, but when she dies, Alex's share automatically goes to his children. Because Ellen's share will go to her kids, the house will probably be sold, and the proceeds divided, when she dies.

Single People

A living trust can be every bit as desirable for a single person as for a couple. Any person, single or not, who wants to avoid probate, can successfully use a living trust.

EXAMPLE: Alina, in her 50s, is a single mother with two teenage children. Alina's major asset is her house, which is mostly paid for. Alina wants to leave all her property equally to her children. She sensibly does not want probate fees paid on the transfer of her house after she dies. So she sets up a living trust and transfers ownership of her house to it. In the trust, she also creates a child's trust for each of her two children. If either child is younger than 35 when Alina dies, that child's trust property will be held in a child's trust until that child reaches age 35. Alina names her sister Natasha to serve as trustee of any child's trust that becomes operational.

Disinheriting a Child

Sometimes people are troubled by deciding how much, if any, property to leave to a child. Legally, you can completely disinherit a child if you want to. (However, those who are accidentally disinherited by their parents can claim part of their parents' estate.) But deciding to disinherit a child is often not emotionally easy to do. Many people decide that something less harsh than disinheritance is desirable. Rather than completely cutting off a child by direct words, they decide that it's wiser to leave some small, lesser amount to this out-of-favor child.

EXAMPLE: Toshiro and Miya have three daughters and a substantial estate. They are very close to two of the daughters, but are bitterly on the outs with the third, Kimiko. Toshiro and Miya had originally intended to leave most of their property to the surviving spouse, and some to the two daughters they're close to. Then, when the surviving spouse dies, the remaining property is to be divided between these two daughters.

But they have second thoughts. Do they really want to cut Kimiko out entirely? If they do, aren't they creating an incentive for her to sue and try to invalidate their estate plan? They decide that good hearts and prudence both dictate the same decision. Each will leave Kimiko $25,000 in their living trust and include a "no-contest" clause in both their wills and trusts. This clause states that if any beneficiary challenges a will or trust, she gets nothing if her challenge is unsuccessful. The parents expect Kimiko to take the certain $50,000 rather than risk an expensive lawsuit she's very likely to lose. Also, Toshiro and Miya are relieved that they haven't had to formally disinherit one of their own children.

If you decide to disinherit a child, you must make that explicitly clear in your will.

Unmarried Couples

Unlike married couples, unmarried couples in most states have no automatic legal right to inherit any of each other's property.

A major concern of most unmarried couples is to ensure that each will inherit property from the other. Happily, people have the right to leave their property by living trust to whomever they want.

> **EXAMPLE:** Ernesto and Teresa have lived together for several years. Aside from a few small gifts to friends or family, each wants to leave all their property to the other after death. They're concerned with efficiency and economy, but above all they want to be sure that their estate plan can't be successfully attacked by several close relatives who have long been hostile to their relationship. Each then prepares a living trust, leaving their property as they desire. They videotape their signing and the notarization of this document to provide additional proof they were both mentally competent and not under duress.

If either member of an unmarried couple has children, they'll want to do specific planning for each child.

> **EXAMPLE:** John and Byron have been together for 15 years. Six years ago, John adopted a son, Max. John and Byron both serve as parents for Max. John and Byron each prepare a living trust, leaving property to Max in a child's trust and naming the other partner as successor trustee of that trust.
>
> In his will, John specifies that if Max is a minor when he dies, he desires that Byron be appointed Max's guardian. John consults an attorney to discuss how he can prepare the most persuasive case for Byron, so that, if the need arises, a judge (who gets the final, official say) will be mostly likely to appoint Byron as guardian.

Same-Sex Couples

Now that the U.S. Supreme Court has declared same-sex marriage legal nationwide, there are fewer caveats or special rules for same-sex couples who want to work on their estate plans.

If you're legally married, your marriage is legal in every U.S. state, every marriage-related right and obligation applies to you, and you can assume that this book's guidance for married couples applies equally to you. If you are part of an unmarried same-sex couple and you have not registered as domestic partners, civil union partners, or reciprocal beneficiaries, then you should plan your estate as an unmarried couple (see above).

However, there is still some gray area for those who have registered their relationships as domestic partners, civil union partners, or reciprocal beneficiaries. Now that same-sex couples can get legally married, states have varied in how they are dealing with such legal statuses—some have eliminated these laws (turning all registered relationships into marriages) and others have left their laws unchanged. These are very state-specific and situation-specific issues. If you have any questions about your marital status, whether you are still in a domestic partnership, or what rights and obligations your registered relationship provides, get help from a local attorney who specializes in estate planning for same-sex couples.

RESOURCE

Learn more about the legal rights of same-sex couples. Nolo offers two unique books about legal issues important to same-sex couples: *A Legal Guide for Lesbian & Gay Couples*, by Frederick Hertz and Lina Guillen, and *Making It Legal: A Guide to Same-Sex Marriage, Domestic Partnerships & Civil Unions*, by Frederick Hertz and Emily Doskow. You can also find a lot of free information on this topic at www.nolo.com.

Communicating Your Decisions to Family and Friends

Most of the examples in this chapter demonstrate my belief that talking can help resolve many potential difficulties with family and friends. But talking is not a panacea. Certainly, there are times when someone doesn't want to listen or talk, or times when communication reveals only a deep and unbridgeable gulf. Still, most of the people I've worked with have been aided by talking openly about what they want to accomplish with their living trusts. If you have a personal problem or two, something to work out on an emotional level, it can require a good deal of thought, understanding, and consideration. For these problems, two or more heads do seem better than one.

Common Questions About Living Trusts

Complexities and doubts sometimes arise between considering a living trust and deciding to prepare one, so before you move into the heart of this book, read through this chapter. It answers a number of questions about living trusts I've been asked over the years, both by clients and by readers of my estate planning books.

Does Everyone Need a Living Trust?

For those who want to plan now to avoid probate, living trusts are often the best probate-avoidance device. Indeed, many people who plan their estates ultimately choose a living trust to transfer most of their property, particularly their big-ticket assets—house, stocks and bonds, and other valuable items.

Given the advantages of avoiding probate, shouldn't every prudent person use a living trust? Actually, no. Some people don't really need to plan now to avoid probate, and others may find more benefit using other probate-avoidance methods.

Generally, you may not need a living trust, at least not right now, if:

- **You are young and healthy.** Your primary goals probably are to be sure your property will be distributed as you want, and to provide financial resources and arrange for someone to care for your minor children, if you have any. A will (perhaps coupled with life insurance) often achieves these goals more easily than a living trust.

  Here's why: A will is simpler to prepare than a living trust. While using a will usually means property goes through probate, probate occurs only after death. As long as you are alive, the fact that probate will be avoided is of no benefit. Because very few healthy younger people die without any warning (and because they often don't yet own enough property that would make probate fees amount to much), it can make good sense to use a will for a number of years. Later in life, when the prospect of death is more imminent and you have accumulated more property, you can create a living trust to avoid probate.

Different Views on Living Trusts for Young People

Some attorneys maintain that living trusts are desirable for younger people because they provide protection if you can no longer manage your estate. If you become incapacitated without having named a person to make decisions for you, a court will have to hold a conservatorship proceeding to appoint a guardian. A living trust could protect against this possibility.

This view may (or may not) make sense for your situation. The risk of a young person's suddenly becoming incapacitated is low. Further, most young people don't own substantial assets or estates that need to be "managed." For these reasons, many young people conclude that they have enough to deal with already, and choose not to create a living trust in their youth. On the other hand, some very cautious young people may decide to plan for incapacity by making a living trust.

An easier way for young people to arrange for someone to have legal authority over their finances is to prepare a durable power of attorney for finances. In this document, you can name a trusted person (called an "agent" or "attorney in fact") to handle finances in the case of your incapacity. If you do become unable to handle your own finances, the person you named will take care of them for you. Learn more about financial powers of attorney at Nolo.com at www.nolo.com/legal-encyclopedia/powers-of-attorney .

- **You can more sensibly transfer your assets, or at least some of them, by other probate-avoidance devices.** Other easy ways to avoid probate include joint tenancy, pay-on-death bank accounts, transfer-on-death securities accounts, life insurance, gifts, and, in some states, transfer-on-death deeds for real estate. In addition, the laws in some states allow certain amounts or types of property (and occasionally all property left to certain classes of beneficiaries, such as a surviving spouse) to be transferred without probate even if a will is used. None of these devices has the breadth of a living trust, which can be used to transfer virtually all types of assets. However, each can be easier to use, and equally efficient, in particular circumstances. It's best to understand all probate-avoidance methods and then to decide which ones will work best for you. (See Chapter 14.)

- **You have complex debt problems.** If you have a serious debt problem, such as a business that has many creditors, probate provides an absolute cutoff time for notified creditors to file claims. If they don't do so in the time permitted (a few months, in most states), your inheritors can take your property free of concern that these creditors will surface later and claim a share. A living trust normally doesn't create any such cutoff period, which means your property could be subject to creditors' claims for a much longer time.

- **Your primary goal is to name a personal guardian to care for your minor children.** A living trust shouldn't be used for this purpose. You do this in your will.

Naming a Guardian for Minor Children in a Living Trust

A few states' laws, such as California's, can be read to allow the appointment of your minor children's personal or property guardian in your living trust. However, this is most definitely not common practice. A judge must confirm the appointment of any acting personal or property guardian. It's unwise to present judges with novel legal documents when important matters are at stake.

A will can always be used to name a personal guardian for your minor children. (See Chapter 15.) If you have a great deal of valuable property, you will probably create a living trust (or another probate-avoidance device) to transfer it. And, in that case, you'll also use a "backup" will, like the one provided by this book, to name a personal guardian for your minor children.

- **Your state has streamlined probate procedures for married or registered couples.** Several states—Alaska, Idaho, Texas, Washington, and Wisconsin—allow a married couple to create a community property agreement that avoids probate for community property left to the surviving spouse. And in California, married couples and registered domestic partners can use simplified procedures to pass property to a spouse or partner, reducing the hassle of probate. If you live in one of these states and plan to leave all or most of your property to your spouse or partner, you may not need a living trust. See "Options in Community Property States" in Chapter 14.

- **Your state allows you to own property with your spouse as "community property with right of survivorship."** Alaska, Arizona, California, Idaho, Nevada, and Wisconsin authorize married couples to own property as community property with right of survivorship. This ownership type allows spouses to retain the benefits of community property while avoiding probate.

- **You are separated but not yet divorced.** To protect the rights of divorcing spouses, your state may have very specific rules about what you can and cannot do with property after separation but before your divorce is final. If you are in the middle of a divorce, see a lawyer before trying to create a living trust or transferring property in or out of one.

- **You own little property.** If you don't have a lot of assets, there isn't much point in bothering with a living trust and probate avoidance, because probate won't cost that much. Often parents in this situation provide money for their young children, in case of a parent's death, by purchasing life insurance. (Insurance proceeds do not go through probate.) However, insurance proceeds (above a minimal amount) cannot be turned over to children younger than 18. So you may need to leave the proceeds under your state's Uniform Transfers to Minors Act (available in all states except South Carolina). Using this act, you name an adult custodian to manage the money for the benefit of the child until the child becomes an adult. (See Chapter 8.)

How large should your estate be before you need to concern yourself with avoiding probate? There's no mathematical rule here. Even a relatively small estate—say $50,000—might cost $1,000 or more to transfer by probate. If you have a small estate, you may want to check out the dollar amount of property your state allows to be transferred by a will without formal probate. This varies widely from state to state.

California, one of the more generous states, allows you to transfer up to $162,250 without probate. (That limit rises every three years to reflect cost-of-living increases.) Most states allow much less. You can find a state-by-state list of each state's rules in the article "Probate Shortcuts in Your State" at www.nolo.com/legal-encyclopedia/executor-probate.

If I Prepare a Living Trust, Do I Need a Will?

Yes. Even if you arrange to transfer almost all your property by a living trust, you should always prepare a backup will. A backup will can serve several purposes. Use your backup will to:

- name beneficiaries for property that is generally not desirable to transfer to a living trust, such as your personal checking account or car
- name beneficiaries for any property that you haven't transferred to your trust or that you may not yet officially own (for example, lottery winnings, a lawsuit settlement, or an inheritance)
- name a personal guardian who will look after your young children, and
- name a property manager who will look after your children's property.

Backup wills are covered in Chapter 15. This book provides will forms in Appendix B and as downloadable forms.

How Can I Leave Trust Property to Children and Young Adults?

Chapter 8 covers how you can use your living trust to leave property to minor children or young adults. Here I cover some basic, preliminary questions.

Providing for Minor Children

You can leave property to minor children (those younger than 18) in your living trust and name an adult to manage that trust property.

If any of your living trust property is left to a beneficiary who's a minor when you die, an adult must manage that property for the minor.

What Your Living Trust Can't Do for Children

Do not use a living trust to name a personal guardian to care for your minor children if you die. Similarly, do not use a living trust to name a general property guardian to manage all property owned by your minor children. You must use your will for those purposes.

Various legal devices can be used to leave property to minors:

- **Small gifts for children's benefit.** If your estate is relatively modest and there is a trusted person to care for the child (usually the other parent), it's often easiest simply to leave property directly to the adult who will care for the child.
- **Larger gifts.** If the gift is larger—as a rough rule, say between $50,000 and $100,000—it can be desirable to leave the property by using the Uniform Transfers to Minors Act (UTMA) in your living trust. You name an adult custodian to manage the property you leave to the child.

  The trust forms in this book have specific provisions allowing you to leave gifts that will be managed under the UTMA. You can use these UTMA provisions in any state except South Carolina.

- **Very large gifts.** The best way to leave even larger gifts—more than $100,000—to minor children is generally by using a child's trust, which allows you to designate the age at which the child will receive the property. Your successor trustee manages the trust property for the child's benefit until the child receives it outright.

The forms in this book allow you to create a child's trust as a part of your living trust. If you die before a minor beneficiary has reached the age you've chosen, that child's trust property is held in a child's trust. If you don't specify an age, the trust provides that the property remains in the child's trust until that child becomes age 35. This trust is irrevocable after your death. If the child has already reached that age when you die, that child receives the property outright, and no child's trust is created.

EXAMPLE: One of the beneficiaries of Edward's living trust is Abigail, age 17. Edward establishes a child's trust for her, as part of his living trust. His trust states that she will receive her trust property when she becomes 35. Edward dies when Abigail is 26. Her property is maintained in the child's trust until she becomes 35.

While a child's trust is operational, the trustee (the successor trustee of your living trust) has broad powers to spend any of that trust's income or principal for the child's health, support, maintenance, or education. When the child reaches the age you specified (or age 35, if you didn't specify an age), the successor trustee turns the trust property over to your child.

Young Adult Beneficiaries Who Can't Handle Money Responsibly Now

A child's trust does not have to be used solely for minors. You can leave a gift in a child's trust for any beneficiary who is younger than 35 when you create your trust.

EXAMPLE: Julio's son Enrique is 22. Julio wants to leave Enrique valuable property, worth more than $250,000. Julio worries (sadly, with good reason) that Enrique isn't mature enough to handle this money responsibly if he inherits it soon. So Julio creates a child's trust for this gift to Enrique, and provides that Enrique will receive the gift outright at age 35.

Will My Living Trust Reduce Estate Taxes?

When some people hear the word "trust," they feel it must mean "tax savings." Not so. Indeed, most living trusts are designed solely to avoid probate, not taxes. A basic trust for a single person (Form 1 in this book), or a shared living trust for a couple (Form 2), will not reduce estate taxes.

That said, very few people need to worry about federal estate taxes, and only a small number of states levy state estate taxes. Chapter 14 provides details about estate taxes, and you can learn the latest estate tax information in the "Estate, Gift and Inheritance Taxes" section of Nolo.com at www.nolo.com/legal-encyclopedia/estate-tax.

Will I Have to Pay Gift Taxes?

Some people worry that by creating a living trust, they'll become enmeshed in gift taxes. Not to worry.

No gift tax is assessed when you transfer property to your living trust. To make a taxable gift, you must relinquish all control over the property. Since you keep complete control over property in your living trust (and you can revoke the trust at any time before you die), you don't make a gift simply by transferring property to the trust. (See Chapter 14 for a discussion of gifts and gift taxes.)

Will a Living Trust Shield My Property From Creditors?

Some people think that a living trust can protect their assets from creditors. No such luck.

While You're Alive

Property in a revocable living trust is not immune from attack by your creditors while you're alive. On the other hand, if property is put in an *irrevocable* trust—and you no longer have any control over it—it's a different legal matter. Property transferred to a bona fide irrevocable trust is immune from your creditors. The key words here are "bona fide." If an irrevocable trust is set up to defraud creditors, it's not bona fide. This book does not include irrevocable trusts.

 SEE AN EXPERT

Keeping creditors away from your property. If you're concerned about protecting your assets from creditors, see a lawyer.

After Your Death

A living trust won't shield your assets from your creditors after your death either, even after the property has been turned over to your beneficiaries.

One advantage claimed for probate is that it ensures that one's debts and taxes are paid before property is distributed to inheritors. If duly notified creditors don't make their claims within an allotted time, they're simply cut off. Does that mean you should worry about how your debts, including estate taxes, get paid if there's no probate and no probate court supervision? In most cases—no.

Many people leave no significant debts, and even if they do, they normally leave sufficient assets to pay them. The most common kinds of large debts—mortgages on real estate or loans on cars—don't have to be paid off when the owner dies. Normally, these kinds of debts are transferred with the asset to an inheritor, who then becomes liable for the mortgage or loan. In other words, mortgages or car loans pass with the property and don't need to be paid off separately.

Your successor trustee (who should also be named as executor of your will) has the legal responsibility of paying your debts. If no probate occurs to cut off creditors' claims, all your property, including all property that was in the living trust, remains liable for your debts. This is true even after the property is transferred to inheritors. If only one person inherits from you, that person will wind up paying your debts and any estate taxes from the inherited property.

If there are several inheritors, who will pay your last debts and taxes might cause more confusion. You can eliminate this problem by designating a specific trust asset—often a bank account or stock market account—to be used to pay your debts. If you don't have a suitable asset available to do this, consider purchasing insurance to provide quick cash to pay debts. (Providing in your trust for payment of your debts is covered in Chapter 9.)

Do I Need a "Catastrophic Illness Clause" in My Trust?

The term "catastrophic illness clause" commonly refers to a clause that, hopefully, prevents assets from being used for the costs of a major illness that strikes you or your spouse when you want government aid to help pay the bills. Many people are concerned with becoming eligible for federal benefits without having to use up all (or even any) of their assets. They don't want their assets counted when eligibility for government aid is determined. Married couples want to protect at least the assets owned by the healthier spouse.

A catastrophic illness clause certainly sounds like a good idea. But unfortunately, no simple clause can protect your assets. Bluntly put, the law doesn't easily allow people to retain their assets and still become eligible for federal aid. There are various, more complex ways of protecting some of your assets if you're faced with huge medical bills, including making gifts, paying children for services, or using certain complex types of trusts.

 RESOURCE

More information on protecting assets. Methods of hanging onto your assets are discussed in *Long-Term Care: How to Plan & Pay for It*, by Joseph Matthews (Nolo).

SEE AN EXPERT

Individualized advice on protecting assets. If you want to take concrete actions to protect your assets from possible medical costs, see a lawyer knowledgeable in this distinct legal area. To help you, a lawyer must be up to date on relevant federal and state statutes and regulations, which can change fast.

How Does Where I Live Affect My Living Trust?

Living trusts are valid under the laws of every state. Still, a number of questions can arise about living trusts and where you live.

Determining Your Legal Residence

In your trust document, you'll name the state where you live; that state's laws govern the document. If you live in one state but work in another, it's the state where you live whose laws apply. You must also sign appropriate documents to transfer property to your trust in that state. (See Chapter 10.)

For most people, the state they reside in (in legalese, their "domicile") is self-evident. But for others, it can be more complex.

If during the course of a year you live in more than one state, your residence is the state with which you have the most significant contacts—where you vote, register vehicles, own valuable property, have bank accounts, or run a business.

If you might be justified in claiming more than one state as your legal residence, you may want to arrange your affairs so that your legal residence is in the state with the most advantageous state inheritance or estate tax laws. Some states impose inheritance and estate taxes, while others do not.

EXAMPLE: Carlo and Sophia, a couple in their 60s, spend about half the year in Florida and the other half in Pennsylvania, which has an inheritance tax. They have bank accounts and real estate in both states. To take advantage of Florida's lack of an inheritance tax, they register their car in Florida, vote there, and move their bank accounts there. This leaves them owning nothing in Pennsylvania but a condominium near where their son lives. They decide to sell him the condo and lease it back six months of every year, severing their last important property ownership contact with Pennsylvania.

SEE AN EXPERT

Advice about your domicile. If you have significant contacts with more than one state, and a substantial estate, it may be worthwhile to have a lawyer with tax and estate planning experience advise you.

If You Live Outside the Country

If you are currently living outside the United States but are a permanent resident of the United States, you can prepare a valid living trust for property physically located within this country—usually real estate.

A problem here can be getting your living trust properly acknowledged (notarized or an equivalent). You need an acknowledgment that is legal in the state where the property is. That state's law may allow acknowledgment by officials outside the country. (California, for example, permits certain diplomatic personnel and foreign judges and notaries to acknowledge signatures.) However, it's risky to rely on a foreign acknowledgment, because title companies or other financial institutions that will be involved with the transfer of trust property after you die may not accept it. A title company may balk at accepting a trust (or deed) that has an unfamiliar kind of acknowledgment, even if it's legal under state law. (And, as an astute lawyer friend put it, "In real estate, the law is whatever a title company says it is.")

This leaves you three options:

- Have your trust notarized in the state where the property is located.
- Check to see whether that state allows foreign acknowledgments. If it does, contact a title company, and any other institution that will be involved in the transfer of in-state property, to see if it will accept a living trust (and real estate deed) with a foreign acknowledgment.
- Leave the property by will, not a living trust.

SEE AN EXPERT

Get help if you don't maintain ties with any particular state. See a lawyer to discuss what state you should declare as your residence.

If you are in the armed forces and living out of the country temporarily, your legal residence is the state you declared as your home of record—the state you lived in before going overseas, or where your spouse or parents live.

If you acquire property, such as real estate, in a foreign country, you must check out that country's laws regarding transfer of real estate on death.

If You Move to Another State or Country

Revocable living trusts are valid and used in every state, and your trust remains valid if you move to a different state. However, if you're married and you move from a community property state to a common law state, or vice versa, you may want to check the marital property ownership laws of your new state. (See "Marital Property Laws" in Chapter 5.) Also, if you leave a gift using the Uniform Transfers to Minors Act and you move to a state that terminates the custodianship at a different age, you'll want to review and possibly amend this portion of your trust.

If you move to another country after creating a living trust, the trust remains valid. Under the 1961 Hague Convention (effective for U.S. citizens since 1981), a document notarized as a valid document in one country is recognized as valid by other countries that agreed to the treaty.

Out-of-State Beneficiaries or Successor Trustee

Your trust beneficiaries and your successor trustee can live in any state or any country.

Registration

Some states require "registration" of living trusts. These requirements are neither a serious burden nor reason not to use a trust. (See "Registering the Trust" in Chapter 11.)

Can I Place Real Estate in a Living Trust?

Generally, it's easy—and quite common—to place valuable real estate (usually your home, whether house or condominium) in a living trust. You simply prepare and record a deed, transferring the real estate from you, personally, to you as trustee of your trust. (See "Real Estate" in Chapter 10.)

Property Tax Reassessment

In some states, certain real estate transfers, such as sales to new owners who aren't family members, result in the property's being immediately reappraised for property tax purposes. By contrast, if the property is not transferred to new owners, it usually won't be reappraised for a set period of years, or is reappraised at a reduced rate.

In states that reappraise property when it's transferred to a new owner, placing title to property in a living trust very rarely, if ever, triggers a property tax reappraisal. For instance, California law (Cal. Rev. & Tax. Code § 62) expressly prohibits reappraisals for transfers to a living trust where the grantor is a trustee. To be absolutely sure that this is true in your state if you're transferring real estate into a living trust, you can check with your local property tax collector to learn exactly what reappraisal rules apply. Just ask the clerk, "Will there be a property tax reassessment if I transfer my house to a living trust?"

Transfer Taxes

Very rarely, if ever, are transfer taxes imposed when you transfer your real estate to your living trust. But to be absolutely safe here, check this out with your county assessor or recorder's office.

Deducting Mortgage Interest

For income tax purposes, the trust doesn't exist. You retain the right to deduct all mortgage interest from your income taxes, even though your home is technically owned by the trustee of your trust.

Insurance Policies

Insurance policies on your home—fire, liability, theft, and other particular policies—do not have to be reregistered in the trust's name. Like the IRS, insurance companies are concerned with the real ownership, not legal technicalities to avoid probate or reduce estate taxes. So there's no reason at all to contact your insurance company when you transfer your home or other real estate to your living trust.

Tax Breaks for Sellers

You have the right to sell your principal home once every two years and exclude $250,000 of profit from income taxation. A couple can exclude all profits up to $500,000. During your life, you retain that right even if you have transferred that home to a living trust. (I.R.C. § 121.)

Homestead Rights

Generally, transferring your home to a living trust does not affect the protection offered by state homestead laws. These laws typically protect a homeowner's equity interest in a home, up to a designated amount, from creditors. The living trust forms in this book each contain a specific statement that the grantor(s) intend to remain eligible for the state homestead exemption they would be entitled to if they still owned the real estate outside the trust.

"Homestead" Defined

A homestead is a legal device, available under the laws of most states, to protect a limited amount of equity in your home from creditors. In some states that allow homesteads, you record a Declaration of Homestead with the county land records office; in others, the protection is automatic. In either case, if you qualify for a homestead, your home is protected against forced sale by creditors (other than mortgage holders) if your equity is below the dollar limit set out in the statute.

However, if you're in debt and concerned that a creditor may try to force a sale of your house, check your state's homestead rules carefully. If you are not seriously in debt, there is no need to worry about this one.

Selling or Refinancing Your House

If you try to sell or refinance a house that is in a living trust, you might encounter some paperwork hassles, but nothing more serious. Some banks balk at refinancing a home that technically is owned by the trustee of a living trust, even if you show them the original trust document. Similarly, some title companies are reluctant to insure sale of a home by a trustee while the grantor is alive. By contrast, once an owner dies and a house is transferred to the beneficiaries, title companies routinely approve the sale of that real estate, even though it is transferred by a successor trustee.

If you encounter a problem trying to sell or refinance a house owned by your trust, you have two options:

- Seek a bank or title company that is reasonable and will allow the transaction in the trustee's name, which is fully legal.
- Transfer the property out of the trustee's name back into your individual name. Then go ahead with the sale or refinancing. Once the refinancing is completed, you can prepare yet another deed, again transferring the property back to the trustee. Convoluted, yes, but not really onerous.

Citations to Federal Statutes
Federal laws are codified in the United States Code, cited as U.S.C. A citation to a law lists the appropriate volume and sections of the U.S.C. For example, in the citation below, you can find the Garn-St. Germain Depository Institutions Act in Volume 12 of the United States Code, Sections 1464 and 1701.
The Internal Revenue Code is contained in Volume 26 of the U.S.C. This volume is often cited simply as I.R.C.

Due-on-Sale Clauses

Federal law expressly prohibits enforcing a "due-on-sale" clause in a mortgage because of a transfer of one's home ("principal residence") to one's own revocable living trust. (The Garn-St. Germain Depository Institutions Act, 12 U.S.C. §§ 1464, 1701.)

No statute expressly prohibits a bank from enforcing a due-on-sale clause when other real estate is transferred to a trust. However, I've never heard of it happening, probably because banks know it wouldn't make sense. After all, the transfer is flatly not a sale. No money changes hands. The IRS doesn't consider the transaction a sale. If a bank did try to claim that a due-on-sale clause was activated by a transfer of, say, investment or commercial real estate to a trust, you could always rescind the transaction and transfer the property back to your individual name.

Some highly cautious lawyers (not me) do obtain a bank's (mortgage holder's) prior consent to transfers of commercial real estate to a living trust. Sometimes banks charge a fee of $100 or $200 for consenting to the transfer.

Transferring Part Interests in Real Estate

Any portion of real estate you own, such as a time-share or percentage of ownership, can be transferred to a living trust. (See "Real Estate" in Chapter 10.)

Owning Real Estate in More Than One State

You must record a transfer deed in the land records office of the county where the real estate is located. So if you own one piece of real estate in Arizona, one in New York, and another in Vermont, you must record transfer deeds in all three states.

Rental (Income) Property

Under federal tax law, net profits received from rental property are "passive income." Losses in passive income cannot be used to offset profits or gains from "active income." However, there is a limited $25,000 exception to this rule for owners who "actively participate" in operation of the rental property. This $25,000 exception remains applicable if the rental property is placed in a living trust. (I.R.C. § 469.)

Contaminated Property

Under federal law, "responsible parties" are liable for the costs of cleaning up contaminated land. Responsible parties include past and current owners of the real estate—whether or not the present owners contributed to the contamination. Contamination includes pollution from various toxic or dangerous substances, such as petroleum products, dry cleaning solvents, and many other chemicals.

SEE AN EXPERT

If you own land that may be contaminated. If you own real estate that you know, or suspect, is contaminated, do not simply leave that property under your living trust, or by other means. You may be leaving someone a massive, very costly problem. See a lawyer experienced with problems of contaminated property.

Can I Sell or Give Away Trust Property While I'm Alive?

You can readily sell, transfer, or give away property in your trust.

Making Gifts

While you are alive, you can give away property held in your living trust. There are no restrictions on your power to make gifts from your trust. However, federal gift tax rules apply to gifts you make from trust property, as well as to gifts you make from your own nontrust property. (See "Federal Gift and Estate Taxes" in Chapter 14.)

Selling Trust Property

You can readily sell any property in your trust. There are two ways to go about it:

- Sell the property directly from the trust, acting in your capacities as grantor and trustee to sign the title document, bill of sale, sales contract, or other document. The trust documents in this book specifically state that the trustee has the power to sell trust property, including stocks or bonds.
- In your capacity as trustee of the living trust, first transfer title of the particular item of trust property back to yourself as an individual, and then sell the property in your own name.

The only reason for using the second option, which requires more paperwork, is if some institution involved in the sale insists you sell it in your own name. This rarely happens. For instance, stockbrokerage companies are familiar with sales by a trustee from a living trust. At most, you might have to point out to some overcautious bureaucrat that the specific trustee powers clause of your trust document specifically gives you authority to make the sale.

Amending Your Trust After Sale or Gift of Trust Property

You should amend your revocable living trust if you sell or give away property that the trust leaves to a particular trust beneficiary. Obviously, the trust document cannot leave property that the trust no longer owns. (Amending living trusts is discussed in Chapter 12.)

Is a Bank Account Held in Trust Insured by the FDIC?

Yes. If the bank is covered by the FDIC, any bank account in the trust's or trustee's name is insured up to the $250,000 maximum per institution.

Banks also offer "pay-on-death" accounts, which function as de facto living trusts for the funds in the accounts, and which also are protected by the FDIC.

Will Property in My Living Trust Get a "Stepped-Up" Tax Basis When I Die?

Yes. Property left through any type of revocable living trust does get a stepped-up tax basis. This is an important concern for many people, who understand that, for inheritors of their property, a stepped-up basis is highly desirable for income tax reasons. Here's how it works.

To understand the concept of stepped-up basis, you must first understand what "basis" means. Put simply, the basis of property is the figure used to determine taxable profit when the property is sold. Usually, the basis of real estate is its purchase price, plus the cost of any capital improvements, less any depreciation. Once you know the basis, you subtract that figure from what you sell the property for. The result is your taxable profit.

> **EXAMPLE:** Phyllis bought a home for $340,000. She puts $25,000 into capital improvements (new roof and foundation). So her basis in the property is $365,000. If she sells the property for $775,000, her profit is $410,000.

Under federal law, the basis of inherited property is increased, or "stepped up," to its market value as of the date the deceased owner died. (This is only fair, as the same property is valued, for estate tax purposes, at its market value as of the date the owner died.) At an owner's death, the inheritors' basis of living trust property becomes the market value of that property at death, not the original acquisition cost. Of course, if the property has declined in value after purchase, the change in basis is a negative. However, given the long-term inflationary economy, property owned for a while usually increases in value. Thus, for most estates, the basis is stepped up.

> **EXAMPLE:** Continuing the example above, Phyllis dies and, through her living trust, leaves the house (with a market value of $775,000) to her niece, Nancy. Nancy's basis in the house is $775,000. If she promptly sells it for that amount, she has no taxable profit.

In community property states (see the list in Chapter 7), both halves of property shared by both spouses receive a stepped-up basis when one spouse dies. This includes property in a shared living trust. In all other states (called "common law" states), only the property of a married person who dies receives a stepped-up basis. The property already owned by the surviving spouse does not get a stepped-up basis; it retains the basis it had. Thus, with a shared trust in a common law state, when one spouse dies, that spouse's trust property receives a stepped-up basis. However, the trust property of the surviving spouse does not.

> **EXAMPLE:** Alexander and Harriet, residents of New York, share ownership of a house with a basis of $400,000. When Alexander dies, the house is worth $800,000. The basis of Alexander's share is stepped up to its value at the time of death. However, Harriet's share retains its original basis, which is one-half of $400,000, or $200,000.
>
> If Alexander and Harriet lived in Texas, a community property state, and had the same property situation, each spouse's share of the house would receive a stepped-up basis to $400,000 when Alexander died.

Who Must Know About My Living Trust?

Normally, the only person who must know about your living trust before you die is your successor trustee. And even the successor trustee need know only where the trust document is, not what's in it. However, most people do show the trust document to their successor trustee. After all, you should fully trust this person. And it should make the job easier to know in advance what property the trust owns, and who gets it after your death.

Whether or not to tell your beneficiaries what's in your trust and who gets what is entirely your personal decision. Personally, I believe it's wisest to inform at least your major beneficiaries of your trust gifts, unless you have a compelling reason not to do so.

What About Free Living Trust Seminars?

You may see advertisements for free living trust seminars or talks. Be cautious about these. Some are given by reputable attorneys or other financial professionals who are seeking new clients and offer legitimate information. Others are given by high-pressure salespeople who pressure you to buy an expensive trust (and perhaps life insurance or an annuity as well). Do not agree to buy anything on the spot. You should never have to rush to prepare a living trust. Take time to be sure you are getting something you need and want.

Could Someone Challenge My Living Trust?

A trust can be challenged in court. In our judicial system, any legal document, including a living trust, can be challenged this way. But theory doesn't matter here, reality does. The important questions to ask are:

- Is there any likelihood someone will challenge my living trust?
- If there is, what can I do to protect myself?

Legal challenges to a living trust are quite rare. You don't need to concern yourself unless you think a close relative might have an axe to grind after your death.

Some people ask about including a "no-contest" clause as a protection against a lawsuit attacking their trust. A no-contest clause doesn't prevent anyone from contesting the validity of your trust. It simply says that if a beneficiary contests your living trust and loses, that person gets nothing. Thus, a no-contest clause will not discourage a nonbeneficiary from suing. Nor will a no-contest clause necessarily deter a disgruntled beneficiary who wants more, and is willing to risk losing your gift by suing.

> **SEE AN EXPERT**
>
> **Adding a no-contest clause.** If you think you need a no-contest clause, it's an indication you have a potentially serious problem—someone who might challenge your trust. See a lawyer.

Following are the kinds of legal challenges that can theoretically be made against a living trust.

Challenges to the Validity of the Trust

Someone who wanted to challenge the validity of your living trust would have to bring a lawsuit and prove either of the following:

- When you made the trust, you were mentally incompetent or unduly influenced by someone.
- The trust document itself is flawed—for example, because the signature was forged.

Proving any of this is not easy. It's generally considered more difficult to successfully challenge a living trust than a will. That's because your continuing involvement with a living trust after its creation (transferring property in and out of the trust, or making amendments) is evidence that you were competent to manage your affairs.

Lawsuits by Spouses

Most married people leave much, if not all, of their property to their spouses. But if you don't leave your spouse at least half of your property, your spouse may have the right to go to court and claim some of your property after your death. Such a challenge wouldn't wipe out your whole living trust, but might take some of the property you had earmarked for other beneficiaries and give it to your spouse.

The rights of spouses vary from state to state. (See "Disinheritance" in Chapter 7.)

Lawsuits by a Child

Children usually have no right to inherit anything from their parents. There are two exceptions: Laws that give minor children certain rights and laws that are designed to protect children who are unintentionally overlooked in a will.

Minor Children

State law may give your spouse and minor children (those younger than age 18) the right to inherit the family residence. The Florida Constitution, for example, prohibits the head of a family from leaving a residence to anyone except the surviving spouse or minor child. (Fla. Const. Art. 10, § 4.)

Overlooked Children

Most state laws protect offspring who appear to have been unintentionally overlooked in a parent's will. The legal term for such an overlooked offspring is a "pretermitted heir." In most states, this term means a child born after the will was signed. Though the law is unclear, it could be argued that a child omitted from a living trust was also a pretermitted heir. Fortunately, it's easy to avoid these problems. See Chapter 7 and Chapter 15.

What Type of Trust Do You Need?

No law specifies the form a living trust must take. As a result, there is no such thing as a standard living trust. Indeed, there are a bewildering variety of living trust forms. Some attorney-created forms contain vast piles of verbiage, most of which serve no real-world purpose except to generate attorneys' fees.

This book offers two types of living trusts, as clear and understandable as I can make them:

- a probate-avoidance trust for an individual, and
- a probate-avoidance trust for a couple that owns property together, called a "shared living trust."

Using More Than One Living Trust

Legally, you can have more than one living trust, for different types of property. Although it isn't necessary for most people, in complex property ownership situations, using more than one trust can make sense. For example, you might set up one trust for your business and another for the rest of your property, if you want one of your business associates to act as successor trustee to handle and transfer your business property, but a spouse, friend, or close relative to distribute your other property.

If You Are Single

If you are single and making a living trust by yourself, use Nolo's living trust for one person (Form 1). If you are a single parent, you can use Form 1 to create a living trust to leave property for your minor children.

You can use this form to leave all of your property, or any part of it, including your share of co-owned property. For instance, if you own a house together with your sister, you simply transfer your share of that house into your trust. Similarly, you can transfer your share of a partnership or shares in a small corporation to your trust, assuming the partnership agreement or corporate charter and bylaws permit it.

With Nolo's individual trust, you can also:

- name your successor trustee or trustees, and
- leave property to minors or young adults— including your own children, of course—through a child's trust, or a gift under the Uniform Transfers to Minors Act. (See Chapter 8.)

EXAMPLE: Alfonso is a single parent of two teenage daughters. His major assets are a house and a solely owned electrical supply business. He creates an individual living trust, and transfers the house and business to it. In the trust, he leaves his property equally to his two daughters. Because they are minors, he creates a child's trust for each daughter to last (if needed) until that daughter becomes 30. He names his sister Grace to be trustee of each trust. He also creates a will, and names Grace to be guardian of his children if he dies before both have become legal adults.

A More Complex Trust

Some single people want to create a trust that does more than avoid probate. For example, a sibling might want to create a "life estate" trust that first avoids probate, then leaves property for the benefit of a brother for his life, and then at the brother's death leaves the property outright to other beneficiaries. Drafting a complex trust requires careful attention to the specifics of your situation. You cannot use Nolo's individual living trust to accomplish these goals. Get help from an experienced estate planning attorney.

If you decide to make an individual trust, go to Chapter 5, which explains what property to put in your living trust.

If You Are Part of a Couple

This book provides two ways for members of a couple to create a living trust:

- Each spouse prepares an individual trust.
- Both spouses prepare one shared living trust.

Both co-owned property and separate property can go into either kind of trust. However, keep in mind that when separate property goes into a shared trust, the non-owner spouse will be a trustee for the other spouse's separate property. This opens up the possibility that the non-owner spouse could fraudulently take advantage of that position to access or control the other spouse's separate property. Hopefully, few couples need to bother about this concern, but if it is a worry to you, then consider doing one of these two things:

- Create an independent living trust for each spouse's separate property.
- For separate-property financial accounts, name the couple's shared trust as the beneficiary for each separate-property account. Doing this does not transfer ownership of these accounts to the trustees of the trust. The account(s) will remain as separate property of one spouse. It also means that the trust will receive funds from that account at the death of the owner.

Terminology for Unmarried Couples
Because most couples who use shared living trusts are married, my discussion of these trusts is cast in terms of "spouses" and "marital property." However, the discussion applies equally to unmarried couples. It's too awkward to restate this point in each sentence or sprinkle the text with terms such as "partners" or "significant others." Please, if you are a member of an unmarried couple, make the necessary semantic substitutions for yourself.

Individual Trusts for Members of a Couple

A member of a couple can legally use one separate, individual trust for all of that person's property or two living trusts: one trust for separately owned property and another trust for property shared with the other spouse. But this is rarely necessary or advisable. As you'll see below, both separately owned and shared property can be conveniently handled in one shared living trust.

Most couples prefer not to create two individual trusts because it requires dividing property they own together, which is often the bulk of their property.

Splitting ownership of co-owned assets can be a clumsy process. For example, to transfer a co-owned house into two separate trusts would require the spouses to sign and record two deeds transferring a half-interest in the house to two separate trusts. And to transfer household furnishings to separate trusts, spouses would have to allocate each item to a trust or do something as silly as each transferring half-interests in a couch to their individual trusts.

In some common law states (see the list in Chapter 5), some attorneys advise couples to go this route. The claimed advantage for this is that it's then easier, upon the death of a spouse, to tell what property each spouse owns. I think this type of caution is unnecessary, and not worth the drawbacks of dividing shared property while both members of the couple are living. With a properly drafted shared trust, there should be no difficulty identifying what property belonged to which spouse.

If, however, you and your spouse own most or all of your property separately, you may each want to make an individual trust. Most couples who want this fit one of these profiles:

- You live in a community property state, and you and your spouse signed an agreement stating that each spouse's property, including earnings and other income, is separate, not community property. (See Chapter 5 for a discussion of community property.)

- You don't want your spouse to have any legal authority as trustee over your separate property in a shared trust, either while you are alive or after your death. (See Chapter 6.)
- You are recently married, have little or no shared or community property, and want to keep future property acquisitions separate. (To accomplish this, you'll both need to sign a written statement of your intentions.)
- You want to create three trusts: a shared one for property both spouses own together, and two individual trusts, one for each spouse's separate property.
- You each own mostly separate property acquired before your marriage (or by gift or inheritance), which you conscientiously keep from being mixed with any shared property you own. Couples who marry later in life and no longer work often fit into this category. Not only is the property they owned before the marriage separate, but Social Security benefits and certain retirement plan benefits are also separate, not shared, or community, property.

> **EXAMPLE:** Howard and Luisa live in Indiana, a common law state. Both have adult children from prior marriages. When they married, they moved into Howard's house. They both have their own separate bank accounts and investments, and one joint checking account that they own as joint tenants with right of survivorship.
>
> Each makes an individual living trust. Howard, who dies first, leaves his house (and furnishings) to Luisa, but his other property to his children. The funds in the joint checking account are not included in his living trust, but pass to Luisa, also without probate, because the account was held in joint tenancy. Howard's other bank accounts go to his children, under the pay-on-death arrangement he has with the bank. (Joint tenancy, pay-on-death accounts, and other probate-avoidance methods are discussed in Chapter 14.)

If you and your spouse decide on separate living trusts, each of you will transfer your separately owned property to your individual trust. If you own some property together—a house, for example—you each transfer your portion of it to your individual trust.

SEE AN EXPERT

Preparing separate trusts. If you and your spouse decide to prepare two separate trusts and do not name each other as successor trustees, you may want to see a lawyer to be as certain as you can that there won't be any conflict between the spouse and the successor trustee.

Shared Living Trusts

If you and your spouse own most or all of your property equally together and don't want to divide it up and transfer it into two separate trusts, you'll probably choose to make one living trust and transfer all of your property—both shared and separately owned—to it. While you live, each of you retains full ownership of all your separate property, as well as your share of jointly owned property.

> **EXAMPLE:** Lorenzo and Marsha are married and own a house together. Marsha also owns, as her own property, some valuable jewels left to her by her mother. Lorenzo owns, as his separate property, some stock his uncle gave him.
>
> Lorenzo and Marsha create one shared living trust and transfer all of their jointly owned property to it. Marsha's jewelry is also placed in this trust, identified as her separate property. Similarly, Lorenzo's stock is placed in this trust, identified as his separate property. Neither loses any ownership rights to her or his separate property by placing it in the shared living trust.

If probate avoidance is your goal, you can use a shared living trust no matter how much all of your property is worth.

How a Shared Trust Works

With this book's shared marital trust, you and your spouse will be cotrustees of your living trust. You'll both have control over your shared ownership property in the trust. In theory, this means either spouse can act alone to sell or give away shared trust property. However, because banks, title companies, and others often have their own rules requiring both spouses' signatures, as a practical matter, the consent of both to sell or transfer shared property is commonly necessary.

> **SEE AN EXPERT**
>
> **If one spouse will not be a trustee.** If for any reason—health, mistrust, whatever—you don't want your spouse to serve with you as a trustee of your shared trust, see a lawyer.

As I've said, each of you retains ownership of your separate property, because in the trust document it's identified and listed as property owned by only one spouse. With your separate trust property, you may:

- sell it, give it away, or leave it in the trust
- in the trust document, name a beneficiary or beneficiaries to inherit that property, or
- amend the trust document to name a new beneficiary or beneficiaries for that property.

Technically, trust amendments require consent of both spouses, but this should be a mere formality where a spouse wants to amend the trust to name new beneficiaries. If the other spouse proves recalcitrant—say the couple is getting divorced—either spouse can revoke the entire trust and prepare a new one.

Each spouse is also free to add separately owned property to the trust later.

In the trust document, both spouses separately name beneficiaries for their share of co-owned property, as well as for all of their own separate property. Commonly, spouses leave all, if not the bulk, of their property to each other. But leaving all or most of your property to your spouse isn't legally required. Each spouse has complete freedom in choosing beneficiaries, except that married couples are subject to legal restrictions in many states that entitle a surviving spouse to claim a certain share of a deceased spouse's estate. (See "Marital Property Laws" in Chapter 5.)

A spouse's separate property is kept separate in a shared trust by means of trust "schedules," which are lists of trust property attached to the trust document. Schedule A lists co-owned property. Property listed on Schedule B is the separate property of one spouse (traditionally, the wife), and all property listed on Schedule C is the separate property of the other spouse (traditionally, the husband).

If spouses want to leave significant amounts of property to each other, a shared living trust provides another big advantage over individual trusts. With a shared trust, property left by one spouse to the survivor automatically stays in the living trust when the first spouse dies. It becomes part of the property the surviving spouse has in what is now the surviving spouse's individual living trust. No formal transfer documents are needed. If separate, individual trusts were used, property left to the surviving spouse would need to be transferred first from the deceased spouse's trust to the name of the surviving spouse and then, to avoid probate, the second spouse would have to transfer it into his or her own living trust.

Either spouse can revoke the trust at any time. If either spouse revokes the trust, the couple's property ownership situation returns to exactly what it was before the trust was formed. Shared property is returned to the ownership of both spouses, and separately owned property goes to the spouse who owned it. By contrast, amendments to the trust document require the consent of both spouses. For example, both must agree to change the successor trustee.

What Happens When One Spouse Dies

When one spouse dies, the shared living trust is split into two trusts, Trust 1 and Trust 2; this is automatic under the terms of the living trust document. The surviving spouse is sole trustee of both trusts. (The surviving spouse's duties are discussed in Chapter 13.)

Trust Contains All Shared Property

1. Husband and wife transfer shared property to trust.

> **Shared Living Trust**
> Husband and wife's shared property is listed on Schedule A.

2. Husband dies. Trust property is divided between Trust 1 and Trust 2.

> **Trust 1** (irrevocable)
> Husband's share of trust property not left to wife.

> **Trust 2** (revocable)
> Wife's share of trust property plus trust property left to wife by husband.

3. Wife, as successor trustee, distributes husband's trust property to his beneficiaries.

> To husband's beneficiaries (other than wife).

Trust Contains Shared and Separate Property

1. Husband and wife transfer shared property to trust. Wife transfers her separate property to trust.

> **Shared Living Trust**
> Husband and wife's shared property is listed on Schedule A.
> Wife's separate property is listed on Schedule B.

2. Wife dies. Trust property is divided between Trust 1 and Trust 2.

> **Trust 1** (irrevocable)
> Wife's share of shared property and any of her separate property not left to husband.

> **Trust 2** (revocable)
> Husband's share of shared property and any other trust property left to him by wife.

3. Husband, as successor trustee, distributes wife's property to her beneficiaries.

> To wife's beneficiaries (other than husband).

Trust 1 contains the deceased spouse's share of trust property, except any trust property left to the surviving spouse. Trust 1 is irrevocable; that is, the surviving spouse can't change its terms, which dictate what happens to the property in it.

Trust 2, the survivor's trust, contains the surviving spouse's share of the trust property, plus any trust property left to the surviving spouse by the deceased spouse. Trust 2 remains revocable—the surviving spouse can make changes to it during the surviving spouse's lifetime. (See "Revising or Revoking Trust 2" in Chapter 13.)

In many situations, since all property is left to the survivor, nothing need be done at this point. However, if the deceased left property in Trust 1 to others, the surviving spouse, as sole trustee of Trust 1, distributes that property to the named beneficiaries.

The trustee simply hands over the property to the beneficiaries, except for gifts left to minors or young adults in a child's trust or through the Uniform Transfers to Minors Act (UTMA). (See Chapter 8.) If the property is left in a child's trust, the surviving spouse manages that trust for the child until the child reaches the age specified by the deceased spouse in the trust document to receive the property outright. If the property is left to a custodian under the UTMA, the custodian manages the property until the child is old enough to be legally entitled to the property.

When all the property in Trust 1 has been distributed to the beneficiaries, including any property placed in a child's trust, Trust 1 ceases to exist. No formal documents need be prepared or filed to officially end the trust. Once its mission is accomplished, it simply evaporates.

Trust 2 (the survivor's trust) is basically a continuation of the original revocable living trust. As discussed, it contains any trust property the survivor inherited from the deceased spouse, as well as the surviving spouse's share of shared trust property and any separately owned trust property that belongs to the survivor. The surviving spouse is free to change or amend Trust 2 if desired. For example, the surviving spouse might name a new successor trustee or name a new beneficiary for property that was to have gone to the deceased spouse.

EXAMPLE: Harry and Maude, a married couple, set up a shared living trust to avoid probate. In their trust document, they name themselves cotrustees and appoint Maude's brother Al as successor trustee, to take over as trustee after they have both died. They transfer much of their shared ownership property—their house, money market accounts, and stocks—to the living trust. Maude also puts some of her family heirlooms, which are her separate property, in the trust.

The trust document states that Maude's brother Al is to receive the heirlooms when she dies; everything else goes to Harry. Harry leaves all his trust property to Maude. Both name their son, Edward, as alternate and residuary beneficiary. (The residuary beneficiary is the person who receives all property not left to other named beneficiaries. See Chapter 7.)

Maude dies first. The shared living trust splits into Trust 1, which contains Maude's heirlooms, and Trust 2, which contains everything else—Harry's half of the co-owned trust property and the trust property he inherits from Maude. Harry becomes the sole trustee of both trusts.

Following the terms of the trust document, Harry distributes Maude's heirlooms (from Trust 1) to Al, without probate. Trust 1 then ceases to exist. Harry doesn't have to do anything with the trust property Maude left him; it's already in Trust 2, his revocable living trust.

Harry later decides that Al is getting too ill and old to be a wise choice as successor trustee for Harry's trust. So Harry amends his trust, naming Edward to be his successor trustee. (See Chapter 12 for how to amend a living trust.)

With a shared trust, when the second spouse dies, the successor trustee takes over as trustee of Trust 2. This successor trustee is responsible for distributing the surviving spouse's trust property to the surviving spouse's beneficiaries, named in the trust document. If any trust property is left to a young beneficiary in a child's trust, the trustee will also manage it. Again, no formal documents are required to terminate Trust 2.

When a spouse dies, the surviving spouse may need to amend his or her living trust to name new beneficiaries or alternate beneficiaries.

> **EXAMPLE:** Continuing with Harry and Maude, after Maude's death, Harry names his son, Edward, as his trust's beneficiary and residuary beneficiary. Harry needs to name new alternate beneficiaries and chooses Edward's two children.

If your combined estate might be large enough to trigger estate taxes, then continue on to the next section. Otherwise, you can to skip to Chapter 5.

AB Trusts

For years, many prosperous couples used AB trusts to reduce or eliminate federal estate taxes. In fact, this book used to contain information and instructions for creating an AB trust. However, because current federal law now exempts almost all estates from tax, AB trusts are now useless for most couples.

Shrinking Concern About Estate Taxes

In 1993, when this book was first published, the federal personal estate tax exemption was $600,000. An estate would owe federal estate tax if it were larger than that amount. Even if each member's estate was under that amount, many couples did have combined estates reaching that threshold. And because couples often leave their property to each other, the estates of surviving spouses were at risk for owing estate tax when that surviving spouse died.

> **EXAMPLE:** A couple in 1993 had a combined estate worth $900,000. Both leave their property to the survivor. When the first spouse died in 1994, his half of the estate was worth $450,000, well under the personal estate tax exemption. But after receiving the spouse's half of the estate, the surviving spouse then had an estate of $900,000. When that spouse died, $300,000 was subject to estate tax.

The AB trust had a fix for this problem. It allowed the first spouse to die to leave property in a life estate trust. The surviving spouse would have the right to receive all income of the trust and to spend the trust principal for "health, education, support, and maintenance, in accord with the surviving spouse's accustomed manner of living." Crucially, under IRS rules, the property in the AB trust did not become owned by the surviving spouse—that property remained owned by the AB trust. When the surviving spouse died, none of the first-to-die spouse's trust property was added to that surviving spouse's estate.

> **EXAMPLE:** Returning to the example above, if the first spouse to die had left his property worth $450,000 in an AB trust with a life estate for his surviving spouse's benefit, that $450,000 would not be legally inherited by the surviving spouse. She would have been able to use the property in the trust for "health, education, support, and maintenance," but it would not have added to the value of her estate and when she died, her estate would not have owed tax.

While AB trusts worked well for many couples, they did have drawbacks. The property left by the deceased spouse had to be legally separate from the property of the surviving spouse. And AB trusts required ongoing maintenance, like obtaining a taxpayer ID, keeping financial records, and filing an annual tax return.

Since the early 90s, Congress has raised the amount of the estate tax exemption several times. Every time the exemption rose, fewer couples needed an AB trust. Then in 2011, Congress introduced "portability'" into federal estate tax law. Portability allows a surviving spouse to use any unused portion of the first-to-die spouse's exemption. In other words, if the estate of the first-to-die spouse did not use its entire personal estate tax exemption, the estate of the surviving spouse could use it—in addition to the surviving spouse's own personal exemption. Now add in another federal estate tax rule—the longstanding "marital deduction" that allows a spouse to leave any amount of money to a surviving spouse tax free. The use of the marital deduction results in the deceased spouse's using almost none of the personal exemption —$11,700,000 in 2021—which can then be used by the surviving spouse. This combination of tax rules—the rising exemption, portability, and the marital deduction—has rendered AB trusts basically pointless for most couples because most couples do not have estates large enough to owe estate taxes.

> **EXAMPLE:** A couple has a combined estate worth $20 million. The wife dies in 2021, leaving her share of $10 million to her husband. All of that $10 million is exempt from estate tax because of the marital deduction, so the wife has not used any of her personal estate tax exemption. The husband's estate is now worth $20 million. He dies later that year. Because of portability, his estate can use all of his wife's $11.7 million exemption and add it to his own. This makes his total exemption $23.4 million, and his estate will not owe estate tax.

When AB Trusts Might Still Be Useful

In some increasingly rare situations, you may still have use for an AB trust. One reason is to guard against state estate taxes. A few states have estate taxes with exemptions that are lower than the federal exemption. So, if you live in one of those states, your estate could owe state estate tax, even if it is not large enough to owe federal estate tax. In this situation, a married couple could use an AB trust to guard against the state tax. (See Chapter 14 for more about state estate taxes.)

Also, unmarried couples have more use for AB trusts than married couples. The estates of unmarried couples cannot use the marital deduction or portability to lower estate tax liabilities. So unmarried couples who have a combined estate of more than $11 million could use an AB trust to keep the first-to-die spouse's property out of the estate of the surviving spouse.

Finally, tax laws continue to change. So, it's possible that Congress will lower the amount of the personal estate tax exemption or repeal portability. If so, AB trusts could become useful once again.

SEE AN EXPERT

See a lawyer if you want to explore using an AB trust. If you think you might want to use an AB trust, get help from an expert estate planning lawyer. These trusts are now high-end work, so be prepared to pay substantial attorneys' fees.

Choosing What Property to Put in Your Living Trust

Okay, it's time to begin hands-on work. In this chapter, you'll make your initial decisions about what property to put in your trust. You can place any amount of property in your trust. However, some types of property are better suited for living trusts than others. This chapter explains which types of property are best for your living trust, and which types of property should be distributed in another way. (Chapter 14 explains some of those other methods.)

For many people, deciding what property to transfer to a living trust is not a difficult matter. They have one, or a few, "big-ticket" items—for example, a house, some stocks, and a money market account—and they know they want to avoid probate of this property. But for many other people, matters aren't quite so simple. Some have questions about different types of property—say, about personal checking accounts, retirement accounts, or more unusual items such as copyrights or patents. And if you're married, you may need to determine which property is shared in equal amounts and which is the separate property of one spouse.

This chapter:

- discusses types of property you'll probably want to put into your trust
- reviews state marital property laws that can require you to leave property to your spouse, and
- provides a property worksheet you can use to make a thorough inventory of what you own and estimate the net value of your property.

Even if you think you know what property you want to put in your trust, read these materials carefully to be sure your decisions pose no potential problems. Of course, you can always revise your decisions before preparing your actual trust document. The point isn't to lock you in now, but to get you started.

Listing the Property to Be Put in Your Trust

You must list, as part of your trust document, each item of property held in trust. Any property you don't list will not go into your living trust and will not pass under the terms of the trust. It may instead have to go through probate.

A list of trust property is called a "schedule" and is attached to the trust document. (This is explained in detail in Chapter 9.) A trust for one person has only one schedule. A shared trust has up to three schedules. There is one for shared-ownership property, one for any separate property of one spouse, and another for any separate property of the other spouse. If a spouse doesn't have any separate property, you can simply eliminate the appropriate schedule.

> ! CAUTION
>
> **You must transfer title to the trustee.** You must also prepare separate documents formally transferring property ownership to the trust. Property with a document of title—like a deed to a house, or a stock account—must be transferred by preparing and signing a new document of title. You do that by placing title in the trustee's or trustees' name(s), "as trustee(s) for the _____[name]_____ Trust." Property without a document of title—such as household goods, jewelry, and clothes—can be transferred simply by listing them on a trust schedule. Preparing these documents is vital, and is explained in detail in Chapter 10. But for right now, your concern is simply to decide which property you want in the trusts and to write down how you'll list that property.

Many people instinctively think of their trust beneficiaries and property together: The antique dresser goes to Mary, the house will be divided between the kids, and so on. But to be thorough and sure you do the job right, I suggest that you separate these two key elements. Here, list your trust property. Then, in the next chapter, you'll learn about naming your trust beneficiaries.

Adding Property to the Living Trust Later

If you acquire valuable property in your name after you create your living trust, you can easily add it to the trust. Also, once you've set up the trust, if you're buying property you intend to keep for a while, you can simply acquire it in the name of the trustee(s) of your trust. Finally, if you mistakenly leave something out of your trust, you can add it later by amending your trust. (See Chapter 12.)

Property You Should Not Put in Your Living Trust

You don't need to put everything you own into a living trust to save money on probate. Property that is of relatively low value (the amount depends on state law) may be exempt from probate or qualify for a streamlined probate procedure that's relatively fast and cheap. And in some states, at least some of the property left to a surviving spouse can probably be transferred without a full-blown probate court proceeding.

Generally, it's better not to include the following types of property in your trust:

- **Your personal checking account.** Unless you want to pay your bills in the name of the trust, it's usually best not to transfer your checking account into your trust. A checking account in the name of a trust can cause raised eyebrows —even refusal to accept the check— by people or institutions who wonder, "Why can't she write the check in her own name? What's this trust business?"

- **Individual retirement accounts.** Retirement accounts such as IRAs, 401(k)s, 403(b)s, and profit-sharing plans should not be put in your trust. Indeed, for some individual retirement accounts, it's not legal to do so. With a retirement account, you name a beneficiary or beneficiaries to receive any money left in the account at your death, without probate. While you could name your trust as beneficiary of these accounts, there's generally no reason to do so. If you want to name that trust to receive funds left in the accounts when you die, see "Naming Your Living Trust as Beneficiary" on the next page.

- **Automobiles.** Some insurance companies won't insure a vehicle owned by a trust. They worry that an unknown number of people could be entitled, under the terms of the trust, to drive the vehicle. Anyway, the value of many people's car or cars isn't so high that they need to worry about transferring them by living trust. Also, most state motor vehicles departments have special forms that conveniently allow cars to be registered in joint tenancy, a handy way to avoid probate for an auto. And many states—

Arizona, Arkansas, California, Colorado, Connecticut, Delaware, Illinois, Indiana, Kansas, Maryland, Minnesota, Missouri, Nebraska, Nevada, Ohio, Oklahoma, Texas, Vermont, and Virginia—allow "transfer-on-death" vehicle registration, where you name, on your vehicle registration, the person who will receive the vehicle upon your death. No probate is necessary.

But if you own a valuable vehicle, or several, it can be worth your while to seek out an insurance company that will allow you to own and transfer them by living trust. Some insurance companies will insure a vehicle owned by a trust. Indeed, some insurance companies simply list the trust as an "additional insured," with no additional fee or premium.

- **Property you buy or sell frequently.** If you don't expect to own the property at your death, there's no compelling reason to transfer it to your living trust. (Remember, the probate process you want to avoid doesn't happen until after your death.)

- **Cash.** You can't put actual cash, hard currency, in a living trust—you can't put a stack of bills into a document. You can, however, transfer a cash money *account* into a trust, and then you can make cash gifts from that trust.

- **Life insurance.** When you buy an insurance policy, you name beneficiaries to receive the proceeds of the policy outside of probate. However, if you want a minor or young adult to be the beneficiary of an insurance policy, you need to name an adult to manage the proceeds in case the insurance is paid out before the beneficiary is a legal adult. One way to accomplish this is to create a child's trust as part of your living trust and then name the trustee as the beneficiary of your life insurance. If the trustee receives the proceeds while the young beneficiary is still a minor, the trustee manages that money for the beneficiary through the trust. If the young beneficiary is old enough to be entitled to receive trust property outright, the trustee can simply give the beneficiary the money. (This is covered in detail in Chapter 8.)

Naming Your Living Trust as Beneficiary of Your Retirement Account

If you have substantial assets in an individual retirement account, you may want those funds to go to your living trust when you die. The usual reason for this is that you want any leftover individual retirement account funds to be distributed according to your trust's beneficiary plan. You can legally do this. But there are some major concerns that you need to consider before deciding to do it.

The first issue is that an individual retirement account is a "wasting asset" (except for a Roth IRA). This means that once you reach age 72 (or 70 ½ for those who turned 70 before July 1, 2019), you must withdraw a certain percentage of your account each year. The withdrawal percentage is calculated on the basis of your statistical life expectancy. (The IRS determines the withdrawal percentage by using what it calls the "Uniform Lifetime Table.") So, if you live a long life, most or all of the funds in your account will have been withdrawn.

Still, you may understandably be concerned with what happens to your retirement account if you die prematurely, or if, for whatever reason, significant funds remain in the account at your death. You can leave these funds to your trust by naming the trust as beneficiary of your account.

You will need to consider how the money will be withdrawn after your death. If all the money in the account will be promptly withdrawn and distributed to beneficiaries, there's no problem. But if a surviving spouse inherits money from an individual retirement account, it can be income tax desirable to take the money out of that account over a period of years. Under IRS rules, there's a required minimum yearly withdrawal. If your spouse is the sole beneficiary of the account and more than ten years younger than you, the required withdrawal rules are calculated on the life expectancies of both you and your spouse. (The IRS determines this withdrawal percentage using what it calls the "Joint Life and Last Survivor Tables.")

Also, if you are considering naming your living trust as the beneficiary of your IRA and that trust has multiple beneficiaries, you should be aware that the IRS rules base the mandatory annual withdrawal for each beneficiary on the oldest beneficiary's life expectancy, which can be undesirable for younger beneficiaries. You may want to name several individual beneficiaries for your IRA, rather than leave that IRA to your trust. That way each beneficiary's mandatory annual withdrawal is based on his or her own life expectancy.

> **SEE AN EXPERT**
>
> **Get expert help before naming your living trust as the beneficiary of your retirement account.** There can be significant financial risks to your beneficiaries if you name your living trust as the beneficiary of your retirement account. If you're wrestling with this issue, get the help of a knowledgeable lawyer or accountant.

However, if you do this and your spouse is more than ten years younger than you, you lose the ability to make withdrawals based on both your life expectancies. Also, if you named your living trust as your retirement account beneficiary, your surviving spouse (if there is one) loses valuable rights to roll over your retirement account fund into the spouse's own account without penalties.

There may be additional paperwork or hassle to complete to validly name your trust as beneficiary of your retirement plan. For example:

- Federal law requires that all funds in a 401(k) or 403(b) plan be left outright to a surviving spouse unless that spouse has given a written waiver of that right.
- 401(k)s and some other retirement plans must adopt an amendment allowing life expectancy, for withdrawal purposes, to be calculated on the basis of the plan owner and the oldest trust beneficiary. The IRS can supply you with a model amendment form.
- Retirement accounts purchased with community property are co-owned equally by both spouses. You may need a written declaration of gift from your spouse.

A thorough explanation of the applicable laws and rules can be found in *IRAs, 401(k)s & Other Retirement Plans: Strategies for Taking Your Money Out*, by Twila Slesnick and John C. Suttle (Nolo).

- **Joint tenancy property.** Property held in joint tenancy does not go through probate, as is explained in Chapter 14. So, generally, there is no need to worry about transferring jointly owned property, including joint bank accounts, into your living trust. However, one possible reason for transferring jointly owned property to the trust is that you cannot name alternate beneficiaries for joint tenancy property. If all owners die simultaneously, each owner's share of the joint tenancy property passes under their will. While you could eliminate this remote possibility by transferring your share to your living trust, making the transfer requires a couple of paper steps that are at least a bit of a hassle (See "Paperwork" in Chapter 10.) Most people understandably don't bother with this level of contingency planning.

- **Pay-on-death bank accounts.** With these accounts, you name a beneficiary or beneficiaries to receive directly, without probate, all funds in the accounts when you die. (See Chapter 14.)

- **Investment and financial accounts.** With financial and investment accounts, you have a choice. You can transfer those accounts into your trust (technically, to yourself as trustee of your trust) or you can name your trust as beneficiary of the account. Use whatever method is easiest and works best for you. With either option, each financial institution holding your account will likely want a copy of your trust. If you don't want to reveal the full contents of your trust to financial institutions, you can give them a "certification of trust" (sometimes called an "abstract of trust") which legally establishes the existence of your trust but omits the personal elements—your property, your beneficiaries, and your successor trustees. See "Certifications of Trust" in Chapter 10.

- **Transfer-on-death real estate deeds.** In many states, you can use a deed to name a beneficiary for real estate. Upon your death, the real estate will be transferred to the beneficiary free of probate. States which allow this are: Alaska, Arizona, Arkansas, California, Colorado, District of Columbia, Hawaii, Illinois, Indiana, Kansas, Maine, Minnesota, Missouri, Montana, Nebraska, Nevada, New Mexico, North Dakota, Ohio, Oklahoma, Oregon, South Dakota, Texas, Utah, Virginia, Washington, West Virginia, Wisconsin, and Wyoming.

  A transfer-on-death deed can work well if you want to name a single beneficiary for your real estate. However, if you want to name multiple beneficiaries or alternate beneficiaries, these deeds do not work as well—use another probate-avoidance tool.

- **Community property with right of survivorship.** Alaska, Arizona, California, Idaho, Nevada, and Wisconsin expressly authorize spouses to own community property in this manner.

- **Digital assets.** You may want to consider planning for what will happen to your digital assets when you die. Digital assets include online accounts as well as files that you store on your computer, in online accounts, or in the cloud. Many digital assets—such as email and social media accounts—aren't property that you can leave to beneficiaries through a living trust or will. However, you may own digital music, digital photos, domain licenses, or other digital assets that could be passed to beneficiaries. You will have to figure this out on a case-by-case basis, looking closely at your account, ownership, or licensing agreements to determine whether the item is transferable. That said, unless a digital asset has significant financial value, it's usually not wise to try to transfer that asset to your living trust or to mention it in your will. Provisions for digital assets can become outdated quickly. Further, it's unclear whether service providers will respect the provisions of a trust or will that transfer ownership of digital assets. In any case, consider leaving instructions for your digital assets for the people who will be wrapping up your estate. They will appreciate having login and password information to access and close your accounts, and you may also want to leave instructions about what to do with your email accounts, memberships, or social media accounts. If you do leave login information and instructions, do it in a separate letter—not in your will or living trust—and store it with your other estate planning documents.

- **Employee stock options.** Some businesses give, or allow employees to purchase, options to buy stock of the company for a set price. Often the company imposes restrictions or prohibitions on employee transfers of the options. Even if the company allows transfer to a living trust, complex IRS rules govern the exercise of this type of stock option and subsequent sale of the stock. Because of these rules, it is normally not a good idea to transfer employee stock options to your living trust. By contrast, you can transfer stock options bought on a recognized stock exchange—for instance, the right to buy 1,000 shares of Apple Inc. for a set price. This contractual right may be transferred to your living trust by Notice of Assignment. (See "Securities" in Chapter 10.) Indeed, if you trade frequently in publicly traded options, you can open an option account in the trust's name.

SEE AN EXPERT

If you decide you must transfer employee stock options to your trust. If you want to transfer employee stock options to your living trust, you'll need a lawyer who's up to date on the complex tax rules, including capital gains tax, that govern the transaction.

- **Contaminated real estate.** Do not transfer to your trust any real estate you know, or suspect, has been chemically polluted.
- **Income or principal from a trust.** If you are the beneficiary of an established trust and have the right to leave any of your interest in this trust to someone else, you cannot do that in your own living trust. The reason is that you cannot transfer title of the trust that benefits you into your own living trust, because you are not the owner of the trust. Your trust cannot give away what it doesn't technically own. You can

leave your rights to this type of trust income property by your will. (See Chapter 15.)

- **Annuities.** Generally you name a beneficiary or beneficiaries in the annuity policy contract. These beneficiaries receive any money in the account when you die, outside of probate.

Property You Can Put in Your Living Trust

Whatever type of trust you create with this book, the primary goal is avoiding probate fees. As a general rule, the more an item is worth, the more it will cost to probate it. That means you should transfer at least your most valuable property items to your living trust—or use some other probate-avoidance device to leave them at your death. Think about including:

- houses and other real estate
- small business interests, including stock in closely held corporations
- money market accounts
- other financial accounts
- stocks, bonds, and other security accounts held by brokers
- royalties, patents, and copyrights
- valuable jewelry, antiques, furs, and furniture
- precious metals
- valuable works of art, and
- valuable collections of stamps, coins, or other objects.

SEE AN EXPERT

Property on which you owe money. Some items of property are commonly not owned free and clear. The most obvious example is a house with a mortgage. When you use your living trust to leave that house to a beneficiary, the beneficiary will receive it subject to the mortgage. Similarly, if you give someone a car subject to a loan and lien, those debts go with the car.

If you have sufficient assets, it's legally possible to use your trust to provide that these debts be paid off. That way, the beneficiary receives a house, car, or other previously debt-encumbered property free and clear. See a lawyer if you want to arrange this.

Real Estate

The most valuable thing most people own is their real estate—their house, condominium, or land. Other types of real estate include property such as a boat marina dock space or a time-share interest in a piece of property, like a vacation house or apartment used twice a year. You can save your beneficiaries substantial probate costs by transferring your real estate through a living trust.

If you own real estate in joint tenancy or tenancy by the entirety, however, you've already arranged to avoid probate for that property, so there's much less reason to transfer it to a living trust. (See Chapter 14.) One advantage of owning real estate in a living trust is that, in a living trust, you can provide for who will receive the real estate in the event that both owners die at the same time. You cannot provide for this with real estate owned in joint tenancy.

If You're Not Sure How You Hold Title

If you own real estate with someone else but aren't sure how the title is held, look at the deed. It should say how the title is held:

- in joint tenancy (sometimes abbreviated JT or JTWROS, for "joint tenancy with right of survivorship")
- tenancy in common
- community property (in community property states; in a community property state, if the deed says the property is owned "as husband and wife," that means community property)
- community property with right of survivorship, or
- tenancy by the entirety.

If it's not clear to you how the title is held, get help from a title company or an attorney.

If you own real estate with someone else, you can transfer only your interest in it to your living trust.

Co-op apartments. If you own shares in a co-op building, you'll need approval from the co-op board to transfer your ownership to your living trust. This may prove challenging, as some co-ops are reluctant to allow a trust—even a living trust controlled by the grantor—to be an owner. First check the co-op's bylaws and rules, to see if they provide any guidance, then work with the board to provide whatever it requires to allow the transfer.

> ! CAUTION
>
> **Retirement co-ops.** Occasionally, an unfortunate technicality is used to deny transfer to a living trust. For instance, some co-op retirement units restrict ownership to people older than a certain age, say 65 or 70. In a few instances, co-op boards have interpreted these rules to prohibit transfer to a trustee of a living trust, claiming that the trust doesn't have an age. While correct, this should be irrelevant. As you know by now, it is not the trust that is the technical owner, but the trustee of the trust. Here, that's the grantor, the person older than 65 or 70 who lives in the co-op. If the IRS can understand that the living trust has no independent legal existence as long as the person who created it is alive, co-op officials should be able to comprehend that, too.

Mobile homes. The rules on when an attached mobile home becomes "real estate" vary in different states. If this matters to you, see a lawyer or look up your state's law. (Legal research is discussed in Chapter 16.)

Time-shares. A time-share is usually an interest in a vacation property, often a condominium. The time-share gives the owner the exclusive right to stay in the property for specific time periods. Technically, ownership of a time-share may be held by deed, contract, or lease. (Sometimes terms such as "vacation license" or "time-share ownership" are used.) If the ownership is by deed, a new deed needs to be prepared transferring the interest to your trust. (If ownership is listed as "vacation license" or "time-share ownership" you'll need to find out if that type of ownership is considered an interest in real estate under state law. If it is, you need to make the transfer by deed.) If ownership of the time-share is held by contract or lease, that contract or lease should be assigned to the trust.

> 💼 SEE AN EXPERT
>
> **Help with transferring a lease.** If you want to transfer your interest in a lease to your living trust, get help from a local attorney. An experienced attorney will be able to advise you on the custom in your state.

Homeowner's Insurance

Don't bother notifying your homeowner's insurance company that you have placed your home in your living trust. As I've explained, as long as you live, you personally are, for all real-world purposes including the IRS and homestead rights, the owner of your home. Your homeowner's policy will still cover your home. But if you tell your insurance company about the transfer, they might raise problems and questions that you'll have to waste time answering. Don't risk the hassles.

Small Business Interests

The delay, expense, and court intrusion of probate can be especially detrimental to an ongoing small business. Using your living trust to transfer business interests to beneficiaries quickly after your death is almost essential if you want the beneficiaries to be able to keep the business running, or even to be able to sell it for a fair price.

SEE AN EXPERT

Controlling management of a business. If you want to impose controls on the long-term management of your business, a revocable living trust is not the right device. See an estate planning lawyer to draft a different kind of trust, with provisions tailored to your situation.

Different kinds of business organizations present different issues when you want to transfer your interest to your living trust.

Sole proprietorships. If you operate your business as a sole proprietorship, with all business assets held in your own name, you can simply transfer your business property to your living trust as you would any other property. You should also list the business's name itself on a trust schedule; that transfers the customer goodwill associated with the name.

Partnership interests. If you operate your business as a partnership with other people, you can probably transfer your partnership share to your living trust. If there is a partnership certificate, it must be changed to show the trust, or you as trustee, as owner of your share.

Some partnership agreements require the people who inherit a deceased partner's share of the business to sell that share to the other partners if they want it. But that happens after death, so it shouldn't affect your ability to transfer the property through a living trust.

It's not common, but a partnership agreement may limit or forbid transfers to a living trust. If yours does, you and your partners may want to see a lawyer before you make any changes. If the other partners won't agree to revise your partnership agreement to allow this transfer, you're stuck.

Solely owned corporations. If you own all the stock of a corporation, you should have no difficulty transferring it to your living trust. All you need do is prepare the appropriate corporate papers—for example, Notice of Meeting of Shareholders, and Resolution of Shareholders (there's only one, remember)—authorizing the transfer of the shares of stock to the living trust. The precise corporate paperwork needed depends on what's required by your articles of incorporation and the bylaws of your corporation.

Closely held corporations, including limited liability companies (LLCs). A closely held corporation is a corporation that doesn't sell shares to the public. A limited liability company is akin to the closely held corporation, except that it is treated as a partnership for tax purposes. All shares or ownership interests are owned by a few people who are usually actively involved in running the business. Normally, you can use a living trust to transfer your interest in an LLC or shares in a closely held corporation by listing the interest or stock in the trust document. With the stock, the certificates must be reissued in the trustee's name.

You'll want to check the corporation's bylaws and articles of incorporation to be sure that if you transfer the shares to a living trust, you will still have voting rights in your capacity as trustee of the living trust; usually, this is not a problem. If it is, you and the other shareholders should be able to amend the corporation's bylaws to allow it.

There may, however, be legal restrictions on your freedom to transfer your shares to a living trust. Check the corporation's bylaws and articles of incorporation, as well as any separate shareholders' agreements or, for LLCs, the operating agreement.

One fairly common rule is that surviving shareholders or LLC owners have the right to buy the shares of a deceased shareholder or owner. In that case, you can still use a living trust to transfer the shares or LLC interest, but the people who inherit them may have to sell them to the other shareholders or owners.

SEE AN EXPERT

Get help with Subchapter S or professional corporations. Special IRS rules apply if you want to transfer shares in a Subchapter S corporation to a living trust. The trust must contain special provisions that make it a "qualified" Subchapter S trust under IRS regulations. To make sure your trust has the right language for your S corp shares, get help from an attorney.

Money Market and Bank Accounts

Money market funds can be readily transferred into your trust. Often, these money market funds contain substantial amounts of cash, so it's wise to place them in your living trust.

It's not difficult to hold bank accounts or credit union accounts (aside from your personal checking account) in your living trust. But you may well decide that you don't need to, because there's another easy way to avoid probate of the funds. With a "pay-on-death" account (sometimes called a Totten Trust, or a "revocable trust account"), you can designate a beneficiary for the funds in a bank account. The beneficiary receives whatever is in your account at your death, without probate.

If you want to put a certificate of deposit (CD) in your trust, check with the issuing bank to see if it will allow the transfer. Some will, and many will not. Your bank may refuse the transfer by claiming that for even technical ownership of a CD to change, it must have matured, and that an early transfer will cost you a penalty. In that case, you can only wait

until the CD matures, and change title to it when or if you roll it over.

Naming Your Living Trust as Beneficiary of a Financial Account

You can name your living trust as the beneficiary of any pay-on-death account, including bank accounts and securities accounts registered in transfer-on-death form. That is often easier than formally transferring ownership of that account (or accounts) into your name as trustee of your trust. However, even to name your trust as the account beneficiary, the financial institution involved may require that you provide a copy of the trust document or a certification of trust.

Stocks and Securities

Stocks and stock accounts can be held in living trusts. Brokerage companies are familiar with living trusts; you can readily transfer an existing stockbrokerage account into your living trust, or create a new trust account. Once your account is in your trust's name (technically, in your name as trustee for your trust), all stocks in that account become owned by the trust, so you can trade as often as you want without additional trust paperwork.

Some financial institutions require that you provide them with a copy of your living trust in order to transfer ownership of the account into the trust or trustee's name. If you are (understandably) reluctant or unwilling to allow employees of financial institutions to read the personal specifics of your trust, you can show them a certification of trust instead of your entire trust document. A certification of trust is a short version of the trust that omits personal details but is legally acceptable proof of a trust's existence. Most states have specific statutes governing what must be in a certification. See Chapter 10 for a list of state statutes and more information on how to use a certification.

In your living trust, you can leave your brokerage accounts however you desire—all to one person, divided by percentage between several people, or specific stocks to specific people.

If you have personal possession of individual stock certificates, you need to get new certificates issued, listing the new owner as trustee of your trust. (See Chapter 10.)

An Alternative: Transfer-On-Death Registration

Every state except Texas allows ownership of securities to be registered in a "transfer-on-death" form. This allows you to designate someone, or your trust, to receive the securities, including mutual funds and brokerage accounts, after your death. No probate will be necessary.

If you have many beneficiaries, it may be best to name your living trust as the beneficiary of your financial accounts. Doing this simplifies your work because instead of naming multiple beneficiaries for each account, you just name your trust as the single beneficiary for each financial account. Then on the property schedule of the trust document, you list "All funds received by the trust as beneficiary of the accounts owned by [*the owner's name*] at the following financial institutions." And in the beneficiary section of the trust document, you name beneficiaries for these accounts and indicate what each beneficiary will receive, defined by dollar amounts, percentages, or some combination of both.

Here is a variation of this for couples: Each member of the couple can name the other as the beneficiary for the couple's financial accounts and then name the trust as the alternate beneficiary to receive the accounts if the other member of the couple is no longer alive.

Cash Accounts

It's common for people to want to leave cash to beneficiaries—for example, to leave $5,000 to a relative, friend, or charity. To accomplish this, you can transfer ownership of a cash account—a savings account, money market account, or certificate of deposit, for example—to your living trust. (Don't transfer a pay-on-death account, since the beneficiary for it is already named.) Then, in the trust document, you can name a beneficiary to receive the contents of the account or any specified sum from it. So if you want to leave $5,000 to cousin Fred, you can put this amount in a bank or money market account, transfer it to your living trust, and name Fred, in the trust document, as the beneficiary. Or you could put an account with a larger amount in your trust, and leave $5,000 from it to Fred and the balance to another beneficiary.

> **EXAMPLE:** Michael would like to leave some modest cash gifts to his two grown nephews, Warren and Brian, whom he's always been fond of. He puts $25,000 into a money market account and then transfers the account into his living trust. In his trust document, he names Warren and Brian as beneficiaries of $5,000 each from that, with whatever is left to go to Michael's wife. After Michael's death, the two nephews will each receive $5,000 from the trust.

If you don't want to set up an account to leave a modest amount of cash to a beneficiary, think about buying a savings bond and leaving it to the beneficiary.

U.S. Treasury Notes or Bonds

You can place U.S. Treasury bonds—such as series EE bonds, I bonds, or other treasury securities—in your living trust. There are no adverse tax consequences. The federal government requires that a specific form be used to make the transfer into the trust. (See Chapter 10.)

Royalties, Copyrights, and Patents

You can transfer your right to future royalties, or copyrights and patents you own, to your living trust. Simply list the royalty, copyright, or patent in your trust property schedule and then transfer your interest in a copyright, patent, or royalty to the trust using the proper legal form. (Instructions are in Chapter 10.)

> **SEE AN EXPERT**
> **Oil, gas, or mineral interests.** If you want to transfer one or more of these interests to your living trust, see a lawyer. Complicated matters, such as possible assignment of leases or handling depletion allowances, can arise that require professional attention.

Other Valuable Property

Many other types of valuable property can also be placed in your trust, including jewelry, antiques, furs, furniture, precious metals, works of art, and collectibles.

The common denominator of all these types of property is that none of them has any formal ownership papers, like a deed for real estate. Some may have papers authenticating them, but these are not documents of title and don't need to be changed. So you can transfer any of these valuables to your trust simply by listing them on the trust schedule. You may also want to prepare an "assignment" form for this property, as is explained in "Paperwork" in Chapter 10.

You need special forms to transfer some types of valuable property to your trust. For example, because all airplanes must be registered with the FAA, you transfer an airplane to your trust by complying with appropriate FAA regulations and forms. Similarly, for large boats registered with the Coast Guard, you need to complete that agency's forms. And for powerboats registered with a state agency, you need the appropriate state form. Less valuable boats—unregistered ones, like a rowboat or canoe—do not have documents of title and can simply be assigned to your trust. (See Chapter 10.)

Marital Property Laws

If you are married, you need to know what property is owned by each spouse separately and what property is held in shared ownership to properly complete your trust. Whether you make separate trusts (because most or all of each spouse's property is owned separately) or a shared trust, you need to clarify which spouse owns what to know which schedule—shared or individual—to list the property on. Each spouse controls, in the trust document, who will inherit his or her own trust property.

To figure out who owns what, you need to know a little about the law of the state where you live (and of any other state in which you own property) regarding marital property. Marital property laws can be divided into two basic groups: community property states and common law states.

Community Property States

Community Property States		
Arizona	Louisiana	Texas
California*	Nevada	Washington*
Idaho	New Mexico	Wisconsin

* Registered domestic partners are also covered by community property laws.

Alaska, South Dakota, and Tennessee allow a married couple to make a written agreement stating that they wish certain property to be treated as community property. (See a lawyer if you want to make this kind of agreement.)

In these states, the general rule is that spouses own everything acquired during the marriage 50-50 unless the spouses agree otherwise. It doesn't matter whose name is on the title slip.

There are a few important exceptions to the general rule. Property acquired before marriage is not community property; it is the separate property of that spouse. Likewise, property given to one spouse, by gift or inheritance, is separate property.

Typically, most property owned by spouses is community property, especially if the couple have been married for a number of years. For example, if while married you bought real estate with money you earned during marriage, your spouse legally owns a half interest in it unless you both signed an agreement keeping it separate.

Community Property Basics	
Community property includes:	Separate property includes:
• money either spouse earns during marriage	• property owned by one spouse before marriage
• things bought with that money, and	• property given to just one spouse, and
• separate property that has become so mixed (commingled) with community property that it can't be identified.	• property inherited by just one spouse.

Married couples living in community property states don't have to accept these rules. They can sign a written agreement that makes community property the separate property of one spouse or that makes separate property become community property.

Sometimes it's not obvious who owns what. For example, are life insurance proceeds shared property or the separate property of the deceased spouse? The answer depends on the source of the funds used to pay for the insurance and the intention of the couple. If the insurance was paid for with shared marital property, the proceeds are co-owned. Similarly, if the couple agreed (in writing) that the proceeds were shared property, no matter who paid for them, that agreement controls. But if the policy was paid for from the separate property of the deceased, with no agreement that it was a shared ownership policy, the proceeds are the separate property of the deceased.

SEE AN EXPERT

Marital property agreements. If you and your spouse have complex property holdings, and there's any question whether any of your property is community or separate, it's wise to prepare a written marital property agreement, defining the nature of each major item of your property. Of course, to prepare the document, you two have to agree how your property should be classified. If you need help with that, see a lawyer or an accountant.

Agreements About Community Property

In all community property states, married couples can choose to turn separate property into community property—this normally must be done in writing. Further, although Alaska, South Dakota, and Tennessee are not community property states, married couples who live in those states can choose to hold property as community property.

Most community property states also allow married couples to make an agreement that leaves all community property to the surviving spouse without probate. These agreements are often called "community property agreements" or CPAs.

In some states, you can use a CPA to accomplish both tasks—that is, to agree that certain property (1) is community property, and (2) should pass to the surviving spouse without probate.

If you want to make a community property agreement, get help from an experienced attorney in your state.

If you move from a common law state to California, Idaho, Washington, or Wisconsin, some of your property may be reclassified as community property. In these states, the rule is that property acquired by a couple during marriage, no matter who owned it in a common law state, is treated as community property, owned equally by each spouse, if it would have been

Uncertain Marital Statuses

Most people are quite certain whether or not they're married. If you're not sure, here's what you need to know.

The divorce decree. You're not divorced until you have a final decree of divorce (or dissolution, as it's called in some states) issued by a state court in the United States.

If you think you're divorced but never saw the final decree, contact the court clerk in the county where you think the divorce was granted. Give the clerk your name, your ex-spouse's name, and the date, as close as you know it, of the divorce.

Legal separation. Even if a court has declared you and your spouse legally separated, and you plan to divorce, you are still married until you get the divorce decree.

Foreign divorces. Divorces issued to U.S. citizens by courts in Mexico, the Dominican Republic, or another country may not be valid if challenged, especially if all the paperwork was handled by mail. In other words, if you or your spouse got a quickie foreign divorce, you may well be still married under the laws of your state. If you think that someone might make a claim to some of your property after your death based on the invalidity of a foreign divorce, see a lawyer.

Common law marriages. In some states, a couple can become legally married by living together, intending to be married, and presenting themselves to the world as a married couple. Even in states that allow such common law marriages, most couples who live together don't have common law marriages. If you really do have a valid common law marriage, you must go to court and get a divorce to end it—there's no such thing as a common law divorce.

Common law marriages can be created in Alabama, Colorado, District of Columbia, Iowa, Kansas, Montana, Rhode Island, Texas, and Utah. (Another handful of states recognize common law marriages created under laws that have since been repealed.) When a couple legally creates a common law marriage and then moves to another state, the couple is still legally married.

Same-sex couples. Now that same-sex marriage is legal in every state, knowing your marital status and understanding what it means is less complicated than it used to be:

- If you are legally married, you're married in every state in the United States and you have the same rights and obligations as any other American married couple.
- If you haven't married or registered your relationship as a domestic partnership, civil union, or reciprocal beneficiary relationship, then you are unmarried.
- If you've registered your relationship, then things might be less clear. Some states continue to recognize and offer relationship registration for same-sex (and different-sex) couples. But others have eliminated those laws and have converted those relationships to marriage. If you are uncertain about the legal status of your marriage or partnership (or if you're unclear about what rights and obligations your marriage or partnership provides), see an attorney for help. A lawyer who specializes in same-sex estate planning in your state will help you sort things out.

If you're confused about your marital status, see a local family law lawyer to help you sort it out.

community property had the couple acquired it in one of these states. The legal term for such property is "quasi-community property." This means each spouse owns half of this property and can leave only that share at death. Wisconsin has a similar concept, called "deferred marital property." When one spouse dies, the survivor is entitled to half the value of deferred marital property owned by both spouses.

EXAMPLE: Cora and Eric Gustafson live in Florida, a common law state. Cora buys some stocks with money she earned while married. She owns the stocks in her own name and is free to leave them by will or trust to whomever she pleases, subject to state law on the inheritance rights of spouses.

Later, Cora and Eric move to California. Because the stocks would have been Cora and Eric's community property if they had been bought in California, they are now "quasi-community property." At death or divorce, the stocks will be treated as community property, owned 50-50 by each spouse. Cora now owns only half and can leave only half in her trust or will.

However, if you move from a community property state to a common law state, your ownership rights in the property already acquired stay the same. The new state's law applies only to property acquired in the new state.

In community property states, separate property may turn into community property if it is mixed ("commingled") with community property. For example, if you deposit separate property funds into a joint bank account and then make more deposits and withdrawals, making it impossible to tell what part of the account is separate money, it's all considered community property.

EXAMPLE: Roberto and Celia live in Nevada, a community property state. They have been married for 20 years. Except for some bonds that Celia inherited from her parents, virtually all their valuable property—house, stocks, car— is owned together. The money they brought to the marriage in separate bank accounts has long since been mixed with community property, making it community property too.

In community property states, there are restrictions on one spouse's freedom to transfer community property. Especially in the case of real estate, the consent of both spouses is necessary for either to sell or give away his or her half-interest in the property. Each spouse can, however, leave his or her half-interest in the property through a will or living trust.

If you live in a community property state, and you and your spouse create a living trust together, property you transfer to the trust will stay community property, even though it is technically owned by the living trust. Separately owned property (property of only one spouse) will also remain separate property. That means that community property transferred to a living trust is still eligible for the favorable tax treatment given community property at one spouse's death. (Both halves of community property left to the surviving spouse get a "stepped-up basis" for income tax purposes; see "Will Property in My Living Trust Get a 'Stepped-Up' Tax Basis When I Die?" in Chapter 3.)

It also means that if either spouse revokes the living trust, ownership of the property will go back to the spouses as it was before the property was transferred to the living trust. Community property goes back to both spouses equally, and separate property goes to the spouse who owned it before ownership was transferred to the trust.

Common Law Property States

Alabama	Kentucky	North Dakota
Alaska	Maine	Ohio
Arkansas	Maryland	Oklahoma
Colorado	Massachusetts	Oregon
Connecticut	Michigan	Pennsylvania
Delaware	Minnesota	Rhode Island
District of Columbia	Mississippi	South Carolina
Florida	Missouri	South Dakota
Georgia	Montana	Tennessee
Hawaii	Nebraska	Utah
Illinois	New Hampshire	Vermont
Indiana	New Jersey	Virginia
Iowa	New York	West Virginia
Kansas	North Carolina	Wyoming

In these states, it's usually fairly easy for spouses to keep track of who owns what. The spouse whose name is on the title document—for example, the deed, brokerage account paper, or title slip—owns it. In these states, if the property doesn't have a title document, it belongs to the spouse who paid for it or received it as a gift. It's possible, though, that if there were a dispute about ownership, a judge could determine, based on the circumstances, that a spouse whose name is not on the title document might own an interest in the property.

Tennessee's Joint Revocable Trust

Tennessee law now allows spouses to create a "joint revocable trust" which turns all their assets into community property held in that trust. Before creating this type of trust, you'll need to consider the benefits and disadvantages of doing so. Consult a Tennessee lawyer who is familiar with this type of trust to learn more.

It's increasingly common for couples, especially if they are older and have children from a prior marriage, to sign an agreement (before or during the marriage) to own property separately. Or they may not make a formal agreement, but carefully avoid mixing their property together.

If you want to co-own property equally, you can do that simply by taking title to property in both names for new property, or preparing a new ownership deed for previously owned property, listing the new owners as both of you. You should also state you own the property "equally, as tenants in common" if you intend to place the property in your living trusts. (For married couples, no state taxes will be assessed because of any transfer of title, because any transfer of property between spouses is free of tax.)

SEE AN EXPERT

n common law states, see a lawyer if you don't want to leave at least half of your living trust property to your spouse. This matter is discussed further in "Disinheritance" in Chapter 7.

Completing the Property Worksheet

On the worksheet in this section, you can list all of your property. This groundwork should make preparing your actual trust document easier. But completing it is not mandatory; use it if you think it will help you.

Even if you plan to leave everything to your spouse or children, you need to describe your property sufficiently on a trust schedule so that it is readily identifiable. In other words, every item (or group of items, in some circumstances) must be specifically described and listed as part of the trust document. (Examples are given in Chapter 9.)

You can list assets that will not be transferred to your living trust, such as retirement accounts, cars, and life insurance policies. Listing all of your property here will help you estimate your net worth, to see if your estate could be subject to estate taxes.

Remember, this worksheet is purely for your convenience. It can be as messy or as neat as you care to make it. Pencil is recommended (unless you're the type who does *The New York Times* crossword puzzle in ink).

You can also download an electronic version of the property worksheet from this book's companion page: www.nolo.com/back-of-book/LITR.html. (See Appendix A.)

Section I: Assets

Column 1—Property Description

Here you write out what you own. How specific you should be depends in part on how you plan to leave your property (who your beneficiaries are), which you'll pin down in Chapter 7. For example, if you're going to leave all of your books to your daughter, there's no need to list them individually. But if you own several rare first editions that you'll leave to separate beneficiaries, list each book.

Column 2—Net Value of Your Ownership

In Column 2, estimate the net value of each item listed. "Net value" means your equity in your share of the property—the market value of your share, less your share of any debts on that share, such as a mortgage on a house or the loan amount due on a car.

If you're a couple, "your share" means the value of both of your interests.

Obviously, listing net values for your property means making estimates. That's fine; there's no need to burden yourself with seeking precise figures. After all, your death taxes, if any, will be based on the net value of your property when you die, not its current worth. For example, if you think the net worth of your house, after you subtract the mortgage, is about $200,000, your car $5,000, and your stamp collection would fetch $2,000 if you put an ad in a philatelists' journal, use those numbers.

If you own property with someone other than a spouse or mate, simply estimate the worth of your share of that property.

> **EXAMPLE:** Paul owns a house with a market value of $380,000 as a tenant in common with his sister Ava; each owns half. Paul computes the net value of his share by first subtracting the amount of mortgages, liens, and past-due taxes from the market value to arrive at the total equity in the property. There's a $100,000 mortgage and a $20,000 lien against the property. The total equity, then, is $380,000 minus $120,000, or $260,000. The net worth of Paul's half of the property is $130,000.

With some common sense, you can probably safely make sensible estimates yourself. Only with more complex types of property, such as business interests, might you want expert help.

> **EXAMPLE:** Stacey is sole owner of the Maltese Falcon Restaurant, a successful business she has run for 20 years. She has only a vague notion of its market value, since she has never been interested in selling it. Making a reasonable estimate of the worth of the business is difficult, since the market value of her restaurant includes the intangible of "goodwill." Stacey talks to an accountant to help her arrive at a sensible estimate of the worth of the restaurant.

Column 3—Who Owns It

Because you need to identify which property is shared and which is separate, indicate that here. Use whatever symbols you want to identify the ownership—for example, O (ours); H (Husband); W (Wife); S (shared); M (Mary); N (Neil).

Column 4—Transfer to Trust

In Column 4, indicate whether you want to transfer this item of property to the trust. For each item you'll put in the trust, put a "T."

Section II: Liabilities

Here, list any liabilities (debts) you haven't already taken into account in Section I. For example, list any significant personal debts—the $10,000 loan from a friend or the $5,000 unsecured advance on a line of credit. Also list all other liabilities, such as tax liens or court judgments, and add up all these liabilities.

Section III: Net Worth

Here's where you calculate your net worth by subtracting your total liabilities (Section II.D) from the total net value of your assets (Section I.G).

Property Worksheet

I. Assets

Description of Your Property	Net Value of Your Ownership	Who Owns It	Transfer to Trust?

A. Liquid Assets

   1. Cash

   2. Savings accounts

   3. Checking accounts

   4. Money market accounts

B. Marketable Securities

   1. Certificates of deposit

   2. Treasury bills or notes

Description of Your Property	Net Value of Your Ownership	Who Owns It	Transfer to Trust?
3. Government bonds and securities			
_____	_____	_____	_____
_____	_____	_____	_____
_____	_____	_____	_____
_____	_____	_____	_____
_____	_____	_____	_____
_____	_____	_____	_____
4. Listed stocks and bonds			
_____	_____	_____	_____
_____	_____	_____	_____
_____	_____	_____	_____
_____	_____	_____	_____
_____	_____	_____	_____
_____	_____	_____	_____
_____	_____	_____	_____
_____	_____	_____	_____
_____	_____	_____	_____
_____	_____	_____	_____
_____	_____	_____	_____
_____	_____	_____	_____
_____	_____	_____	_____

C. Other Personal Property (all your property except liquid assets, business interests, and real estate)

1. Automobiles and other vehicles, including planes, boats, and recreational vehicles

_____	_____	_____	_____
_____	_____	_____	_____
_____	_____	_____	_____
_____	_____	_____	_____

2. Household goods

_____	_____	_____	_____
_____	_____	_____	_____
_____	_____	_____	_____
_____	_____	_____	_____
_____	_____	_____	_____
_____	_____	_____	_____
_____	_____	_____	_____
_____	_____	_____	_____

Description of Your Property	Net Value of Your Ownership	Who Owns It	Transfer to Trust?
3. Clothing			
4. Jewelry and furs			
5. Artworks, collectibles, and antiques			
6. Tools and equipment			

Description of Your Property	Net Value of Your Ownership	Who Owns It	Transfer to Trust?
7. Valuable livestock/animals			
8. Life insurance (proceeds payable on death)			
9. Retirement accounts, including IRAs, 401(k)s, and profit-sharing plans			
10. Unlisted (private) stocks and bonds			
11. Promissory notes (owed to you)			
12. Precious metals			
13. Digital assets			
14. Other valuable personal property			

Description of Your Property	Net Value of Your Ownership	Who Owns It	Transfer to Trust?

D. Miscellaneous Receivables

   (mortgages, deeds of trust, or promissory notes held by you; any rents due from income property owned by you; and any payments due for professional or personal services, or property sold by you that are not fully paid by the purchaser)

E. Real Estate

   1. Address

   2. Address

   3. Address

   4. Address

   5. Address

Description of Your Property	Net Value of Your Ownership	Who Owns It	Transfer to Trust?

F. Business Interests

1. Sole proprietorships

_____ _____ _____ _____
_____ _____ _____ _____
_____ _____ _____ _____
_____ _____ _____ _____

2. Partnership interests

_____ _____ _____ _____
_____ _____ _____ _____
_____ _____ _____ _____
_____ _____ _____ _____

3. Shares in limited partnerships

_____ _____ _____ _____
_____ _____ _____ _____
_____ _____ _____ _____
_____ _____ _____ _____

4. Shares in limited liability companies

_____ _____ _____ _____
_____ _____ _____ _____
_____ _____ _____ _____
_____ _____ _____ _____

5. Shares in corporations, including Subchapter S corporations

_____ _____ _____ _____
_____ _____ _____ _____
_____ _____ _____ _____
_____ _____ _____ _____

6. Other business interests

_____ _____ _____ _____
_____ _____ _____ _____
_____ _____ _____ _____
_____ _____ _____ _____

G. Total Net Value of Your Assets $ _____

II. Liabilities

To Whom Debt Is Owed   Amount

A. Personal Property Debts

1. Personal loans (banks, major credit cards, etc.)

2. Other personal debts

B. Taxes (include only taxes past and currently due; do not include taxes due in the future)

C. Any Other Liabilities (legal judgments, accrued child support, etc.)

D. Total Liabilities (excluding those liabilities already deducted in Section I)

$ _____

III. Net Worth (Total Net Value of Your Assets, from Section I.G, above, minus Total Liabilities, from Section II.D, above)

$ _____

Trustees

To be legally valid, your living trust must have a trustee—someone responsible for managing the property in the trust. The trust property is actually held in the trustee's name. When you create a trust from this book, you are the initial trustee. If you create a shared living trust, you and your spouse are cotrustees.

When the initial trustee, or both trustees, have died, the "successor trustee" you have named in the trust document takes over. This person is responsible for transferring trust property to the beneficiaries and handling any other matters required by the trust— such as managing a child's trust, or filing federal tax returns. Technically, the executor of your will is responsible for filing tax returns, but normally, the executor and successor trustee are the same person. If not, the executor and successor trustee will have to work together.

For many people, the decision of who to name as successor trustee is clear, but for others, complexities and uncertainties can arise.

The Initial Trustee

A key to how a living trust works is that you, or you and your spouse, are the initial trustees. Understanding this point is essential to understanding what a living trust is—a device that allows you to absolutely control your own property while you are alive, and at the same time avoid probate of the property after you die.

SEE AN EXPERT

Naming someone else as initial trustee. If you want to name someone besides yourself to be your initial trustee because you don't want to, or cannot, continue to manage your own assets, see a lawyer; don't use the trust forms in this book. When you make somebody else your initial trustee, you create a more complicated trust, often necessitating much more detailed controls on the trustee's powers to act. In addition, under IRS rules, if you aren't a trustee of your own living trust, separate trust records must be maintained, and a fiduciary trust tax return (Form 1041) filed each year.

Your Responsibilities as Trustee

You won't have any special duties as trustee of your trust. As a day-to-day, practical matter, it makes no difference that you now manage your property as trustee, rather than in your own name. You do not need to file a separate income tax return for the living trust. As long as you are trustee, any income the trust property generates must be reported on your personal income tax return, as if the trust did not exist. (IRS Reg. 26 CFR § 1.671-4.) Likewise, you don't have to obtain a trust taxpayer ID number or keep separate trust records.

You have the same freedom to sell, mortgage, or give away trust property as you did before you put that property into the living trust. (Thus, one spouse does not have rights over the other spouse's separate property.) Normally, the only difference is that you must now sign documents in your capacity as trustee. It's that easy.

> **EXAMPLE:** Celeste and Angelo want to sell a piece of land that is owned in the name of their living trust. They prepare a deed transferring ownership of the land from the trustees of the trust to the new owner. They sign the deed as "Celeste Tornetti and Angelo Tornetti, trustees of the Celeste Tornetti and Angelo Tornetti Living Trust dated February 4, 20xx."

If you make a shared living trust, it's important to realize that once shared property belongs to the trust, either trustee (spouse) has authority over it. Legally, either spouse can sell or give away any of the shared trust property. In practice, however, both spouses will probably have to consent (in writing) to transfer shared real estate out of the living trust. Especially in community property states, buyers and title insurance companies usually insist on both spouses' signatures on transfer documents.

SEE AN EXPERT

Naming only one spouse as trustee. If you want only one spouse to be the original trustee of a shared living trust, there's an unusual—and unequal—distribution of authority over shared property, and you should see a lawyer.

Naming a Cotrustee

If you think you'll want or need someone else to manage your trust property for you, but don't want the hassles of having a separate trustee, you can consider naming yourself and another person to both be the initial trustees of your trust. Both of you would have authority to act on the trust's behalf. No fiduciary trust tax return is required, since *one* of the trustees is the original grantor.

> **EXAMPLE:** Beatrice is in her 80s. She doesn't want to abandon control over her property but has difficulty managing things—keeping track of bills and payments, for example. So she creates a living trust, naming herself and her daughter Polly as initial cotrustees. Either trustee can act for the trust. Because Beatrice is one of the initial trustees, she does not have to keep separate records or file a trust tax return. As a practical matter, Polly can handle most trust transactions on her own.

SEE AN EXPERT

Get help if you want initial cotrustees. If you want to have a cotrustee to serve with you, it's best to see a lawyer, so the authority of the trustees is clearly defined and specifically geared to your situation. Don't rely on the forms in this book.

The Trustee After One Spouse's Death or Incapacity

If you create a shared living trust, when one spouse dies or becomes incapacitated and unable to manage financial affairs, the other becomes sole trustee.

Using the trust forms in this book, a spouse's physical or mental incapacity is determined by the vote of people you've chosen to make that decision (discussed below). If one spouse is incapacitated, the other spouse, as sole trustee, takes over management of both spouses' trust property. As trustee, that's the extent of the surviving spouse's authority; the living trust does not give the surviving spouse power over property of the incapacitated spouse not owned by the living trust, and it does not give the surviving spouse authority to make health care decisions for the incapacitated spouse. For this reason, it's also wise for each spouse to create documents called durable powers of attorney and health care directives, giving the other spouse authority to manage property not owned by the trust and to make health care decisions for an incapacitated spouse. (See "Planning for Incapacity" in Chapter 14.)

The duties of a surviving spouse as trustee under a trust prepared with this book are summarized below. They are discussed in more detail in Chapter 4.

The Successor Trustee

Your trust document must name a successor trustee. The successor trustee takes over after you have died, or, for a shared trust, after both members of the couple have died. The successor trustee also takes over if you, or both you and your spouse, become incapacitated and are unable to manage the trust property.

Incapacity means the inability to manage your affairs. For a shared trust, the successor trustee has no authority to act if one spouse is alive and capable of managing trust property.

Picking your successor trustee is an important decision. Not only must you pick someone you trust who can do the job and is willing to do it, you also probably don't want to ruffle any family feathers when making your choice. You can name successor cotrustees, if this fits your needs.

When you decide on your successor trustee, your job isn't done. You should also name an alternate successor trustee, in case the successor trustee dies before you do or can't serve for some other reason. If you named two or more successor trustees, the alternate won't become trustee unless none of your original choices can serve. (See "Naming More Than One Successor Trustee," below.)

The Surviving Spouse's Trustee Duties

In a shared trust, the surviving spouse, as trustee, is responsible for distributing the trust property of the deceased spouse as the trust document directs. Trust property left by the deceased spouse to the surviving spouse does not require any actual distribution, since the trust form specifies that such property remains in the revocable living trust. So no further steps need to be taken to legally transfer this property to the surviving spouse.

The surviving spouse manages, as sole trustee, the ongoing revocable trust that contains the surviving spouse's property, including trust property inherited from the deceased spouse.

For information about the duties of a successor trustee, including information about a surviving spouse's role as sole trustee, see "The Trustee's Duties" in Chapter 13.

Choosing Your Successor Trustee

Your successor trustee will play a vital role in carrying out the aims of your living trust.

In most situations, the successor trustee does not need extensive experience in financial management; common sense, dependability, and complete honesty are usually enough. A successor trustee who may have long-term responsibility over a young beneficiary's trust property probably needs more management and financial skills than a successor trustee whose only job is to distribute trust property. But as I've said, the successor trustee does have authority, under the terms of the trust document, to get any reasonably necessary professional help—from an accountant, a lawyer, or a tax preparer, perhaps—and pay for it out of trust assets.

Your successor trustee should be whoever you feel is most trustworthy to do the job, who's willing to do it, and can actually do it. Often a major beneficiary, such as a spouse or an adult child, is named as successor trustee. However, you don't have to name a beneficiary as trustee. If you believe the beneficiary

(much as you love that person) will be troubled by having to handle the practical details and paperwork, it is preferable to name someone else, often another family member. Or as a last resort, consider naming an institution as trustee.

If you are married or partnered and create a shared trust, keep in mind that the successor trustee does not take over until both spouses have died (or become incapacitated). That means that after one spouse's death, the surviving spouse may have time to amend the trust document and name a different successor trustee if desired.

Naming an Out-of-State Trustee

Your successor trustee does not have to live in the same state as you do. But someone close by will probably have an easier job, especially with real estate transfers. For transfers of property such as securities and bank accounts, it usually won't make much difference where the successor trustee lives.

Naming More Than One Successor Trustee

Legally, you can name as many successor cotrustees as you want, to serve together with power divided among them as you specify. However, as a general rule, because of coordination problems and possible conflicts among multiple trustees, it's generally best to name just one successor trustee. This isn't invariably true, however. For example, a parent may not want to be seen to favor one child over others, and to avoid this could name two or more children as successor cotrustees. This can be especially appropriate if the children are equal beneficiaries of the trust. If the children all get along, it rarely causes a problem.

When appointing cotrustees, you must decide how authority is shared among them—whether each can act separately for the trust, or all must agree in writing to act for the trust. Consider giving each the power to act for the trust without the formal written consent of the others. Especially if they live far away from one another or travel often, this could speed up the eventual property transfer process, avoiding delays that might otherwise be caused if one cotrustee were temporarily unavailable.

But what is most important is that you have complete confidence that all your successor trustees will get along. Do be cautious here. Power and property can lead to unexpected results (ask King Lear). If the cotrustees are prone to conflict, you may well create serious problems (and are doing none of them a favor) by having them share power as trustees.

If the cotrustees can't agree, it could hold up the distribution of trust property to your beneficiaries. In extreme situations, the other trustees might even have to go to court to get a recalcitrant trustee removed so that your instructions can be carried out. The result might be much worse, and generate much more bad feeling, than if you had just picked one person to be trustee in the first place.

Having more than one successor trustee is especially risky if the successor trustees may be in charge of property you have left to a young beneficiary in a child's trust. The trustees may have to manage a young beneficiary's property for many years, and will have many decisions to make about how to spend the money—greatly increasing the potential for conflict. (Children's trusts are discussed in Chapter 8.)

If you name more than one successor trustee, and one of them can't serve, the others will serve. Only if none of them can serve will the alternate successor trustee you name take over.

Naming a Bank or Trust Company as Successor Trustee

It's possible to name a bank or trust company as successor trustee. However, in my experience, it is far wiser to name a trusted person.

Institutional trustees are more likely to be impersonal and indifferent to the needs of the beneficiaries. They also charge hefty fees, which come out of the trust property, leaving less for your family and friends. Additionally, many small institutions probably won't even be interested in small living trusts—ones that contain less than several hundred thousand dollars' worth of property. When possible, it's better to leave your trust in the hands of a dependable human.

That said, under some circumstances, you may want to consider naming a bank or trust company as successor trustee. For example, if there is no person you believe will act honestly and competently as your successor trustee, a financial institution can get the job done. Or if your family is embroiled in conflict, an impartial institutional trustee may cause the least amount of familial strife. If you decide to name an institutional trustee, obtain the agreement of the institution before you do so.

An additional possibility is to name a person and an institution as successor cotrustees. The bank or trust company can do most of the paperwork, and the person can keep an eye on things and approve all transactions.

Naming a Sole Beneficiary as Successor Trustee

It's perfectly legal to name a beneficiary of the trust as successor trustee. In fact, it's common.

> **EXAMPLE:** Santiago names his only child, Jaime, to be his sole trust beneficiary. Santiago also names Jaime as successor trustee. So when Santiago dies, Jaime's only task is to turn the trust property over to himself.

> **TIP**
> **Talk with the person you choose.** Confer with the person you've chosen to be your successor trustee to be sure your choice is willing to serve. If you don't, you risk creating problems down the line. No one can be unwillingly drafted to serve as a successor trustee. The person you've chosen may not want to serve, for a variety of reasons. And even if the person would be willing, if the named successor trustee isn't familiar with the responsibilities of a trustee, transfer of trust property after your death could be delayed.

The Job of the Successor Trustee

Obviously, when you choose your successor trustee, it helps for you both to understand what the job entails. The primary job of the successor trustee is to turn trust property over to the beneficiaries you named in the trust document. This is normally not difficult if the property and beneficiaries are clearly identified. Still, some effort is required.

Usually, the successor trustee obtains several certified copies of the death certificate of the grantor. Then the successor trustee presents a copy of the death certificate and a copy of the living trust document, along with proof of identity, to financial institutions, brokers, and other organizations that have possession of the trust assets. They will then release the property to the successor trustee, who will then turn that property over to the beneficiaries. If any documents of title (ownership) must be prepared to transfer trust property to the beneficiaries, the successor trustee prepares them. For example, to transfer real estate owned by a living trust to the beneficiaries after the death of the grantor, the successor trustee prepares, signs, and records (in the local land records office) a deed from himself or herself, as trustee of the living trust, to the specified beneficiaries. No court or agency approval is required.

What happens if an institution won't cooperate with the successor trustee? Happily, such problems are unlikely. Institutions that deal with financial assets—from title companies to county land records offices to stockbrokers—are familiar with living trusts and how they work.

Documents Required of the Successor Trustee

The surviving spouse of a shared living trust must record one or more documents with the county recording office to establish her or his legal authority as sole trustee. This authority allows the surviving spouse to transfer the deceased grantor's trust property to trust beneficiaries. The document(s) required vary by state. See "Trust Administration After Death of a Grantor" in Chapter 13. Also, the surviving spouse should get help from a lawyer to revise or amend Trust 2. See "Revising or Revoking Trust 2" in Chapter 13.

It's even easier for the trustee to distribute trust assets that don't have documents of title—household furnishings, jewelry, heirlooms, collectibles—to the appropriate beneficiaries. The trustee just turns the property over to the beneficiaries.

When all beneficiaries have received the trust property left to them in the trust document, the successor trustee's job is over, and the trust ends.

In some situations, additional tasks may be required of the successor trustee.

- **Managing trust property if the trust grantor or grantors become incapacitated.** With Nolo living trusts, if the grantor becomes (or grantors become) incapacitated and can no longer manage the trust property, the successor trustee manages the trust until the grantor dies or regains capacity. The term "incapacity" is not defined in the trust document. In commonsense terms, it means that the grantor has become mentally or physically unable to handle financial affairs.

In this book's trust forms, you name three people who can determine, by majority vote, whether or not you have become incapacitated, if the issue ever arises. Name any three persons you trust and who are likely to be around (both alive and accessible) longer than you.

Don't, however, name as your successor trustee a person who may determine incapacity. You don't want your successor trustee wearing two hats—participating in the decision about control, and then taking over. This could create at least the appearance of a conflict of interest, which might mean that financial institutions would be hesitant to accept your successor trustee's authority.

SEE AN EXPERT
Keep track of the people you've named to make incapacity decisions. If one or more of the people you've chosen to make a decision about your (possible) incapacity become unavailable, for whatever reason, you should amend your trust to name a new person. (See Chapter 12 for more on amending your living trust.) If the need for a determination ever arises (hopefully it will not), you want three people involved in making that decision. Not only are three heads better than two or one, but you also want to avoid the risk of having only two people, who might disagree. A tie vote over whether you have become incapacitated would not be good.

Having a Doctor Make the Determination

In our culture, doctors are often called upon to determine someone's mental capacity, even though this is not strictly a medical determination. With living trusts, one possible method for determining incapacity is by a doctor's statement. But there are possible problems with this. As anyone who has visited a doctor's office in the last few years has learned, federal law (the Health Insurance Portability and Accountability Act, commonly referred to as HIPAA, 42 U.S.C. § 1320(d)), gives patients the right to privacy when it comes to medical information. HIPAA severely restricts the release of a patient's medical information.

This creates a catch-22 when it comes to getting a doctor to issue a statement about someone's capacity to handle financial affairs. If your successor trustee goes to a doctor and asks for a statement saying you are incapacitated and can no longer manage the trust, the doctor could well be precluded, by HIPAA, from giving it.

 SEE AN EXPERT

Get help from a lawyer if you want a doctor to be able to determine your capacity—and thus when your successor trustee is entitled to take over. In that case, your trust document must specifically authorize doctors to use and release any of your medical records needed or used in making that determination. Granting that authorization isn't simple; you'll need a lawyer to prepare the correct release forms. HIPAA is a federal law, but some states have their own, even more stringent, patient privacy laws. For example, California law requires a medical release to be in 14-point type and cover several matters not required under federal law. (Civ. Code §§ 56.10–56.16.) Be sure to find a lawyer who's knowledgeable about both federal law and your state's requirements.

With Nolo's shared trust, the successor trustee could wind up managing both spouses' trusts if both spouses are alive but incapacitated. When a successor trustee takes over for an incapacitated grantor, the job is basically financial. The successor trustee must become (rapidly) familiar with the grantor's financial resources and needs, and handle all money matters and problems as they arise.

- **Preparing and filing estate tax returns.** If a federal estate tax return must be filed after a grantor's death, and taxes paid, the successor trustee is responsible for these tasks. Also, a final income tax return must be filed for the deceased grantor. The successor trustee must also file a state inheritance tax return if one is required. The executor you name in your backup will (see Chapter 15) shares legal responsibility for filing these tax returns. Usually, the same person is appointed as the successor trustee and executor.

- **Managing children's trusts.** The trust forms in this book allow you to leave trust property to young beneficiaries (younger than 35 when you die) in simple child's trusts. (See Chapter 8.) If you die before any child reaches the age you've specified, your successor trustee will manage trust property left for the benefit of that child until the child reaches that age. Thus, the successor trustee can have ongoing management responsibilities for a child's trust. Annual trust income tax returns are required for each operational child's trust and are the responsibility of the successor trustee.

The tasks required of a successor trustee are discussed in more depth in Chapter 13. Specific, state-by-state instructions for trustee tasks are provided in *The Executor's Guide: Settling a Loved One's Estate or Trust*, by Mary Randolph (Nolo), and *The Trustee's Legal Companion*, by Liza Hanks and Carol Elias Zolla (Nolo).

The Successor Trustee's Authority

The trust forms in this book spell out the specific powers granted to the successor trustee.

The Successor Trustee's Powers

The living trust forms in this book give the successor trustee all powers permitted under state law. The forms also define certain specific powers—for example, that the trustee has authority to buy and sell real estate and stocks. Some banks, title companies, stockbrokerage companies, or other financial institutions demand this level of detail before approving a trust transaction, even though such authority is clearly included in a general grant of power under state law.

The living trust forms also give the successor trustee broad authority to manage any child's trust, including the power to spend any amount of each child's trust income or principal for that child's "health, support, maintenance, or education." As long as you trust your successor trustee, defining the power to manage young beneficiaries' trust property in this broad way is the best approach.

Once in a while, a financial institution gets quirky and demands that a trust specifically authorize some relatively unusual transaction the trustee wants to engage in. For example, a brokerage company may claim that some very sophisticated maneuver isn't authorized by the trustee's powers clause in your trust. The general trustee powers clause should give you all the authorization you need. But if a financial institution proves recalcitrant, you have two options:

- Transfer the property from your trust to yourself, personally. Then go ahead and make the transaction. When it's done, transfer that property back to your trust.
- Amend the trustee's powers clause of your trust to add whatever specific language the financial institution insists upon.

The Successor Trustee's Duty to Act Responsibly

The successor trustee must manage any trust property, including any property in a child's trust, in a "prudent manner." This means the trustee must always act honestly and in the best interests of the beneficiary. For example, the trustee must not make risky investments with trust property.

Legally, the trustee cannot personally profit or benefit from a transaction (this is called "self-dealing"). Basically, this means personally profiting or benefiting from a transaction involving trust property, such as buying a house from the trust. But remember, legal restrictions can be enforced only by a lawsuit. Be sure you have someone you trust as successor trustee, to minimize the possibility of litigation.

The successor trustee has authority to get professional assistance if necessary and pay for it with trust money. For example, the successor trustee might want to pay a tax preparer for help with the child's trust income tax return, or to consult a financial planner for investment advice.

Payment of the Successor Trustee

Often, the successor trustee of a basic probate-avoidance living trust isn't paid. This is because the successor trustee's duty is to distribute the deceased grantor's trust property, which is not normally an arduous job. More importantly, the successor trustee is usually a major beneficiary of the trust. For these reasons, the trust forms in this book provide that no compensation be paid except when the successor trustee is:

- managing any trust when the grantor or grantors have become incapacitated, or
- managing an ongoing child's trust.

The trust forms provide that in these situations a successor trustee is entitled, without court approval, to "reasonable" compensation for services. The successor trustee decides what is reasonable and takes it from the appropriate trust property, either from the living trust or the child's trust.

In these situations, the successor trustee might have to actively manage the trust property for some time, so some pay for that work seems fair. The duties and burdens of a successor trustee who manages a child's trust can be substantial. The trust can last for decades and entail extensive financial responsibilities. If you have more than one trust, the job can become even more demanding.

Notifying Trust Beneficiaries

In a number of states, a successor trustee of a living trust is specifically required by statute to provide basic information about the trust to trust beneficiaries. This duty includes notifying trust beneficiaries that the trust has become irrevocable and possibly providing a copy of the trust document. In all states, it's wise for the successor trustee to give this information to beneficiaries, even if a specific statute does not compel it. A successor trustee should understand and accept this responsibility. The good news is that it shouldn't be hard to do—a simple letter setting out basic trust information should suffice.

RESOURCE

Get state-by-state details about the successor trustee's duties. *The Executor's Guide: Settling a Loved One's Estate or Trust*, by Mary Randolph (Nolo), and *The Trustee's Legal Companion*, by Liza Hanks and Carol Elias Zolla (Nolo), list every state's rules regarding a successor trustee's duties. If a state imposes specific duties, the citation to that state's statute is provided.

SEE AN EXPERT

See a lawyer to restrict the trustee's authority. Consult a lawyer if you are uneasy about:

- the broad grant of powers to the successor trustee
- the successor trustee's authority to sell trust property, regardless of the desires of other beneficiaries
- the lack of specific restrictions on the successor trustee
- the successor trustee's authority to manage and invest trust funds, or
- allowing open-ended compensation for managing a child's trust or Trust A.

Such a concern may well indicate potential serious problems, which require careful professional attention.

Also, if you decide that you want your successor trustee to be compensated for tasks entailed in transferring trust property to adult beneficiaries, see a lawyer. Compensation might be appropriate if your estate is large and you have complex beneficiary provisions.

Choosing Your Beneficiaries

After deciding what property you'll put in your trust and who will be your successor trustee, your next step is to decide who will be your trust's beneficiaries. Who gets what? This is the heart of preparing your living trust.

This chapter raises some important concerns about choosing beneficiaries and provides a worksheet on which you can list each beneficiary and what property you want to leave him, her, or it. You can name any person or institution you want as a beneficiary. A beneficiary does not have to be a U.S. citizen or resident. An institution does not have to be located in the United States.

Even if you believe your beneficiary decisions are cut-and-dried, please resist any temptation to skip this chapter. It contains important information you should take into account even if you have already decided who will inherit your property. For instance, you may initially think you don't want to bother naming alternate beneficiaries. But to make that decision sensibly, you should understand how alternate beneficiaries are used in living trusts, and why it's often wise to name them.

> **TIP**
> **Keeping a list of your beneficiaries.** Consider keeping a list of your beneficiaries' addresses and contact information. Your successor trustee will need to contact each of your beneficiaries to arrange for the transfer of the property you left them. It will be a big help to your successor trustee if you have prepared a list of your beneficiaries' names and contact information (and have kept that list up-to-date). Store the list with your estate-planning documents.

Kinds of Trust Beneficiaries

Several different classes of trust beneficiaries are used in trusts in this book:

- **Primary beneficiaries.** Beneficiaries whom you name to receive specific property. Primary beneficiaries include individuals, institutions, and groups who receive property together.

- **Alternate beneficiaries.** Beneficiaries whom you name to receive property left to a primary beneficiary if that primary beneficiary predeceases (dies before) you.

- **Residuary beneficiaries (and alternate residuary beneficiaries).** Beneficiaries who receive all trust property not left to primary or alternate beneficiaries (including when both predecease you). You can, if you choose, leave all trust property to your residuary beneficiary, and not name any primary or alternate beneficiaries.

Keep It Simple

Some living trust books argue that you:

- cannot be trusted to choose your beneficiaries without professional help, and
- need to create all sorts of complex beneficiary provisions to cover all sorts of contingencies, such as providing for what happens if a child's needs change long after you die, or a spouse remarries.

It's not hard to dream up remote possibilities about beneficiaries. While this certainly makes work for lawyers, it isn't what most people want. Most folks realize that it's rarely sensible to try to impose post-death controls over property given to beneficiaries.

"My life has been full of terrible misfortunes, most of which never happened." —Mark Twain

This book assumes you'll leave property outright, with no strings attached (except for gifts to minors or young adults, discussed in Chapter 8).

> **CAUTION**
> **Conditions on gifts.** If you do want to impose conditions on gifts—for instance, distributing money in three installments, or varying the amount left to a beneficiary depending on future needs—see a lawyer.

Unmarried Couples

Because most couples who use shared living trusts are married—and to simplify the instructions—throughout this chapter I use the term "spouse." However, the instructions apply equally to unmarried couples. If you are part of an unmarried couple, simply replace the term "spouse" with "partner" or whatever term you prefer.

Naming Your Primary Beneficiaries

For single people, or couples using a shared living trust, choosing your primary beneficiaries is often the heart of making your trust. Deciding on your primary beneficiaries is entirely up to you. Your beneficiaries can include a spouse, mate, friends, young adults, children, or charitable or other institutions.

Property Received by Beneficiaries Is Not Subject to Income Tax

Beneficiaries who inherit property are not liable for any federal income tax on that property. Of course, very large estates may have to pay federal estate taxes and possibly state estate or inheritance taxes, but once those have been paid, the recipient of a gift is not subject to income tax on its value. That said, if that gift generates income in the future, the beneficiary is responsible for paying income tax on that.

In your trust document, you do not have to use the full legal names of your beneficiaries. You can use the names by which they are commonly known. What's crucial is that your successor trustee(s) can identify who each beneficiary is. Remember, because there will be no judge involved in the distribution of your trust property, there will be no nit-picking authority incorrectly trying to insist that full legal names are legally required.

CAUTION

Disinheriting a spouse or child. If you are married and live in a common law state and you don't plan to leave at least half of what you own to your spouse, consult a lawyer experienced in estate planning. (See list of common law states below.) Whatever your wishes, state law entitles your spouse to some of your estate, possibly including some of the property in your living trust. In most circumstances, you don't have to leave anything to your children. But if you want to disinherit a child, you should state that expressly in your will. See "Disinheritance," below.

For individual trusts, naming beneficiaries is simple. Just list on the worksheet, and later on Form 1, whomever you want to receive your trust property. That's it!

EXAMPLE: Ruth has three grown children and two grandchildren. She also has a brother she is close to, and she's been a long-time contributor to Doctors Without Borders. She names the following primary beneficiaries for her trust property:

- Each child receives 21%.
- Each grandchild receives 7%.
- Her brother receives 14%.
- Doctors Without Borders receives 9%.

For shared trusts, each spouse names beneficiaries separately, because each spouse's share of trust property is distributed when that spouse dies. When the first spouse dies, that spouse's trust property is distributed to the beneficiaries named in the trust document. Property left to the other spouse stays in the ongoing revocable trust of the surviving spouse. When the second spouse dies, all the property in that trust is distributed to the second spouse's beneficiaries.

EXAMPLE 1: Roger and Marilyn Foster create a shared living trust. Each puts shared, equally owned property and separately owned property in the trust. When Roger dies, Marilyn takes over as sole trustee. The property Roger left to Marilyn stays in the trust. Marilyn distributes the trust property Roger left to other beneficiaries. When Marilyn dies, her trust property will be distributed by her successor trustee to her beneficiaries.

EXAMPLE 2: Marcia and Perry transfer all the property they own together into their shared living trust. Marcia names Perry as the beneficiary of all her interest in the trust property. Perry names Marcia to inherit all of his half except his half-interest in their vacation cabin, which he leaves to his son from a previous marriage, Eric. If Perry dies first, Perry's half-interest in the cabin will go to Eric, who will co-own it with Marcia.

Some Thoughts About Gifts

Before plunging into technical concerns about how to name beneficiaries or shared gifts, let's pull back for a moment and consider what gifts are. In our predominantly commercial culture, gifts are special, whether they are made during life or at death. Gifts are free, voluntary transfers of property, made without any requirement or expectation of receiving anything in return. The essence of gift giving is generosity, an open spirit. To say one makes gifts "with strings attached" is not a compliment.

Much of the real pleasure of estate planning comes from contemplating the positive effects that your gifts will have on those you love. Sometimes, these pleasures are focused—you know how much Judith has always liked your mahogany table, and now she'll get to enjoy it. Others are more general—your son will be able to buy a house with the money you leave him, which will relieve some of the financial pressure that has been weighing on him.

I mention the spirit of giving here because it's easy to get bogged down by the mechanics of preparing a living trust and lose sight of your real purpose. So, if technicalities and legalities start to get to you, take a break and remember to whom you're giving your property, and why. And if you wish to explore in profound depth what gift giving is or can mean, read Lewis Hyde's *The Gift* (Vintage/Random House), a brilliant exploration of how gifts work in many cultures.

Simultaneous Death Clauses

The statistical probability of simultaneous death is very low, but still it's one of the first things many couples ask about when preparing a shared living trust: "What happens if we're both killed in a plane crash?"

If you leave all your trust property directly to your spouse, your trust document doesn't have a clause to cover simultaneous death, and you and your spouse die in circumstances that make it difficult to tell who died first, your property could pass to your spouse, and then immediately to your spouse's inheritors. That might not be the result either of you wants.

Note: The forms in this book—the shared living trust and the will for a member of a couple—contain a simultaneous death clause to prevent this. These clauses are worded slightly differently depending on the form, because the trust is a joint form used by both spouses and the will is a separate form for each spouse. But each clause achieves the same result: If both spouses die simultaneously, or if it's difficult or impossible to tell who died first, the property of each spouse is disposed of as if each spouse had survived the other.

> **EXAMPLE:** In their shared living trust, Edith and Archie leave much of their property to each other. However, Archie wants his property to go to his daughter from his first marriage if Edith dies before he does. Edith wants her property to go to her sister if Archie dies before she does. Edith and Archie are killed in a car crash. Under the living trust's simultaneous death clause, Archie's property would go to his daughter, and Edith's to her sister.

You may ask, "How, logically, can simultaneous death clauses work? How can I be presumed to have outlived my spouse when she's also presumed to have outlived me?" Yes, it is a paradox, but it does work. Under the law, each person's trust and will property is handled independently of the other. This allows both spouses to achieve the results each wants in the event of simultaneous death. (As Oliver Wendell Holmes put it, "The life of the law has not been logic; it has been experience.")

Shared Gifts

You can name more than one beneficiary (primary, alternate, residuary, or final) to inherit any item of trust property. For instance, parents frequently want to make shared gifts to their children.

When making a gift to be shared by two or more beneficiaries, always include the beneficiaries' actual names; don't just use collective terms such as "my children." It's not always clear who is included in such descriptions. And there can be serious confusion if one of the people originally included as a beneficiary dies before you do; the law may give the beneficiary's children the right to inherit their parent's share, which may not be the result you intend.

Obviously, if you name shared beneficiaries for a piece of property that can't be physically divided—a house, for example—give some thought to whether or not the beneficiaries are likely to get along. If they are incompatible, disagreements could arise over taking care of property or deciding whether or not to sell it.

You need to resolve these important questions before naming cobeneficiaries:

- What percentage of ownership will each beneficiary receive?
- What happens down the line if the beneficiaries can't agree on how to use the property?
- What happens if one beneficiary dies before you do?

The rest of this section discusses these concerns.

Percentage of Ownership

The key here is to say in your living trust document how ownership is to be shared between the beneficiaries. If you don't specify shares of ownership, it's generally presumed that you intended equal shares, but this rule isn't ironclad, so if you want a gift shared equally, say so.

Here are two examples of what the language in your trust document might look like:

> The grantor's three children, Anne Pasquez, Rob Pasquez, and Tony Pasquez, shall be given the house at 1123 Elm Street, Centerville, Iowa, in equal shares.
>
> The grantor's granddaughters, Maxine Jones and Simone Beal, shall be given all stock accounts, in equal shares.

The beneficiaries can share ownership any way you want. For instance:

> The grantor's spouse and children shall be given all the grantor's interest in the grantor's house and real estate known as 111 57th Street, Muncy, Iowa, in the following shares:
>
> - 50% to the grantor's spouse, Mary O'Rourke
> - 25% to the grantor's son, Jon O'Rourke, and
> - 25% to the grantor's daughter, Mildred O'Rourke.

You can also leave beneficiaries different percentages of different trust assets. Here's an example:

> The grantor's grandchildren shall be given the house at 65 Swan Lane, Springfield, Iowa, in the following shares:
>
> - 40% to Brandon Otto
> - 30% to Elaine Otto Rubenstein, and
> - 30% to Martha Otto.
>
> All jewelry held in the trust shall be given as follows:
>
> - 50% to Elaine Otto Rubenstein, and
> - 50% to Martha Otto.

Notice that the beneficiaries' shares are defined by percentages, not dollar amounts. When you prepare your living trust, you can't know precisely how much your house, stocks, jewelry, or other property will be worth at your death. So if you leave each beneficiary a dollar amount, it creates inevitable problems. At your death, the property may not be worth enough to pay all the dollar amounts. Or there may be money left over after the dollar amounts are paid. If you want to leave someone a set dollar amount, do it from a trust liquid asset, like a bank account or money market fund—and make sure there's always enough in the account to cover it.

Conflict

Shared ownership creates the risk of conflict between beneficiaries. Suppose the people to whom you've left property disagree about how to use it. In most states, any co-owner can go to court and force a partition and sale, with the net proceeds divided by percentage of ownership. Let's say, for example, you leave your house to your three children. Suppose two want to sell it, and one doesn't. The house would be sold even if one child wanted to live in it.

If you are apprehensive, discuss it with the proposed beneficiaries. If there's genuine agreement among them, potential problems are less likely to become real ones. If you conclude there's no risk of conflict, you can simply make the shared gift without any conditions or directions, leaving it up to the beneficiaries to resolve any problems.

It's possible to put provisions governing what the shared owners can do in your trust document. For instance, you could state, "The house cannot be sold unless all three of my children agree on it." But often other problems follow. If two want to sell the house, but one doesn't, who manages the house? Does it have to be rented at market value? Can the child who wants to keep the house live in it? If so, must that child pay the others rent? And what happens if one child dies? The difficulties of dealing with these types of complications are why it's usually more sensible not to specify details of long-term control of property you leave beneficiaries. Let them work it out. If you don't think the beneficiaries can work out any such problems, a shared gift probably isn't appropriate.

SEE AN EXPERT

Imposing controls on cobeneficiaries.
If you fear conflict between cobeneficiaries and want to impose controls on the use of the property you leave them, see a lawyer.

One solution would be to allow the trustee to sell a shared gift if the beneficiaries can't agree how to dispose of it. The trustee would then divide the sale profits to beneficiaries, as defined by the trust grantor. But even this apparently simple solution can raise problems. How and when does it become clear that the beneficiaries can't agree? Suppose all beneficiaries agree property should be sold, but don't agree on the timing of the sale? Or the minimum price required? If you are concerned about a conflict over a shared gift left to beneficiaries, you need the attention and expertise of an experienced estate planning lawyer.

What Happens If a Beneficiary Dies Before You Do

You can name alternate beneficiaries for each primary beneficiary. If the primary beneficiary dies before you do, the alternate will get the share of your property that would have gone to the primary beneficiary. See "Naming Alternate Beneficiaries," below.

Some Common Concerns About Beneficiaries

Here are some common concerns and choices you may face when choosing your beneficiaries.

One Primary Beneficiary

With an individual trust, you can name as many primary beneficiaries as you want. Similarly, with a shared living trust, each spouse can name as many primary beneficiaries as she or he wants. With either type of trust, you can name one person as your sole primary beneficiary either by listing that person as the primary beneficiary or by leaving everything to that person as the residuary beneficiary. See "Residuary Beneficiaries," below.

Married Beneficiaries

When you leave property to someone who's married, the gift is that person's individual or separate property if you make the gift solely in that person's name. For example, suppose your trust document says: "Mary Kestor shall be given the account at FG Financial" or "Mary Kestor shall be given the grantor's interest in the house at 279 18th Street, San Francisco." Mary would be entitled to the entire gift as separate property. As long as the gift is kept separate from, not commingled (mixed) with, her marital property, the gift would not be the property of her spouse.

If you want to emphasize your wishes, you could say: "Mary Kestor shall be given the grantor's antique clock as her separate property." But if Mary later commingles the gift with shared marital property, it may lose its separate property status. This is proof once again that you have, at best, limited control over what happens to your property after your beneficiary receives it.

If you want to make a gift to a member of a couple and have it remain that person's separate property, note that on the beneficiary worksheet, to remind you that when you prepare your living trust in Chapter 9, you should expressly state that using the phrasing above.

By contrast, if you wish to make a gift to a married couple, simply make it in both their names. For example: "Edna and Fred Whitman shall be given the grantor's silver bowl." Again, you can provide clarity by expressly stating your intent: "Edna and Fred Whitman shall be given the grantor's silver bowl as co-owners."

Children From Prior Marriages

If you or your spouse have children from a prior marriage, you have a few options for leaving gifts to them. You can:

- Leave them gifts outright using a shared living trust (Form 2).
- Create a more complex trust with sophisticated beneficiary provisions, such as leaving children money in several installments over time or leaving them different amounts depending on their ages. Get help from a lawyer for this.
- Create a trust that imposes more restrictions on the power of the surviving spouse to use and spend trust principal. Get help from a lawyer for this.
- Give them gifts while you are alive.
- Disinherit them. (See "Disinheritance," below.)

 SEE AN EXPERT

See a lawyer if you anticipate a conflict between a surviving spouse and children. If there is a risk of conflict after your death between your surviving spouse and your children, see a lawyer.

EXAMPLE: Marshall, age 67, and Lisa, age 71, marry. Lisa has a son, Nick, age 32, from a prior marriage. Lisa owns a paid-for house that she and Marshall will live in, and she has $280,000 worth of other assets. She creates a trust that allows Marshall to live in the house if she dies before he does, but doesn't allow him to sell it, rent it, or borrow against it. Nick will receive the house free and clear when Marshall dies.

SEE AN EXPERT

See a lawyer to draft a trust restricting the rights of your spouse. Creating this kind of trust is discussed further in Chapter 14. As explained there, many individual questions need to be resolved to set up such a trust, which must be prepared by a knowledgeable lawyer.

Minors or Young Adults

If a beneficiary you name is a minor (younger than 18) or a young adult who can't yet manage property without responsible adult supervision, you must arrange for an adult to manage the trust property for the beneficiary. The management will take effect only if the beneficiary is still too young to sensibly manage the inherited property. (See Chapter 8.)

Your Successor Trustee as a Beneficiary

It's very common and perfectly legal to leave trust property to the person you named to be successor trustee—the person who will distribute trust property after you (or if you are making a trust with your spouse, you and your spouse) die.

EXAMPLE: Nora and Sean name their son Liam as successor trustee of their shared living trust. Both spouses name each other as sole beneficiaries of their own trust property, and both name Liam as alternate beneficiary. When Nora dies, her trust property goes to Sean and stays in the trust. Unless Sean amends the trust document to name someone else as successor trustee, after Sean's death, Liam, acting as trustee, will transfer ownership of the trust property from the trust to himself.

Pets

As a part of their estate planning, many pet owners arrange informally for a friend or relative to care for a pet. But you can make more formal arrangements. Here are a few things to keep in mind:

- You can use your living trust (or will) to leave your pets, and perhaps some money for expenses, to someone you trust to look out for them. Don't make the gift of an animal a surprise—make sure the people you've chosen are really willing and able to care for your pets.
- You can't leave money or property outright to a pet. The law says animals are property, and one piece of property simply can't own another piece. In most states, if you do name a pet as a beneficiary in your will or living trust, whatever property you tried to leave it will probably go to the residuary beneficiary instead. If you have not named a residuary beneficiary, the property will be distributed according to state law.
- Consider making arrangements for emergency care for your animals in case you suddenly can't care for them.
- In all states, you can establish a trust for your pet. A trustee you name will manage the trust. In the trust document, you direct how your pet is to be cared for. Pet trusts can be desirable if you'd prefer not to leave your pet outright to someone. But creating a pet trust is more costly and complicated than simply leaving your pet to someone as a gift.

SEE AN EXPERT

You'll need an attorney to prepare a pet trust. Laws about pet trusts are complicated and state specific. You'll need to hire an attorney to draft one.

RESOURCE

More about pets and the law. You can read more about how to make a plan for the care of your pets in the "Pets and Estate Planning" section of Nolo.com at www.nolo.com/legal-encyclopedia/pets-estate-planning.

Naming Alternate Beneficiaries

You can name an alternate beneficiary, or beneficiaries, for each gift made to a primary beneficiary. The alternate beneficiary receives the gift if the primary beneficiary predeceases you (dies before you) and you haven't amended your trust to name a new primary beneficiary for that gift.

Naming alternate beneficiaries can be sensible, for a number of reasons. Examples of when you might name an alternate beneficiary include:

- You've left property to older people or to people in poor health.
- You're a cautious person.
- You don't want the bother of amending your trust document if a beneficiary does die before you.
- You're concerned that you might not have time, before your own death, to revise your estate plan after a beneficiary dies.

Here are two examples of how alternate beneficiaries are named in a trust document:

> The grantor's children, Bert Wemby and Cherrie Wemby, shall be given the grantor's interest in the house at 221 Maple Avenue, Winton, New York. If one beneficiary doesn't survive the grantor, the house shall be given to the other. If neither survives the grantor, the house shall be given to Kamal Abram.

Mike McGowan shall be given the grantor's outboard motor and boat. If he doesn't survive the grantor, they shall be given to Mike's son, Pat McGowan.

On the other hand, some people decide they don't want to name alternate beneficiaries—maybe because they don't want the morbid bother of worrying about their beneficiaries dying before they do. These folks may leave their property to beneficiaries considerably younger than themselves, and they count on having time to modify the trust to name a new beneficiary if a beneficiary dies before they do.

You don't have to name an alternate for a charity or another institution you name as a beneficiary. If the institution is well established, it seems safe to assume that it will still exist at your death.

If You Don't Have Any Person You Want to Name as Alternate Beneficiary

Although it's not common, sometimes the maker of a living trust has only a single beneficiary, and does not want to name anyone else as alternate beneficiary.

For example, a single mother has one son, her beneficiary, and there is no one she wants to name as alternate if her son predeceases her. The problem in this situation is that if tragedy strikes and the son dies first, there is no alternate for her estate and it could end up with relatives to whom she would not have wanted to give the property or with the state if there are no relatives.

If you can't think of another person that you'd want to name as an alternate, consider naming a charity or a cause you like instead. That way, in the worst-case scenario, your property will at least go to an institution you believe in.

With a shared living trust, each spouse makes separate gifts, and each spouse has the right to name alternate beneficiaries for those gifts. These choices do not need to be the same as the other spouse's choices.

EXAMPLE: Larry and Louisa create a shared trust. Each leaves a one-half interest in their house to the other. Larry names his two children from a previous marriage as alternate beneficiaries for his half-interest in the house. Louisa names her sister as her alternate beneficiary for her gift.

Naming More Than One Alternate Beneficiary

You can name more than one person or institution as alternate beneficiaries. If you do, you must define how these coalternate beneficiaries will share the property.

EXAMPLE 1: Rosa names her husband, Ramon, as beneficiary of her interest in their house, which they have transferred to their shared living trust. As alternate beneficiaries, she names their three children, Miguel, Constanza, and Guillermo, to share equally.

Ramon dies just before she does, leaving his half of the house to Rosa. Under the terms of the trust document, it stays in the living trust. At Rosa's death, the house goes to the three children, because Ramon is not living. All three own equal shares in all of it. If they sell the property, each will be entitled to a third of the proceeds.

EXAMPLE 2: Benjamin names Bela, his wife, as his primary beneficiary of his interest in their house. He names their children, Susan and Zelda, as alternate beneficiaries. However, Benjamin and Bela have paid many thousands of dollars to help Zelda through medical school. Susan has been self-supporting since she left college. So Benjamin and Bela decide to leave Susan 75% of the house and Zelda 25%, and state this in the trust document when naming them as alternate beneficiaries.

Naming Alternate Beneficiaries for Cobeneficiaries

Things become complicated if you decide to move on to the next level of contingencies—naming alternate beneficiaries for a shared gift. Say you want to leave your house to your three children. What if you want to name alternate beneficiaries? Your options are:

- You can specify that a deceased child's share is to be shared by the remaining beneficiaries.

  Here's a clause specifying that the other beneficiaries of a shared gift share the interest of a deceased beneficiary:

  > Mollie Rainey, Allen Rainey, and Barbara Rainey Smithson shall be given the grantor's house at 1701 Clay Street, Peoria, Illinois. If any of them fails to survive the grantor, that person's interest in the grantor's house shall be shared equally by the survivors.

- You can provide that a deceased child's share is to be shared equally by that beneficiary's own children, and, if there are none, then between the remaining beneficiaries.
- You can name an "outside" alternate beneficiary (a friend or another relative) to receive the interest of any child who dies before you do.
- You can name separate alternate beneficiaries, one for each child—for example, each of their spouses.

Before plunging into complexities about alternate beneficiary provisions for a shared gift, consider whether or not you really want to worry about this contingency. Some people don't like to consider the possibility of one of their children dying before them (and you can always revise your trust if that remote possibility occurs). And once you get started worrying about these kinds of possibilities, where do you stop? You could also worry about what happens if all your alternate beneficiaries, as well as your beneficiaries themselves, die before you. There's no total security, no matter how many levels of alternate beneficiaries you name.

Imposing a Survivorship Period

Some people want to impose what is called a "survivorship period" on gifts made to primary and/or alternate beneficiaries. This means that the beneficiary must outlive the grantor by a set period of time, defined in the living trust, to receive the gift. If the beneficiary doesn't live this long, the gift goes to the alternate beneficiary.

The reason to include a survivorship period is this: If a beneficiary of your property dies soon after you do, the property that you left to that person will go to that person's beneficiaries. With a survivorship clause, in order to pass what was your property on to someone else, a beneficiary must survive you for a certain amount of time.

The trust forms in this book do not impose a survivorship period. Many people (including me) think they are unnecessarily cautious. And people who do want them differ widely as to how long the period should be.

If you decide you do want to impose a survivorship period on your primary beneficiaries, you can add one to the trust document. (I explain how to do this in Chapter 9.) I recommend a relatively short period, between 15 and 45 days. Imposing a longer period normally just unnecessarily delays distribution of gifts to the primary beneficiaries.

> **EXAMPLE:** In Laura's shared living trust, she imposes a 15-day survivorship requirement on all her beneficiaries.
>
> Laura leaves all her trust property to her husband, Juan-Carlos, and names her daughter from a previous marriage as alternate beneficiary. Laura and Juan-Carlos are seriously injured in a car accident; Juan-Carlos dies four days after Laura does. Because Juan-Carlos did not survive Laura by at least 15 days, the trust property he would have inherited from Laura goes to Laura's daughter instead.

If there had been no survivorship requirement, Laura's trust property would have gone to Juan-Carlos. When he died four days later, it would have gone to beneficiaries he had named in the trust document.

Residuary Beneficiaries

Residuary beneficiaries are the person, persons, or institutions you name to receive trust property that isn't given, for whatever reason, to a primary beneficiary or an alternate. For example, if a primary beneficiary predeceases you or can't be located, and you didn't name an alternate, the property would go to the residuary beneficiary.

With a living trust for one person, you should always name a residuary beneficiary and an alternate residuary beneficiary who will inherit if the residuary beneficiary dies before you.

With a shared living trust, both spouses individually name a residuary beneficiary and alternate residuary beneficiary. They may name different people.

> **EXAMPLE:** Peter leaves a house to his wife, Jane, or, if Jane dies before him, to Jane's sister Carolyn. He names his sister Julie as residuary beneficiary. Jane and Carolyn are killed in a car crash three days before Peter dies. Because the primary and alternate beneficiaries are dead, the house goes to Julie. (Pretty cheerful example of how living trusts can work, huh?)

You can name coresiduary beneficiaries, and co-alternate residuary beneficiaries as well. But if you do, you must handle all the potential problems of naming cobeneficiaries (discussed above).

For instance, a person could split the bulk of her estate among her children by leaving it all to the children as residuary beneficiaries. For example, she could name as her residuary beneficiaries: "Henry McCormick, Aaron McCormick, and Joanne Guiliam, in equal shares."

Another approach is to make a few relatively minor gifts and leave the bulk of your property to your residuary beneficiary.

> **EXAMPLE 1:** Jennifer wants to leave her two Tiffany lamps to her friend Linda, $5,000 in a money market account to her niece Martha, and her car to her sister Joan. She wants to leave all the rest of her extensive estate—houses, stocks, limited partnerships—to her long-time partner, Paul. She can simply name Paul as her residuary beneficiary, after listing the three specific gifts. She names Joan as her alternate residuary beneficiary.

> **EXAMPLE 2:** Claudia and Hank are in their second marriage. They have no children together. Each has children from their first marriages—Claudia's are Wendy and Linus, Hank's are Krystin, Phil, and Gary. Claudia and Hank each name the other as residuary beneficiary. But as alternate residuary beneficiaries, Claudia names Wendy and Linus. Hank names Krystin, Phil, and Gary.

The residuary beneficiary of a living trust for a single person, or of one person's portion of a shared living trust, will receive:

- any trust property for which both the primary and alternate beneficiaries you named die before you do
- any trust property that you didn't leave to a named beneficiary (this could include property you transferred to the trust later but didn't name a beneficiary for, and trust property that your spouse owned and left to you)
- any property you leave to your living trust through a "pour-over" will (however, because property left through a pour-over will doesn't avoid probate, there's usually no reason to use one; see Chapter 14), and
- any property that you actually transferred to your living trust but didn't list in the trust document.

Disinheritance

You can disinherit most people simply by not leaving them anything in your living trust or will. If you don't leave someone any of your property, she or he has no rights to it, period. However, you can disinherit your spouse only if you live in one of the nine community property states. When it comes to your children, you should either leave them something or expressly disinherit them in your will.

Disinheriting a Spouse

Whether or not you can legally disinherit a spouse (not that many people want to) depends on whether you live in a community property state or common law state.

Community Property States		
Arizona	Louisiana	Texas
California*	Nevada	Washington*
Idaho	New Mexico	Wisconsin

* Registered domestic partners are also covered by community property laws.

Alaska, South Dakota, and Tennessee allow a married couple to make a written agreement stating that they wish certain property treated as community property. (See a lawyer if you want to make this kind of agreement.)

In community property states (listed above), the general rule is that spouses together own all property that either acquires during the marriage, except property one spouse acquires by gift or inheritance. Each spouse owns a half-interest in this "community property."

You are free to leave your separate property and your half of the community property to anyone you choose. Your spouse—who already owns half of all the community property—has no right to inherit any of your half.

In contrast, in a common law state, a surviving spouse who doesn't receive a set portion of the deceased spouse's property (through a will, a living trust, or another method) is entitled to insist upon that share of the property. The exact share depends on state law. A spouse who doesn't receive the minimum to which the spouse is entitled under state law (the "statutory share") can claim some of the property in your living trust. To be safe, give your spouse at least half your property in your trust.

Even property given away before death may legally belong to the surviving spouse under these laws. For example, take the case of a man who set up joint bank accounts with his children from a previous marriage.

After his death, his widow sued to recover her interest in the accounts. She won; the Kentucky Supreme Court ruled that under Kentucky law, a spouse is entitled to a half-interest in the other spouse's personal property (everything but real estate). Her husband had not had the legal right to give away her interest in the money in the accounts. (*Harris v. Rock*, 799 S.W.2d 10 (Ky. 1990).) Most noncommunity property states have similar laws, called "dower" or "curtesy" laws.

Common Law States		
Alabama	Kentucky	North Dakota
Alaska	Maine	Ohio
Arkansas	Maryland	Oklahoma
Colorado	Massachusetts	Oregon
Connecticut	Michigan	Pennsylvania
Delaware	Minnesota	Rhode Island
District of Columbia	Mississippi	South Carolina
Florida	Missouri	South Dakota
Georgia	Montana	Tennessee
Hawaii	Nebraska	Utah
Illinois	New Hampshire	Vermont
Indiana	New Jersey	Virginia
Iowa	New York	West Virginia
Kansas	North Carolina	Wyoming

Unmarried Couples

Unmarried couples living together have no right to inherit any of each other's property (except registered domestic partners, in some states). In short, each person can leave property to anyone. However, if an unmarried couple has created a valid contract that gives each one the specific right to inherit specific property, that contract will normally be enforced if the person who feels cheated goes to court.

For detailed information about such contracts (and much more), see *Living Together: A Legal Guide for Unmarried Couples*, by Frederick Hertz & Lina Guillen (Nolo).

State law may also give your spouse the right to inherit the family residence, or at least use it for life. The Florida Constitution, for example, gives a surviving spouse the deceased spouse's residence, no matter what the deceased spouse's will or trust says. (Fla. Const. Art. 10, § 4.)

SEE AN EXPERT

Get expert legal advice about disinheriting your spouse. If you live in a common law state and you want to leave your spouse less than half of your property from a shared trust, see a lawyer.

Disinheriting a Child

With rare exceptions, it is legal to disinherit a child. (The Florida Constitution prohibits the head of a family from leaving that person's residence to anyone except that person's spouse or child, if any (Fla. Const. Art. 10, § 4).)

You do not have to leave your child anything in your living trust. But to completely disinherit a child (or the children of a deceased child), your state laws require you to do so in your *will*, even if you transfer all your property by a living trust.

There are two ways to disinherit a child in a will. One is to expressly disinherit the child in the will, by stating that you aren't leaving that child anything. The other is to leave the child a minimal amount, which ensures the child cannot successfully claim to have been overlooked or accidentally omitted. If you don't mention a child in your will, state law may give that child the right to a certain share of your property.

The will forms in this book require you to list all your children. The forms then state that if you haven't left any property to a listed child, that failure to do so is intentional. So, if you leave a child nothing (by will or otherwise), this functions as a disinheritance clause.

Children Born After a Will or Trust Is Prepared

Most state laws protect offspring who were born after a parent's will was prepared. Although these laws mention only wills, not living trusts, it's possible that a court could apply them to a living trust, reasoning that the living trust is serving the function of a will.

These laws presume that the parent didn't mean to disinherit a child who is born after the parent's will has been signed, and thus is not mentioned in a parent's will. (Such children are called "pretermitted heirs," in legalese.) The law assumes that the parent simply hadn't yet gotten around to writing a new will. Such a child is legally entitled to a share (the size is determined by state law) of the deceased parent's estate, which may include property in a living trust.

The easy solution to this problem is to amend your living trust after a child is born. Most parents want to provide for a new child, so it's simply a matter of getting the work done. Amending your trust to provide for a new beneficiary is not difficult. (See Chapter 12.)

Posthumously Conceived Children

Medical technology now makes it possible for a child to be conceived after the biological mother or father has died. Inheritance rights for such children have been litigated in several states, with inconsistent results. Several states have passed laws about posthumously conceived children. Basically, these laws set a limit on the amount of time a child who was conceived after the parent's death has to seek to be legally declared as a child of that parent. Without such a limit, there's a possibility that a child born many years after his parent's death could suddenly claim to be legally entitled to inherit part of that parent's estate—a legal nightmare. Examples of these statutes include: California Probate Code, S 249.5; Iowa Code Ann. § 633.220A; Delaware, 13 Del. Code § 8-707. More states are likely to follow. If your plans include the possibility of a posthumously conceived child, you'll want to know your state's laws (if any) on this subject, and to figure out what you think is best. Discuss this matter with a knowledgeable estate planning lawyer.

Grandchildren

Grandchildren have no right to inherit from their grandparents unless their parent has died. In that case, the grandchildren essentially take the place of the deceased child and are entitled to whatever the deceased child would have been legally entitled to.

General Disinheritance Clauses

You may have heard that some lawyers recommend leaving $1 to close relatives in your trust or will. This is not legally necessary—and it's a bad idea. There's no need to mention anyone but your spouse and perhaps your children in your trust. No one else has a legal right to any of your property. Moreover, your successor trustee must track down each beneficiary to whom you leave a dollar and procure an acknowledgment that the beneficiary received the dollar. That's a lot of work, especially when there's no point to it.

Lawsuits contesting a living trust are very rare. A relative could conceivably try to contest your trust by claiming that you, the grantor, were mentally incompetent when you prepared your trust, and were duped by someone into leaving most or all of your property to them while you really wanted to leave it to this relative.

SEE AN EXPERT

Head off contests by relatives. If you think a relative might try to contest your trust, see a lawyer to determine the wisest course of action.

No-Contest Clauses

A "no-contest clause" in a living trust (or a will) is a device used to discourage beneficiaries of your trust or will from suing to void the trust or will and claiming they are entitled to more than you left them. Under a no-contest clause, a beneficiary who challenges a living trust or will and loses forfeits all any inheritance under that document. Without a no-contest clause, a beneficiary of a living trust can sue, lose, and still collect the amount gifted by the trust.

EXAMPLE: Pip leaves his daughter Estelle $10,000 in his living trust, and includes a no-contest clause in that document. If Estelle challenges the trust and loses, she does not receive the $10,000.

No-contest clauses can be sensible if there's a risk a beneficiary might challenge your estate plan. On the other hand, many people do not like to include a no-contest clause in their estate planning documents, because it seems to imply a suspicion of their beneficiaries that they don't actually feel. The trust and will forms in this book do not contain no-contest clauses.

SEE AN EXPERT

See a lawyer to add a no-contest clause. If you think you may need a no-contest clause, that's an indication of a potential serious problem. See a lawyer to discuss how to handle the risk of a court fight; often, a no-contest clause is just one part of a larger strategy.

Putting Conditions on Beneficiaries

Occasionally, a person wants to make a gift with restrictions or conditions on it. The trust forms in this book do not allow you to make conditional gifts. (You can, however, appoint someone to manage trust property inherited by a minor child or young adult. See Chapter 8.)

EXAMPLE: Ravi wants to leave money to his nephew, Monir, if he goes to veterinary school but if he doesn't, to his niece Sheela. This may sound simple, but it's not. Here are just a few problems inherent in this approach: How soon must Monir go to veterinary school? What happens if he applies in good faith but fails to get in? Who decides if he's really studying? What happens to the money before Monir goes to veterinary school? What happens if Monir goes to veterinary school but drops out after a year and says he'll go back eventually? What happens if he graduates but doesn't become a vet?

Imposing restrictions and controls on beneficiaries is sometimes called "dead-hand control." The obvious risk of dead-hand control is that circumstances can change, so you must try to anticipate what is likely—or even possible—to occur in the future, and provide for it. This, at best, is complex work, and helps to enrich estate planning lawyers.

SEE AN EXPERT

Get expert advice about long-term trusts. Except for a child's trust, you cannot create long-term trusts using this book. Some major types of long-term trusts are discussed in Chapter 14. You'll need a lawyer's help if you want to prepare one.

Property That Is No Longer in Your Trust at Your Death

If you make a gift of specific property in your trust, but then remove that property from your trust before you die—that is, you sell it or give it to someone—the beneficiary for that gift will probably be out of luck, and is likely to be quite upset. So, if you do transfer property from your trust, be sure to amend your trust document and formally delete the provision that left it to a beneficiary. (I explain how to amend your trust document in Chapter 12.)

Beneficiary Worksheets

On one of the following worksheets, list your beneficiaries and the property you want to leave to each:

- Use Worksheet 1 for an individual living trust.
- Use Worksheet 2 for a shared living trust. Each spouse names beneficiaries separately.

To get started, go back to the Property Worksheet in Chapter 5 where you listed what items you will transfer to your trust. On these worksheets, you will name a beneficiary for each item. If you're making a gift to cobeneficiaries and naming alternate cobeneficiaries, you need to decide what share each cobeneficiary receives.

You can also find these worksheets in Appendix B and as downloadable forms on this book's companion page: www.nolo.com/back-of-book/LITR.html. (See Appendix A.)

Beneficiary Worksheet 1: Individual Living Trust

1. Specific Gifts

_____
Item of Property

_____
Primary Beneficiary

_____
Alternate Beneficiary

_____
Item of Property

_____
Primary Beneficiary

_____
Alternate Beneficiary

_____
Item of Property

_____
Primary Beneficiary

_____
Alternate Beneficiary

_____
Item of Property

_____
Primary Beneficiary

_____
Alternate Beneficiary

_____
Item of Property

_____
Primary Beneficiary

_____
Alternate Beneficiary

_____
Item of Property

_____
Primary Beneficiary

_____
Alternate Beneficiary

_____
Item of Property

_____
Primary Beneficiary

_____
Alternate Beneficiary

_____
Item of Property

_____
Primary Beneficiary

_____
Alternate Beneficiary

_____
Item of Property

_____
Primary Beneficiary

_____
Alternate Beneficiary

_____
Item of Property

_____
Primary Beneficiary

_____
Alternate Beneficiary

2. Residuary Beneficiary or Beneficiaries

_____
Residuary Beneficiary(ies)

_____

_____

_____
Alternate Residuary Beneficiary(ies)

_____

Beneficiary Worksheet 2: Shared Living Trust

Wife's Beneficiaries

1. Specific Gifts

Item of Property

Primary Beneficiary

Alternate Beneficiary

Item of Property

Primary Beneficiary

Alternate Beneficiary

Item of Property

Primary Beneficiary

Alternate Beneficiary

Item of Property

Primary Beneficiary

Alternate Beneficiary

Item of Property

Primary Beneficiary

Alternate Beneficiary

Item of Property

Primary Beneficiary

Alternate Beneficiary

Item of Property

Primary Beneficiary

Alternate Beneficiary

Item of Property

Primary Beneficiary

Alternate Beneficiary

Item of Property

Primary Beneficiary

Alternate Beneficiary

Item of Property

Primary Beneficiary

Alternate Beneficiary

2. Residuary Beneficiary or Beneficiaries

Residuary Beneficiary(ies)

Alternate Residuary Beneficiary(ies)

Beneficiary Worksheet 2: Shared Living Trust (continued)

Husband's Beneficiaries

1. Specific Gifts

_____
Item of Property

_____
Primary Beneficiary

_____
Alternate Beneficiary

_____
Item of Property

_____
Primary Beneficiary

_____
Alternate Beneficiary

_____
Item of Property

_____
Primary Beneficiary

_____
Alternate Beneficiary

_____
Item of Property

_____
Primary Beneficiary

_____
Alternate Beneficiary

_____
Item of Property

_____
Primary Beneficiary

_____
Alternate Beneficiary

_____
Item of Property

_____
Primary Beneficiary

_____
Alternate Beneficiary

_____
Item of Property

_____
Primary Beneficiary

_____
Alternate Beneficiary

_____
Item of Property

_____
Primary Beneficiary

_____
Alternate Beneficiary

_____
Item of Property

_____
Primary Beneficiary

_____
Alternate Beneficiary

2. Residuary Beneficiary or Beneficiaries

_____
Residuary Beneficiary(ies)

_____

_____

_____
Alternate Residuary Beneficiary(ies)

_____

Property Left to Minor Children or Young Adults

f any of the beneficiaries you've named (including alternate, residuary, or final beneficiaries) might inherit trust property before they are able to manage it responsibly, you'll want to arrange for an adult to manage that beneficiary's property.

If your young beneficiaries won't inherit anything of great value—that is, if you're leaving them objects that have more sentimental than monetary value— you don't need to arrange for an adult to manage the property.

Here are the beneficiaries you should arrange management for:

- **Any beneficiary now younger than 18.** Legally, children younger than 18 cannot own outright or directly manage substantial amounts of money—roughly, anything more than $2,500 to $5,000, depending on state law.

  If a minor inherits valuable trust property, and you have not arranged for the property to be managed by an adult, a court-appointed guardian will have to manage the property. Contrary to what you might expect, a child's parent does not automatically have legal authority to manage any property the child inherits. A child's parent will have to ask the court to grant the parent that authority, and will be subject to the court's supervision. If neither of the beneficiary's parents are alive, there may be no obvious person for the court to appoint as property guardian. In that case, it may be even more important for you to name someone in your living trust.

TIP

Use your will to name a personal guardian. If you have a child under age 18, you must nominate a personal guardian—the adult responsible for raising the child—in your will, like the one provided by this book. You can't do this in your living trust.

- **Any beneficiary older than 18 you believe is not mature enough to responsibly handle your gift.** If a beneficiary is older than 18 when the beneficiary inherits trust property, you do not legally need to have anyone manage the

property on the beneficiary's behalf. If you don't make any arrangements, the beneficiary will get the property with no strings attached. But with the forms in this book, you can arrange for property management to last until a young adult beneficiary turns any age up to 35—that is, you can choose any age between 19 and 35 when the young adult receives the property outright.

Why 35?

We've created a rule that any beneficiary must receive a gift made from a Nolo living trust outright by age 35 at the latest. We've chosen 35 for the cutoff age because it seems reasonable to conclude that an adult who can't manage financial matters responsibly by that age may never be able to do so. If you want someone else to manage the trust property of a beneficiary who's older than 35, you'll probably want to see a lawyer to create a special type of trust, usually called a "spendthrift trust," and resolve specific problems, such as who will be the trustee many years down the line if the beneficiary survives to old age.

Whether or not you want to provide for management of property inherited by a young adult beneficiary is a personal decision. Some young adults are fully capable of managing money at age 21, while others at the same age might indulge recklessly, even disastrously, if they received a large inheritance outright.

Property Management Options

If you want to provide for property management for a gift to a minor or young adult beneficiary, you have several options:

- **Leave the property directly to an adult to use for the child.** Many people don't leave property directly to a child. Instead, they leave it to the child's parent or to the person they expect to have care and custody of the child if neither parent is available. There's no formal legal arrangement, but they trust the adult to use the property for the child's benefit.

- **Create child's trusts.** You can establish one or more child's trusts in your living trust. Technically, a child's trust is a subtrust of the overall living trust. You create a separate child's trust for each young beneficiary. If you establish child's trusts, your successor trustee will manage the trust property you left each child or young adult and spend it for that child's education, health, and other needs. If you create a shared living trust, the surviving spouse will manage property left to minors by the deceased spouse; the successor trustee will act only after both spouses die. Each child's trust ends at whatever age you designate for that child (between 18 and 35), and any remaining property is then turned over to the beneficiary outright.

- **Name a custodian under the Uniform Transfers to Minors Act (UTMA).** This is a model law written by a national panel of experts. All states but South Carolina have adopted this law, sometimes with minor modifications. In states with the UTMA, you can use your living trust to name a "custodian" to manage property you leave a child, until the child reaches 18 or 21, or up to 30 in some states, depending on state law. If you don't need management to last beyond the age your state law allows, a custodianship is often preferable to a child's trust.

RESOURCE

Children with special needs. These property management options are not designed to provide long-term property management for a child or young adult with serious disabilities. *Special Needs Trusts,* by Kevin Urbatsch and Michele Fuller-Urbatsch (Nolo), explains how you can create a trust that provides for your loved one without interfering with that person's eligibility for SSI or Medicaid benefits.

Which Method Is Better for You: Child's Trust or Custodianship?

Both a child's trust and a custodianship are safe, efficient ways of managing trust property that a young person inherits. Under either system, the

Age Limits for Property Management in UTMA States			
State	**Age at which minor gets property**	**State**	**Age at which minor gets property**
Alabama	21	Montana	21
Alaska	18–25	Nebraska	21
Arizona	21	Nevada	18–25
Arkansas	18–21	New Hampshire	21
California	18–25	New Jersey	18–21
Colorado	21	New Mexico	21
Connecticut	21	New York	21
Delaware	21	North Carolina	18–21
Dist. of Columbia	18–21	North Dakota	21
Florida	21–25*	Ohio	21–25
Georgia	21	Oklahoma	18–21
Hawaii	21	Oregon	21–25
Idaho	21	Pennsylvania	21–25
Illinois	21	Rhode Island	21
Indiana	21	South Dakota	18
Iowa	21	Tennessee	21–25
Kansas	21	Texas	21
Kentucky	18	Utah	21
Maine	18–21	Vermont	21
Maryland	21	Virginia	18, 21, or 25
Massachusetts	21	Washington	21 or 25
Michigan	18–21	West Virginia	21
Minnesota	21	Wisconsin	21
Mississippi	21	Wyoming	21–30
Missouri	21		

* In Florida and Virginia, the minor can choose to receive UTMA funds at age 21, even if the account is set to terminate at a later age.

person in charge of the young beneficiary's property has the same responsibility to use the property for the beneficiary's support, education, and health. For example, you can leave a gift of life insurance by using a child's trust or by naming a custodian under the UTMA, and in either case, the proceeds will be held in trust by an adult for benefit of the child you name to be the beneficiary. So use whichever method works better for you, and don't get hung up worrying about technicalities or puzzling over possible legal intricacies.

Florida and Virginia Unique UTMA Rules

In Florida and Virginia, you can create an UTMA custodianship that will end when a young beneficiary reaches age 21 or 25. However, if you choose age 25, the custodian must give the beneficiary the opportunity to terminate the custodianship (and receive custodial property outright) within a month of the beneficiary's 21st birthday. In other words, even if you want a young beneficiary's property management to end at age 25, the beneficiary can choose to take the gift four years earlier. To avoid this possibility, use a child's trust instead, or get help from an experienced Florida estate planning attorney. (Fla. Stat. § 710.123.) (Va. Code § 64.2-1908 and § 64.2-1919.)

The most significant difference between a child's trust and an UTMA gift is that a child's trust can last longer than a custodianship, which must end by age 21 in most states (or up to 30 in some states). For that reason, a child's trust is a good choice when it's conceivable that a young person could inherit a large amount of property, and you want the money handled by a more mature person, at least through the child's middle 20s.

An UTMA custodianship is usually preferable to a child's trust if the beneficiary will inherit an amount that is likely to be used up for living expenses by the time the child reaches age 18 or 21—the ages when UTMA custodianship ends in most states. For example, if your state allows the UTMA gift to be kept in custodianship until the child is 21 or older, an amount up to $100,000 could surely be consumed by four years of college costs. In this situation, there's probably no need to create a child's trust to last beyond the UTMA cutoff age.

A custodianship can have other advantages as well:

- Handling a beneficiary's property can be easier with a custodianship than with a trust. A custodian's powers are written into state law, and most institutions, such as banks and insurance companies, are familiar with the rules. Trusts, on the other hand, vary in their terms. So before a bank lets a trustee act on behalf of a beneficiary, it may demand to see and analyze a copy of the trust document.

- You can name whomever you wish to be a custodian, and you can name different custodians for different beneficiaries. So if you want to arrange custodianships for grandchildren, for example, you could name each child's parent as custodian. A child's trust is not so flexible: The surviving spouse, or the successor trustee, will be the trustee of all child's trusts created for your young beneficiaries.

- A custodianship may offer better income tax rates than a trust. In 2021, a trust is taxed at 10% on retained income up to $2,650 annually, with the top rate reaching 37% on income of more than $13,050. By contrast, property managed by an UTMA custodian is taxed as income above $2,200 paid directly to the child, often a lower rate than paid by a trust. (This can get complicated, because income paid to a child younger than 19, or a dependent full- time student younger than 24, is taxed at the child's parents' tax rate.)

Tax-Saving Educational Investment Plans

Beyond leaving property to children, you should know that federal law provides three different plans you can use to save for the educational expenses of children. These plans could affect your living trust planning because if you establish one of these plans for your own children, you should have less worry about future educational expenses draining your estate.

529 Plans

A 529 plan is an investment account established to pay for the higher education of a named beneficiary. The beneficiary must be a "family member," who can range from your own children to cousins. Income accumulates in a 529 plan free of taxes. More importantly, no income tax is assessed on money paid from a 529 plan for the beneficiary's tuition, books, fees, supplies, and equipment necessary to attend college, graduate school, or approved vocational institutions. Authorized expenses can also include special needs services for a student with disabilities.

There are two basic types of 529 plans:

- **A savings plan.** You make contributions to the plan, which are then invested as you, within the plan limits, decide. Whatever money has accumulated is available for the beneficiary when the beneficiary goes to college.
- **A prepaid plan.** You can prepay all or part of the costs of in-state college education. You pay the money directly to the educational institution. There's also an Independent 529 plan, a prepaid plan for private colleges.

Generally, an individual can give each beneficiary up to $15,000 per year free from gift tax. Contributions can be made only in cash. Couples can combine their gifts to give each beneficiary up to $30,000 per year. However, 529 plans allow you to aggregate five years of gift tax allowance on a one-time gift. For example, you could make a one-time payment of $75,000 ($150,000 per couple). That gift would not be subject to tax, but you would not be able to make any additional tax-free gifts to the account for the next five years. Gifts made in excess of these limits are subject to federal gift tax. (See "Federal Gift and Estate Taxes" in Chapter 14.)

These plans are called "529" plans because they were created by that section of the Internal Revenue Code. (They are also sometimes called "qualified tuition programs.") Under federal law, you can invest only in a state-authorized plan. Each state now has its own separate plan, managed by an investment company or companies selected by that state. Managers range from TIAA-CREF to Vanguard to J.P. Morgan to various lesser-known financial institutions.

Some state plans allow you to invest only if you live in that state. Also, about half the states allow residents to deduct 529 contributions from their state income tax, which could be a major incentive to buy a home-grown 529 plan. On the other hand, the majority of 529 plans allow anyone to invest in them. Indeed, you could invest in more than one. If you're seeking the best plan for your investment needs and beliefs, you have a rather bewildering array of plans to choose from.

However you choose to invest in a 529 plan, you are basically investing in securities—stocks and bonds—that come with the stock market pitfalls we've all become aware of. Crucially, some state's 529 managers have a far more aggressive (risky) investment strategy than do managers of other state's plans. So you'll need to do quite a bit of homework before selecting a 529 plan that's right for you.

If a beneficiary does not attend college, you can name a new beneficiary from the eligible family group. But if you wind up taking money out of a 529 plan for noneducational purposes, taxes and penalties apply.

RESOURCE

Learn more about 529 plans from the SEC. You'll find lots of free information about 529 Plans online, including the U.S Securities and Exchange Commission's publication, *An Introduction to 529 Plans*, at www.sec.gov.

TIP

Funds in a 529 plan are considered a parental asset, not a child's. For college financial aid purposes, having funds in a parent's 529 plan, rather than in the child's name, can be very desirable. The federal formula for college aid requires students to contribute 20% of their assets to their education. For parents, the figure ranges from 0% to 5.64%.

ABLE Accounts

The federal Achieving a Better Life Experience Act (ABLE Act) allows states to establish a type of 529 account for individuals who became disabled before age 26. Most states have created these accounts. The few states that have not are likely to follow. Also, most states that provide ABLE accounts allow nonresidents to use them if they are otherwise qualified.

Unlike standard 529 accounts, tax-free distributions from an ABLE account can be made for qualified disability expenses, as well as for education costs. However, an ABLE account can contain no more than a total of $100,000. If the account is over that limit, the excess is counted as a resource of the disabled person for purpose of determining eligibility for government assistance. Also, under IRS regulations, the total annual contributions to an ABLE account cannot exceed the gift tax-exempt limit. In 2021, this means that no account can receive more than $15,000 per year. And any funds remaining in an ABLE account are subject to Medicaid "payback" when the owner dies. You can learn more about ABLE accounts and keep track of legislative changes in the Special Needs Estate Planning section of Nolo.com or on the website for the ABLE National Resource Center (www.ablenrc.org).

Coverdell Accounts

Coverdell accounts allow you to set aside $2,000 per beneficiary (younger than 30 years of age) per year to pay for that person's elementary, secondary, or higher education. There is no limit on the number of accounts permitted for any beneficiary, but the yearly maximum applies per beneficiary, from all contributors, for all accounts. In other words, a grandparent and a parent can each open a Coverdell account for the same child, but the total contributions to all accounts for that child in any year cannot exceed $2,000.

Contributions to Coverdell accounts are restricted by income. An individual taxpayer earning less than $95,000 a year can fully contribute. Contribution limits are lowered for a taxpayer with net earnings between $95,000 and $110,000. A taxpayer with net earnings of more than $110,000 cannot contribute. Taxpayers filing jointly with earnings of less than $190,000 can fully contribute. Contribution limits are lowered for taxpayers filing jointly with incomes between $190,000 and $220,000. Taxpayers filing jointly who earn more than $220,000 cannot contribute.

Contributions are not tax deductible when you make them. But money in the account is not taxed when (or if) it grows, and no tax is due when you make qualified withdrawals from the account to pay for a young person's education expenses.

Obviously, the $2,000 limit decreases the appeal of a Coverdell account, and more parents use 529 plans to save for their children's education. But a Coverdell account can still be useful in the right circumstances. For example, a grandparent or another relation could establish Coverdell accounts for your children, while you invest in a 529 account or save in other ways for education costs.

> **TIP**
>
> **IRS resource.** IRS Publication 970, *Tax Benefits for Education*, covers a number of different federal tax benefits and options for children's education expenses.

Child's Trusts

As I've stressed, if you leave any trust property to minors or to young adults who cannot responsibly manage property, you can create, within your living trust, a separate child's trust for each such beneficiary. Your surviving spouse or successor trustee manages all child's trusts.

How a Child's Trust Is Created

The first step is to make your gifts in your living trust document, including gifts left to any children or young adults. One common example is life insurance proceeds made payable to your living trust. You name your child or children as beneficiaries for all proceeds turned over to the trust. Then you complete another clause in your trust document, the child's trust clause, where you list each child's name and the age (from 19 to 35) at which this beneficiary is to receive trust property outright. If, at your death, the beneficiary is younger than the age you specified, a trust will be created for that beneficiary. If the beneficiary is older, the beneficiary gets the trust property with no strings attached, and no trust is created. (Leaving life insurance through your trust is discussed in more detail below.)

> **EXAMPLE:** In their shared living trust, Roger and Victoria each leave their trust property to the other. They name their daughters, who are 22 and 25, as alternate beneficiaries, and arrange for any trust property they may inherit, including their life insurance proceeds, to stay in children's trusts until each daughter reaches 30. They name Victoria's sister, Antoinette, as successor trustee.
>
> Roger and Victoria die in a car accident when one daughter is 28 and the other is 31. The 28-year-old's half of the trust property stays in a children's trust, managed by Antoinette, until she turns 30. The 31-year-old gets her half outright; no trust is created for her.

How a Child's Trust Works

Grantor sets up living trust, leaving some trust property to three children. Grantor dies. Terms of the trust require property to be distributed this way:

33-year-old: Gets property outright.	8-year-old: Property goes into child's trust until child turns 21.	22-year-old: Property goes into child's trust until child turns 25.

If a child's trust becomes operational, your successor trustee (or surviving spouse, if you made a trust together) must obtain a separate trust taxpayer ID number for each child's trust, file separate tax returns, and keep separate accountings and records for each trust. The successor trustee must manage each trust individually. So an operational child's trust is both a component of the overall living trust and a distinct entity. If light can be both a wave and a particle, surely this kind of duality is acceptable. And indeed it is, in the real world of the IRS, banks, and trust beneficiaries.

> **EXAMPLE:** In his individual living trust, Stanley names his 14-year-old son Michael as beneficiary for a stock account currently worth $275,000. He specifies that any stock Michael inherits when Stanley dies should be kept in a trust until Michael is 30, subject to the trustee's right to spend it on Michael's behalf.
>
> Stanley dies when Michael is 19. The stock goes into the child's trust for him, managed by the successor trustee of Stanley's living trust. The trustee is free to use the stock (and the income it produces) to pay for Michael's education and support. Michael will receive what's left of the stock when he turns 30.

You can create a separate child's trust for each young beneficiary you list. If these trusts ever become operational, Nolo's living trust forms provide that each one is given the name of its particular beneficiary. This allows each child's trust to be readily identified and managed in the real world.

> **EXAMPLE:** Leo Goldstein's living trust creates child's trusts for his grandchildren, Janet and John Ronninger, which are to last until each is 30. Leo dies while Janet and John are minors. Leo's successor trustee manages the children's trusts, one of which is called "The Leo Goldstein Living Trust, The Janet Ronninger Child's Trust" and the other of which is called "The Leo Goldstein Living Trust, The John Ronninger Child's Trust." Thus these trusts are identified as independent entities, while technically they are part of the original living trust as well.

Who Serves as the Trustee

The trustee for each child's trust is your successor trustee, or, with a shared trust after both spouses are deceased, the successor trustee takes over any operational child's trusts. The trust forms in this book do not allow you to name another person to be a trustee for a child's trust.

The reason is that naming separate trustees creates serious paperwork and practical problems. Which trustee gets the original of your living trust document? Do you create several originals? Besides, it's usually hard enough to find one competent person who'll serve as trustee for all child's trusts. If you really want to name someone other than your successor trustee to be custodian for a gift to a minor, consider using the UTMA. (See "Custodianships," below.)

SEE AN EXPERT

See an expert if you want to name someone else to be trustee of a child's trust. If you want to have child's trusts managed by someone other than your surviving spouse or your successor trustee, see a lawyer.

The Trustee's Duties

The trustee's powers and responsibilities are spelled out in the trust document. The trust trustee must:

- Manage each child's trust's property until that trust's beneficiary reaches the age set out in the trust document—which can take years.
- Use each trust's property or income to pay for that trust beneficiary's expenses, such as support, education, and health care.
- Keep separate records of trust transactions and file income tax returns for each trust.
- A very few states require periodic reports to the beneficiary of a child's trust. However, in most cases, it doesn't matter whether or not it's done, since everything is within the family.

A trustee who needs to hire an accountant, a tax lawyer, or another expert to help manage a trust can use that trust's assets to pay a reasonable amount for the help.

The trust document also provides that the trustee of a child's trust is entitled to reasonable compensation for work as trustee. The trustee decides what is a reasonable amount without court approval; the compensation is paid from the assets of the particular trust involved.

When the beneficiary reaches the age designated by the trust document, up to 35, the trustee must give the beneficiary what remains of that child's trust property.

Leaving Life Insurance Proceeds Through a Child's Trust

If you name minor children as beneficiaries, or alternate beneficiaries, of your life insurance, you need to create some type of adult management for the proceeds. You may also want mature adult management while the children are younger adults.

One sensible way to accomplish this is to name your living trust as the beneficiary of your life insurance. Then in the trust document, you name each child as a beneficiary of the proceeds, specifying the percentage or amount each child is to receive. Finally, within your living trust, you create a separate child's trust for each child.

Your living trust does not become the owner of the life insurance policy. You remain the owner. If you die while the child or children are younger than the age you specified in your living trust, the money will be managed for the child by your successor trustee until the child is old enough to receive the money outright.

Another possible approach for life insurance with child beneficiaries is to create a custodianship for each child, and name each child's custodian as beneficiary in specified portions for the insurance. (See "Custodianships," below.) A problem with this approach is that in most states, the custodian must turn over all property to the child when the child reaches 21 or 25; in a number of states, the age is 18. With a child's trust, you can extend the age the child must reach before gaining unfettered control of the property.

Technically, passing the proceeds of a life insurance policy through your living trust is a bit more complicated than leaving other property this way. You must take two steps:

1. Name the trustee, as trustee of the child's trust of the living trust, as the beneficiary of your life insurance policy. Your insurance agent will have a form that lets you change the beneficiary of the policy. Tell the agent what you want to do and make sure you have forms that are acceptable to the insurance company.

2. When you list property items in the living trust document (that is, property owned by the trust), list the proceeds of the policy, not the

policy itself. (Chapter 9 contains an example of how to list beneficiaries for insurance proceeds left to your trust.)

Custodianships

Creating a custodianship for a gift under your state's Uniform Transfers to Minors Act (UTMA) may be a preferable alternative to creating children's trusts.

You can create an UTMA custodianship in any state except South Carolina.

How a Custodianship Is Created

After you make all your gifts in your living trust, in a separate section of the trust form you can create as many custodianships as you want for minor or young adult beneficiaries. You do this by identifying the property and the beneficiary it is left to, and appointing a custodian to be responsible for supervising that property. The form provides that the custodian is to act "under the [*your state*] Uniform Transfers to Minors Act." You can also name an alternate custodian in case your first choice can't do the job. Finally, you list the age at which the minor is to receive the property outright, using the list above as your guide. In most states, you have no choice and must list the age that state's UTMA decrees. In a few states, you can choose an age in a set range.

The custodian manages any trust property the young beneficiary inherits until the beneficiary reaches the age at which state law says the custodianship must end. (See the chart that shows when UTMA ends in each state, above.)

EXAMPLE: Sandra and Don make a shared living trust. Sandra leaves 100 shares of Starbucks stock to her niece Jennifer. She names Hazel, Jennifer's mother, as custodian under the Illinois Uniform Transfers to Minors Act. At Sandra's death, Jennifer is 13. So Don, as trustee of the living trust, turns the stock over to the custodian, Hazel. She will manage it for Jennifer until Jennifer turns 21, the age at which Illinois law says she must be given the property outright.

As discussed, in some states, you can specify—within limits—the age at which custodianship will end. If your state allows this, you must state the age at which the custodianship will terminate.

Other Types of Trusts for Minors or Young Adult Beneficiaries

In some situations, you may want a different type of child's trust than the individual trusts you can create with this book's living trust forms. Consult a lawyer if you want to:

- place extensive controls over the use of property in the trust—for example, if you place real estate in the trust and you want it managed in a specific way

- create a trust for a person with special needs who receives SSI or Medicaid benefits. *Special Needs Trusts*, by Kevin Urbatsch and Michele Fuller-Urbatsch (Nolo), explains how these trusts work.

- create a trust for any beneficiary who is already over age 35, or

- combine property for different children into a single trust (often called a "family pot" trust). In this type of trust, the trustee doles out money to different children as the trustee sees fit, according to their needs. If the children are far apart in age, establishing this type of trust may not be a good idea because the older children will not receive trust funds outright until the youngest child reaches the designated age. On the other hand, for young children in a family group, this sort of trust may be sensible, so that the trustee can spend, as a parent would, according to the children's needs.

EXAMPLE: Alexis and Jonathan, who live in New Jersey, make a shared living trust. They leave most of their trust property to each other and leave some property to their young children, Ian and Noel. They both specify, in the trust document, that any trust property the children inherit should be managed by the other spouse as custodian, under the New Jersey Uniform Transfers to Minors Act, until the boys turn 21. Under New Jersey law, they could have specified any age from 18 to 21. As alternate custodian, both name Jonathan's sister.

Alexis and Jonathan die simultaneously in an accident. Jonathan's sister, as custodian, takes over management of the trust property left to the children. When each boy turns 21, he will receive whatever of his property hasn't been used for his support or education.

How a Custodianship Works

Grantor sets up living trust, leaving trust property to adults and two children. After Grantor dies, terms of the trust require property to be distributed this way:

To adult beneficiaries	Custodianship #1 created	Custodianship #2 created
	Beneficiary #1 reaches the age set out in trust document. Receives property from custodian.	Beneficiary #2 reaches the age set out in trust document. Receives property from custodian.

Changes in State Law

States are free to change their rules about the age at which custodianships terminate. If your state does this after you make your living trust, it could affect any custodianships you have set up, though not in any drastic way:

- If your state raises the age at which custodianships terminate, the new age will determine when your beneficiary's custodianship ends.

- If your state adopts a flexible scheme allowing you to choose the age at which the custodianship ends, you can amend your living trust document to designate an age. If you don't amend it, the custodianship will end when the beneficiary reaches the youngest age allowed under the law.

If You Move

If you make arrangements to use your state's UTMA and then you move to a different state, you'll want to review your trust to see if you should amend the UTMA provision to reflect your new state's rules.

If you move to South Carolina, which has not adopted the UTMA, you'll need to change your provision to use that state's Uniform Gifts to Minors Act. However, if the beneficiary of the gift, or the custodian for it, remains in a state that has an UTMA, you can still use that law for your gift.

See Chapter 12 for a discussion on how to amend your living trust.

The Custodian's Responsibilities

A custodian has roughly the same responsibility as the trustee of a child's trust: To manage the beneficiary's property wisely and honestly. The custodian's authority and duties are clearly set out by the Uniform Transfers to Minors Act, as enacted by your state. No court directly supervises the custodian.

The custodian must:

- Manage the property until the beneficiary reaches the age at which, by law, the beneficiary gets the property outright. If the child is quite young at your death, this can be a number of years.

- Use the property or income to pay for the young beneficiary's support, education, and health care.

- Keep the property separate from the custodian's own property.

- Keep separate records of trust transactions. The custodian does not have to file a separate income tax return; income from the property can be reported on the young beneficiary's return. (By comparison, the trustee of a child's trust must file a separate tax return for the subtrust.)

A custodian who needs to hire an accountant, a tax lawyer, or another expert can use the property to pay a reasonable amount for the help.

If state law allows it, the custodian is entitled to reasonable compensation and reimbursement for reasonable expenses. The payment, if any is taken, comes from the property the custodian manages for the beneficiary. If this concerns you, check out your state's laws or see a lawyer. (See Chapter 16.)

Choosing a Custodian

In most cases, you should name as custodian the person who will have physical custody of the minor child. That's almost always one of the child's parents. If the beneficiary is your child, name the child's other parent, unless you have serious reservations about that person's ability to handle the property for the child.

Only one person can be named as custodian for one beneficiary. You can, however, name an alternate custodian to take over if your first choice is unable to serve. And you can name different custodians for different beneficiaries.

> **EXAMPLE:** Elaine, in her living trust, leaves property to two young nephews, Jerry and Mark, and one young niece, Reyna. She names Jerry and Reyna's mother, Alice, as custodian for their gifts. She names Mark's mother, Angela, as custodian for his gift.

Preparing Your Living Trust Document

Now it's time to actually prepare your living trust document. This chapter explains how to do it, step-by-step, when you use one of the trust forms in this book.

Please read this entire chapter carefully so you understand the choices you will make. Take your time and reread as much as you need to.

Checklist for Preparing Your Living Trust Document

☐ **1. Decide which trust form to use.**

☐ **2. Prepare your trust document.**

    A. Using a form from Appendix B.

    ☐ Remove the form you need from Appendix B.

    ☐ Fill in the form by hand, following the step-by-step instructions in this chapter.

    ☐ Type and proofread a final version of the completed form using a computer or typewriter.

    B. Using a downloadable form.

    For instructions on how to access and edit the downloadable forms that come with this book, see Appendix A.

    ☐ Download the form you need.

    ☐ Use your word processor's "Save As" command to rename and save the document to a convenient place on your computer.

    ☐ Fill in the form by following the step-by-step instructions in this chapter.

    ☐ Save, print out, and proofread your final document.

☐ **3. Finalize your document.** Sign and date your trust document in front of a notary public in the state where you live.

☐ **4. Transfer property into the trust.** (See Chapter 10.)

☐ **5. Store your document in a safe place.** (See Chapter 11.)

Choosing the Right Trust Form

This book provides two living trust forms:

- **Form 1:** Basic probate-avoidance living trust for one person.
- **Form 2:** Basic probate-avoidance shared living trust for a couple (married or not) with shared ownership property.

Generally, you should use only one trust. However, in a few special situations you may decide it's preferable to use more than one. (See Chapter 4 for a discussion.)

TIP

If you use forms from the back of the book, make a few copies. Many people need to make only one draft before they type up their final document. But having extra copies of the form certainly can't hurt, and may be useful if you need to prepare more than one draft. Use a pencil to make corrections easier, and go through the form slowly and carefully.

Making Changes to a Trust Form

These Nolo trusts are intended to be used with the language we give to you, except for minor, commonsense variations, or where the directions specifically allow you a choice of what to include. Generally, it's risky to make changes to the trust forms. Changes in the language create the possibility of confusion and contradiction regarding what you intend with your trust. If you are inclined to make many changes to the form language, this may indicate that our form does not suit you, and you need to see a lawyer.

That said, most people who use these forms may need to make minor word changes. For example, if you want to name cosuccessor trustees, you'll need to change the word "trustee" to "trustees" at various places in the form.

> **CAUTION**
>
> **Be very cautious about making changes.**
> You will have to use your common sense to decide whether or not minor changes in the form are needed. But do be very careful. Don't stray far from the language of the form, and be sure you understand the effect of any changes you make.

Step-by-Step Instructions

Important: These instructions are keyed to numbers on the trust forms. For example, Step 1 tells you how to fill in your name(s) and how to name your living trust. On the trust form, each time your name, or names, are called for, you'll see a ①. (If you prepare your trust using the downloadable forms, the numbers will appear in parentheses rather than in a circle.)

The steps are set out in the most logical order. However, the circled numbers on the forms do not always proceed sequentially; for example, number ①, the name of your trust, appears at the beginning of the form and also later, after other circled numbers. This is because the information called for is needed in more than one place in your trust form. Other numbers appear out of sequence because the information called for is necessary only for that one form, so the number given comes after the numbers and information common to all forms. Just remember the basic principle: *The circled number refers you to the specific step in this section that explains how to fill in this blank.*

Some simple information you must fill in is not keyed to a circled number because no instructions seem necessary. For instance, where you see a blank and "he/she" printed underneath, put in either "he" or "she," depending on whether the person referred to (which will be clear in the context) is male or female. Similarly, where you see a blank with "your state" printed underneath, fill in the state where you live.

When you have completed the form, proofread it carefully. Then proceed, as explained in the last three sections of the chapter, to finalize your trust document.

For couples. For the most part, the same decisions must be made whether you're preparing a living trust for one person or for a couple, so the instructions are just about the same. However, some instructions apply only to the two shared living trusts. They are identified by this symbol:

Special Instructions for Unmarried Couples

Form 2 is written using the traditional terms "husband" and "wife." Unmarried couples and same-sex couples will need to replace some terms to reflect their relationship type.

You can use a term that seems most suitable to you and your situation. For example, women in a same-sex marriage may want to change each instance of "husband" and "wife" to "Wife 1" and "Wife 2" or "Spouse 1" and "Spouse 2." Unmarried couples can also choose to replace the word "spouse" with a more accurate term. For example, both shared trusts use the term "surviving spouse," and unmarried couples may want to change it to "surviving grantor" or "surviving partner."

Though making these word changes does require some extra work, it's really just a matter of "find and replace," which hopefully you won't find onerous.

Step ① : Name Your Living Trust

You must give your living trust a name. Normally, you simply use your own name—for example, "The Denis Clifford Living Trust." It's legal to use more inventive names, for reasons ranging from a desire for privacy to nostalgia. (I once had a client who created the "Rue de Rivoli Living Trust.") Also, if you create more than one trust, you will want to distinguish them. One way to do this is to use numbers, particularly Roman numerals, to prevent any confusion in a shared trust, which splits into Trust #1 and Trust #2 on the death of a spouse. For example, "The Denis Clifford Living Trust #I,"

"The Denis Clifford Living Trust #II," and so on. You could also sign the trusts on different days and identify each trust by the date signed—for example, "The Denis Clifford Living Trust, 3/19/20xx"; "The Denis Clifford Living Trust, 4/7/20xx."

Use only one name per person; don't enter various versions of your name joined by "aka" (also known as).

If you go by more than one name, be sure that the name you use for your living trust is the one that appears on the ownership documents for property you plan to transfer to the trust. If it isn't, it could cause confusion later, and you should change the name on your ownership documents before you transfer the property to the trust.

> **EXAMPLE:** You use the name William Dix for your trust, but own real estate in your former name of William Geicherwitz. You should prepare and sign a new deed, changing the name of the real estate owner to William Dix before you prepare another deed to transfer the property from you (William Dix) to your living trust.

COUPLES

Couples who make shared living trusts normally use both their names to identify their trusts— for example, "The Kay and Ornette Lewison Living Trust" or "The Cynthia Duffy and Mike O'Mally Living Trust." As with a trust for an individual, a couple can give their shared trust a fanciful name.

If you use your name or names for your trust, insert it every time there is a **1** on the living trust form.

If you don't use your own name, you'll need to determine, each time you see a **1** , whether your own name or the trust's name is required. For example, when naming the original trustees, you'll put in your own name(s), not the trust's name.

Step **2** : Decide How Many Property Schedules Your Trust Needs

By this time, you should have decided which items of your property you will place in your living trust and which you will leave by other means. (See Chapter 5.) Now you need to list all property that you will transfer to the trust on a "schedule" or "schedules," which will be attached to your trust document. How to list the property on a trust schedule is explained in Step 3.

As you can see by looking at the trust forms, a trust schedule is nothing more than a blank sheet of paper.

First, you must decide how many trust schedules you want to use. If you're creating a trust for one person (Form 1), you will use only one schedule, "Schedule A," even if several—or many—different types of property will be transferred to the trust.

> **EXAMPLE:** Mrs. Johnson wants to transfer her house, stock accounts, jewelry, and household possessions to her living trust. She lists all this property on one trust schedule, Schedule A.

For a couple, there are these:
- Schedule A, Shared Property Placed in Trust
- Schedule B, Wife's Separate Property Placed in Trust, and
- Schedule C, Husband's Separate Property Placed in Trust.

COUPLES

The shared trust form (Form 2) has three schedules, A, B, and C. Schedule A is for the couple's shared ownership property. On Schedule A, you need to identify the character of shared ownership property such as "community property" or "tenants in common." (This is discussed in detail in Step 4, below.) Schedule B is for the wife's separate property, and C is for the husband's separate property. If you have shared property and each spouse has separate property, you will use all three schedules.

EXAMPLE: Mrs. and Mr. Andrezly, in their 60s, have been married for 15 years. Each has children from a former marriage. When they got married, each owned property that they agreed would remain each one's separate property. Since they married, they have acquired shared property, including a home. In their shared living trust, they both want their separate property to go to their children from their first marriages and their shared property to go to the surviving spouse.

They list their property in the shared living trust by using three schedules: Schedule A for the shared property, Schedule B for Mrs. Andrezly's separate property, and Schedule C for Mr. Andrezly's separate property.

If the Andrezlys created three separate trusts —a shared living trust for the shared marital property and two individual living trusts for each spouse's separate property—they would use only Schedule A of the shared trust for their shared marital property.

If one or both spouses do not have separate property, you won't use Schedule B, Schedule C, or both of them. You'll also need to delete references in the trust document to that spouse's (or both spouses') separate property. The paragraphs you may need to change are listed below.

EXAMPLE: Tau and Lien Yu prepare a shared living trust. They own shared property. Lien also owns separate property; Tau does not. So they omit Schedule C from their trust and using Form 2, they edit Sections II(D)1 and II(D)2 as shown below.

---

1. Shared Property

All trust property listed on Schedule A was shared property:

4 *owned as community property of the grantors and shall retain that character after being*
~~identify the character of shared property listed in Schedule A~~

transferred to this trust. If the trust is revoked, this property shall be returned to the grantors

as their community property.

2. Separate Property

The trust property listed on Schedule B shall retain its character as the separate property of

Lien Yu ~~. The trust property listed on Schedule C~~
wife's name

~~shall retain its character as the separate property of~~ _____ .
husband's name

Changes to Trust Form 2 If Separate Property Is Not Included

If either spouse doesn't transfer separate property to a shared trust, you'll need to make appropriate changes on Form 2 by deleting the irrelevant material from the following sections:

- Section II, Paragraph A, refers to Schedules A, B, and C. Thus, if neither spouse has separate property, delete "B and C." If a wife has separate property and her husband does not, this would become "Schedules A and B."
- Section II, Paragraph B(1), refers to the wife's separate property.
- Section II, Paragraph B(2), refers to the husband's separate property.
- In Section II, Paragraph D(2), the first sentence refers first to the wife's separate property on Schedule B. The second sentence refers to the husband's separate property on Schedule C.
- Section IV(A) of Form 2 refers to Schedules A and C; Section IV(B) refers to Schedules A and B.
- Section V(B) of Form 2 refers to Schedules A, B, and C.

Step ③ : List Your Trust Property on the Trust Schedule(s)

After you've decided how many schedules to use, list your trust property on them. Listing the trust property on a schedule does not give that property to beneficiaries. You list the property to make clear what property you have transferred to the trust and is owned by the trust. Then, in your trust document, you name your beneficiaries—that is, specify who will inherit the trust property after your death (Step 7, below).

> ⚠ **CAUTION**
>
> **Transferring property to the trust.** To complete the transfer of property to the trust, you also must reregister title to that property in the trustee's or trustees' name(s). This absolutely essential process is explained in detail in Chapter 10.

When listing trust property on a trust schedule, generally you can use the same wording you used on the worksheet in Chapter 5. Just describe each item clearly enough so that the surviving spouse or successor trustee can identify it and transfer it to the right person. No magic legal words are required. Remember, this isn't a document that will be picked over by lawyers and courts. It's a document for the real world; what's important is that your successor trustee, family, and other beneficiaries are clear on what you've done and what you want.

Identifying Ownership of Trust Property

Don't use "my" or "our" when listing trust property on a schedule. For example, don't enter "my books" or "my stereo system." That's because once the property is in the living trust, technically it doesn't belong to you anymore—it belongs to the living trust, and is held in the name of the trustee.

If you need to refer to yourself or your property in a trust schedule, do so in the third person, by calling yourself "the grantor" or "grantors" rather than using "I" or "we." Sometimes, to clarify what property is owned by the trust, it helps to state on the schedule that identified property was "formerly" or "previously" owned by the grantor.

For example, on a trust schedule, you list: "The three-quarter carat diamond bracelet formerly owned by the grantor."

A variation of this is to identify and list property "in the possession of the grantor," for example, "All golf equipment in the possession of the grantor."

Think about who will ultimately inherit the property. If you're leaving everything to one person, or a few major items to be parceled out among a few people, there's less need to list property in great detail. But if there will be a number of trust beneficiaries, and objects could be confused, be more precise about each one. When in doubt, err on the side of including more information.

When you name the beneficiaries for the trust property in your trust document (Step 7), your gifts must, of course, be consistent with the property listed on the trust schedule(s). You can't leave someone something that isn't listed on a trust property schedule. But the schedule does not have to be as detailed as your gifts. For example, on a schedule you could list "the house, furnishings, and personal possessions at [*street address*]." You can leave all this property to one beneficiary, or you could divide it, naming one beneficiary for the house and another for the furnishings and possessions, or break it down still further into many separate gifts.

Real Estate

A house can be listed by its street address—for example, "The house and real estate at 10001 Lakeway Drive, Seaview, Florida." Similarly, unimproved property can usually be listed by its common name: "The lots previously owned by the grantor on 50 to 80 Alligator Road, Seaview, Florida."

Usually, the street address is enough. It's not necessary to use the "legal description" found on the deed, which gives a subdivision plat number or a metes-and-bounds description. But if the property has no street address or common name—for example, if it is undeveloped land, off-road, out in the country—you need to designate exactly what land you're referring to. So carefully copy the full legal description, word for word, from your deed.

If you own a house and an adjacent lot (or several), it's a good idea to indicate that you are transferring the entire parcel to your living trust by describing the land as well as the house.

EXAMPLE:

> The house at 390 Normal Road, Montclair, New Jersey, and all unimproved land between 390 Normal Road and 320 Normal Road.

Real estate often contains items that are properly classified as personal property. For instance, farms are often sold with tools and animals. If you intend to leave both real estate and personal property together to a beneficiary, make clear what this "together" consists of. It's best to specify the large-ticket items

(tractor, cattle) and refer generally to the rest of the items as "personal property." For example:

> - 240-acre truck farm on Route 11, in Whitman County, Iowa, with all tools, animals, tractors, threshers, and other machines and all other personal property located there.
> - Fishing cabin on the Wild River in Washington County, Maine, with all the fishing gear, furniture, tools, and other personal property found there.
> - The house at 442 Wanaha Bay Road, Island of Hawaii, Hawaii, and all personal possessions and household furnishings in the house.
> - The mobile home permanently located at E-Z motor camp, Kalispell, Montana, and all possessions and furnishings contained in it.

If you own real estate with someone else and are transferring only your share to the trust, you don't need to specify how big a share you own. Just describe the property. The trust schedules then state that you are transferring all your interest in the property, whatever share that is, to the living trust.

EXAMPLE: Rhea owns a one-fifth interest in an apartment house located in Atlanta, Georgia. She prepares a deed transferring her one-fifth interest to her living trust's name. On the trust schedule, she simply writes:

> The interest in the apartment house at 434 Madison Street, Atlanta, Georgia, previously owned by the grantor.

Time-shares. A time-share in a house or an apartment can be transferred to the trust. You can describe your interest as "the grantor's share in ___(*address*)___," or "the grantor's right to three weeks per year use of ___(*address*)___."

You also need to formally reregister title to a time-share in the trust. Depending on your state law, the time-share may be considered real estate, and so must be transferred by recorded deed. Otherwise, the time-share may be transferred with a simple notice of assignment. (See Chapter 10.)

Furnishings and Household Items

Household furnishings can be listed generally:

> The house and real estate at 12 High Street, Chicago, Illinois, and all household furnishings and personal possessions in it.

> All the grantor's household goods and personal possessions located at 82 West Avenue, Chicago, Illinois.

Or you can get more specific:

> All the furniture normally kept in the house at 44123 Derby Avenue, Ross, Kentucky.

> All furniture and household items normally kept in the house at 869 Hopkins Street, Great Falls, Montana.

You can also list individual items, if you plan to leave them separately. For example:

> The antique brass bed in the master bedroom in the house at 33 Walker Avenue, Fort Lee, New Jersey.

> Daumier print captioned "Les beaux jours de la vie."

> Two Victorian rocking chairs in the living room at 75 Washington Street, Jefferson, Montana.

Bank and Money Market Accounts

You can list bank accounts by any means sufficient to identify them. Generally, it makes sense to list the account number:

> Bank account # 78-144212-8068 at Oceanside Savings, Miami, Florida, Market Street. Branch.

> Savings Account No. 9384-387, Arlington Bank, Arlington, Minnesota.

> Money Market Account 47-223 at Charles Schwab & Co., Inc., San Francisco, California.

Cash

You cannot transfer cash to a living trust simply by stating a dollar figure on the schedule. For example, if you list "$25,000" on Schedule A, this doesn't transfer that amount of cash to the trust, because no source for these funds is given. Instead, list a specific source of cash. You can then make specific cash gifts from this source when you name your trust beneficiaries. Here are some examples:

> Bank account #33-931007-6214 at Bonanza Thrift, Miami, Florida.

> $25,000 from the grantor's stash in his desk.
> (This is obviously risky. If the money is removed from the desk, technically it is no longer owned by the trust.)

Securities

Securities, including mutual fund accounts, need to be listed clearly so there is no question what property is referred to:

> Mutual fund account #6D-32 2240001, at International Monetary Inc., Chicago, Illinois.

> All stock and any other assets in account #144-16-4124, at Morgan Stanley, 1290 Avenue of the Americas, NY 10104.

> 100 shares of General Motors common stock.

> Mutual funds in account # 55-144-2001-7, Calvert Social Responsibility Fund, Boston, Massachusetts.

Sole Proprietorship Business Property

With a sole proprietorship business that has not been incorporated, the proprietor is the legal owner of all assets of the business, including the business name and any "goodwill." So you can simply list all assets of that business as a single item of trust property. For example:

> All assets of the grantor doing business as Mulligan's Fish Market, 44 Wellington Street, Wymouth, Kentucky.

> All assets of the grantor doing business as Fourth Street Vinyl Records, 10 Piper's Lane, Hoboken, New Jersey.

> All assets of the grantor doing business as Jim Pine Plumbing, 477 Market Street, Fort Lauderdale, Florida.

You can also divide up the business assets if you're leaving different parts to different people. For example:

> All accounts receivable of the business known as Garcia's Restaurant, 988 17th Street, Atlanta, Georgia.

> The business name, goodwill, lease, and all food and food preparation and storage equipment, including refrigerator, freezer, hand mixers, and slicer, used at Garcia's Restaurant, 988 17th Street, Atlanta, Georgia.

Shares in a Closely Held Corporation

> The stock of ABC Hardware, Inc., formerly owned by the grantors.

Partnership Interest

Because a partnership is a legal entity that can own property, you don't need to list items of property owned by the partnership. Just list your partnership interest:

> All the grantor's interest in Don and Dan's Bait Shop, a partnership, Belmore, Oregon.

Shares in a Solely Owned Corporation

> All shares in XYZ Corporation.

> All stock in Fern's Olde Antique Shoppe, Inc., 23 Turnbridge Court, Danbury, Connecticut.

Membership Interest in a Limited Liability Company

> The grantor's membership interest in the Goat-Cheese-and-Wine LLC.

Miscellaneous Items of Personal Property

There are various ways you can list items of personal property on a trust schedule, depending primarily on whether you want to leave separate items to different beneficiaries, or all of one type of item to a sole (or group of) beneficiaries.

For items of significant monetary or sentimental value, you may want to list them individually. For example:

> HP Pavilion laptop (serial number 129311).

> The medical textbooks in the grantor's office at 1702 Parker Towers, San Francisco, California.

> The photograph collection usually kept at 321 Glen Street, Omaha, Nebraska.

> The collection of European stamps, usually kept at 440 Loma Prieta Boulevard, #450, San Jose, California. (*Describe any particularly valuable stamps.*)

> The Martin D-35 acoustic guitar, serial number 477597.

> The signed 1960 Ernie Banks baseball card kept in safe deposit box 234, First National Bank of Augusta, Augusta, Illinois.

> The Baldwin upright piano kept at 985 Dawson Court, South Brenly, Massachusetts.

> Gold earrings with small rubies in them, purchased from Charles Shreve and Co. in 1971.

If you are like most people, you have all sorts of minor personal possessions you don't want to bother itemizing. To deal with them, you can group a number of items in one category, such as:

- all carpenter's tools, including power saws, in possession of the grantor
- all dolls
- baseball cards
- records, tapes, and compact discs, or
- sports equipment.

Of course, some items without large monetary value can have great emotional worth to you and your family—for example, a photo album, an old music box, a treasured chair. These can be separately listed as you desire.

If you're leaving all these groups of personal items to one beneficiary, there's no need to separately list them, even as groups. You can simply conclude your list with one catch-all item, such as "all personal property previously owned by the grantor."

Sample Schedule A for Shared Property

Below is a sample of a draft Schedule A for shared property for Form 2, a shared trust. When the final trust form is typed, the schedule is likewise typed, eliminating the printed instructions on the form. The final typed schedule is attached to the trust document.

Sample

Schedule A

Shared property placed in trust:

> The house and real estate at 428 Dubuque Drive, Alameda, California.

> All shares of stock in the Mo-To Corporation, Alameda, California.

> The grand piano located at 428 Dubuque Drive, Alameda, California.

> The Diebenkorn painting located at 428 Dubuque Drive, Alameda, California.

> All other household possessions and furnishings located at 428 Dubuque Drive, Alameda, California.

> Money market account #7033372, Bank of America, Boston, Massachusetts.

> Certificate of Deposit No. 10235, Lighthouse Savings and Loan Association, Oakland, California.

> All copyrights and rights to royalties previously owned by the grantors in these books, currently published by Fly High Press, Berkeley, California:

> > *Dunk It: You Can Learn to Dunk a Basketball; Winning Through Whining, a Self-Help Guide; Watch It! How to Survive Urban Life*

Step 4 : Identify the Nature of Shared Trust Property (Form 2 Only)

If you and your spouse are creating a trust together, you should state in the trust document that all shared property transferred to the trust (listed on Schedule A) retains the legal character it had before. That means that it stays community property if you live in a community property state. If you live in a common law state, all shared property transferred to the trust should be owned equally by the couple as tenants in common, not as joint tenants or tenants by the entirety. (See "Paperwork" in Chapter 10. Also see Chapter 5 for a discussion of community property states and common law states.)

If you don't share ownership 50-50, be sure to list each person's percentage of ownership.

If you are an unmarried couple that owns property together, you can likewise state that shared ownership property on Schedule A be returned to you two in the percentages of ownership you define in the schedule, and in this clause, if the trust is ever revoked.

To define the nature of shared trust property, insert one of the following clauses directly after the words, "All trust property listed on Schedule A was shared property":

If you live in a common law state:

> co-owned equally by the grantors as tenants in common and shall retain that character after being transferred to this trust. If the trust is revoked, this property shall be returned to the grantors as co-owned equally by them as tenants in common.

If you live in a community property state:

> owned as community property of the grantors and shall retain that character after being transferred to this trust. If the trust is revoked, this property shall be returned to grantors as their community property.

If you are an unmarried couple:

> co-owned equally by the grantors as tenants in common. Any power reserved to the grantors to alter, amend, modify, or revoke this trust, as to the property listed in Schedule A, must be exercised by both grantors, in writing, to be effective. If this trust is revoked, this property shall be returned to the grantors as co-owned equally by them as tenants in common.

If you are married, you can change ownership of trust property without any possible gift tax consequences—for example, to convert one spouse's separately owned property to shared or community property or vice versa.

Step 5: Decide Whether You Want Management of Trust Property If You Become Incapacitated (Both Forms)

Form 1 provides that the successor trustee takes over management of the trust if you (the grantor) become incapacitated and unable to manage trust property. These provisions eliminate any need for court proceedings to appoint a guardian or custodian for trust property if you become incapacitated.

COUPLES

Incapacity under the shared trust. The shared trust (Form 2) provides that if both spouses become incapacitated, or if the survivor becomes incapacitated after one spouse dies, the trust property is managed by the successor trustee for the grantor's (or grantors') benefit.

Specifically, each trust form provides that if the grantor or grantors become incapacitated, the successor trustee "shall pay trust income at least annually to, or for the benefit of, the grantor(s) and may also spend any amount of trust principal necessary in the trustee's discretion for the needs of the grantor(s)." In other words, the successor trustee has a duty to make sure the incapacitated grantor(s) are properly cared for. If the annual income from the trust is higher than the expenses of the incapacitated grantor(s), the trustee can simply put the surplus in the grantors' bank account, thus using this money "for the benefit of the grantor(s)."

It's sensible and standard to provide for management of trust property if you become incapacitated. This book's trust forms ask you to name three people whom you want to determine your capacity to manage the trust if the question ever arises. If at least two of the three you named determine that you're not able to manage the trust—for example, because you're ill and hospitalized—they can authorize the successor trustee to take over. This way, there will be someone with power to make sure your trust affairs are taken care of.

Pick three people you trust, and who are likely to remain available throughout your life. If one or more of them later becomes unable to do this task, you can amend your trust to name a new person.

The three should sign a single document recording their decision about your capacity. The successor trustee will likely need such a document to prove to financial or other institutions that the successor trustee has the authority to manage the trust. There is no standard legal form for this document. Below is a sample of what it might look like.

Allowing your successor trustee to step in and manage trust property doesn't give your successor trustee legal authority over property that's not in your living trust. To give someone that power, you need a document called a "durable power of attorney for finances."

If you don't prepare a durable power of attorney for finances and you become incapacitated, property not transferred to your living trust will need to be managed by a court-appointed conservator or guardian.

For this reason (and because you may receive other property or income in the future that doesn't make it into the trust), I strongly suggest that you also create a durable power of attorney for finances. See "Planning for Incapacity" in Chapter 14.

Step 6 : Name Your Successor Trustee

In the blanks with the 6 on the trust forms, name your successor trustee and your alternate successor trustee. (Choosing your successor trustee is discussed in Chapter 6.) You've already named yourself as the original trustee, or trustees.

EXAMPLE: Using Form 2, a couple completes Section III(E), Successor Trustee, as follows:

> Upon the death or incapacity of the surviving spouse, or the incapacity of both spouses, the successor trustee shall be Vicki J. Benoit. If she is unable to serve or to continue serving as successor trustee, the next successor trustee shall be B. J. Benoit.

Naming More Than One Successor Trustee

If you name more than one successor trustee or more than one alternate successor trustee, you need to specify in your trust document how the authority of the cotrustees is to be shared. Clearly, this is your personal decision, depending on how well the cotrustees get along and whether or not you think it's safe to let any of them act individually for the trust.

Sample Determination of Incapacity

Determination of Incapacity

Each of the signers below has determined that Lois H. Fulbright, grantor of the Lois H. Fulbright Revocable Living Trust dated June 5, 20xx, has become incapacitated and is no longer reasonably able to manage the trust.

Each signer's determination was made on the basis of that signer's knowledge of the grantor's circumstances and condition.

Under the terms of the trust document, this determination allows the successor trustee named in that document to serve as trustee.

_____ Date: _____

_____ Date: _____

_____ Date: _____

So, depending on your needs, immediately after you name your successor trustees and alternate successor trustees, you'll insert one of the following clauses from the form:

> Any of the successor trustees has full and independent authority to act for and represent the trust.

or

> All the successor trustees must agree in writing to any transaction involving the trust or trust property.

If you have only one successor trustee, you'll need to delete all this material from the form.

Listing Specific Trustee Powers

The trust forms give the trustee "all authority and powers" your state's laws allow. But the trust forms also list specific powers, including the power to sell trust real estate, buy or sell stocks, and several other detailed powers. All of these specific powers are normally included in the general authority conferred on a trustee under state law. But banks, title companies, stockbrokerage companies, and other financial institutions have been known to insist that a trustee be specifically authorized by the trust document to engage in a transaction involving their institution. So, often, spelling out these powers makes the successor trustee's work much easier in the real world.

Bonds

The forms provide that no trustee has to post a bond. A bond is basically an insurance policy guaranteeing that a person will honestly carry out the trustee's duties; it pays off up to a stated amount if the trustee fails to do so. Bonding companies, which are normally divisions of insurance companies, issue a bond in exchange for a premium, usually about 10% of the face amount of the bond.

If you select a trustworthy successor trustee, there's no reason for a bond. In almost all situations, the question never comes up. Since the successor trustee handles the trust outside any court system, there's no forum where a demand for a bond could be raised. But just in case the question is somehow raised in a lawsuit (very unlikely), it's sensible to have waived any bond requirement. The cost of a bond would have to be paid for by your estate, and your beneficiaries would then receive less. Also, it's difficult for an individual to even get a bond in many states.

SEE AN EXPERT

See a lawyer to require a bond. If you do want your successor trustee to post a bond, see a lawyer.

Step 7 : Name the Primary and Alternate Trust Beneficiaries

Now you enter the names of your trust beneficiaries, naming who gets what.

With a trust for an individual (Form 1) or a shared living trust (Form 2), insert their names and descriptions of property given them in the blanks where you see 7 . You can make as many separate gifts as you need to. The forms have spaces for five; if you have more, use another sheet of paper.

Reminder for unmarried couples: If you are an unmarried couple and use Form 2, you'll need to change the printed form's references to spouses. For example, "Husband's Beneficiaries" or "Wife's Beneficiaries" can be changed to the appropriate individual's name. Example: "Al Smith's Beneficiaries" instead of "Husband's Beneficiaries."

Changing Forms 1 or 2 If You Don't Leave Specific Gifts

If you, your spouse, or both of you choose not to leave any specific gifts, but instead leave all trust property to each other, you'll need to eliminate the provisions in Form 2 for making specific gifts, and also make any necessary revisions to the beneficiaries section.

Similarly, if you use Form 1 and don't make any specific gifts but leave all property to your residuary beneficiary, you'll need to eliminate the specific gift provisions from your trust.

> ⚠ **CAUTION**
>
> **The example below shows only how to revise a trust form if you do not want to leave specific gifts.** Some portions of the trust forms in the back of this book have been omitted from the following example.

With Form 2, this may involve deleting Section IV(A)1 and/or Section IV(B)2.

EXAMPLE 1, FORM 2: Lola and Malcolm Decamp use Form 2. Lola leaves two specific gifts, Malcolm leaves none. They revise the Beneficiaries section of the form as shown below.

IV. Beneficiaries

(A) Husband's Primary and Alternate Beneficiaries

Upon the death of _____,
_{husband's name}

trust property owned by _____,
_{husband's name}

as his share of the trust property listed on Schedule A and any separate property listed on Schedule C,

shall be distributed as specified to the beneficiaries named in this section.

1. Husband's Specific Beneficiaries

a. **7** _____ shall be given
_{beneficiary}

_____ .
_{property identified}

If _____
_{beneficiary}

does not survive _____,
_{husband's name}

that property shall be given to _____ .
_{alternate beneficiary}

[All specific husband's beneficiary provisions deleted]

(A)   ~~2.~~ **Husband's Residuary Beneficiary**

The residuary beneficiary of any trust property owned by _____ *Malcolm Decamp* _____
husband's name

_____ as his share of the trust property listed on Schedule A or any separate property

listed on Schedule C, and not specifically and validly disposed of by Section IV, Paragraph (A)1, shall be

8 _____ *Lola Decamp* _____ .
~~residuary beneficiary~~

If _____ *Lola Decamp* _____ does not
~~residuary beneficiary~~

survive _____ *Malcolm Decamp* _____
~~husband's name~~

that property shall be given to **8** ____ *Ted and Linda Decamp, in equal shares* ____ .
~~alternate residuary beneficiary~~

(B) Wife's Primary and Alternate Beneficiaries

Upon the death of ____ *Lola Decamp* _____ ,
~~wife's name~~

trust property owned by ____ *Lola Decamp* _____ ,
~~wife's name~~

as her share of the trust property listed on Schedule A and any separate property listed on Schedule B,

shall be distributed as specified to the beneficiaries named in this section.

1. Wife's Specific Beneficiaries

a. **7** ____ *Susan Fergis* _____ shall be given
~~beneficiary~~

all trust gold jewelry formerly owned by Lola Decamp _____ .
~~property identified~~

If ____ *Susan Fergis* _____
~~beneficiary~~

does not survive ____ *Lola Decamp* _____ ,
~~wife's name~~

that property shall be given to ____ *Jean Fergis* _____ .
~~alternate beneficiary~~

b. **7** ____ *John Fergis* _____ shall be given
~~beneficiary~~

the autographed photo of Willie Mays _____ .
~~property identified~~

If ____ *John Fergis* _____
~~beneficiary~~

does not survive ____ *Lola Decamp* _____ ,
~~wife's name~~

that property shall be given to ____ *the residuary beneficiary* _____ .
~~alternate beneficiary~~

c. **7** _____ shall be given
beneficiary

_____ .
property identified

If _____
beneficiary

does not survive _____ ,
wife's name

that property shall be given to _____ .

2. Wife's Residuary Beneficiary

The residuary beneficiary of any trust property owned by _____ *Lola Decamp* _____
wife's name

_____ as her share of the trust property listed on Schedule A or any separate property

listed on Schedule C, and not specifically and validly disposed of by Section IV, Paragraph (B)1, shall be

8 _____ *Malcolm Decamp* _____ .
residuary beneficiary

If _____ *Malcolm Decamp* _____ does not
residuary beneficiary

survive _____ *Lola Decamp* _____ ,
wife's name

that property shall be given to **8** _____ *Ted and Linda Decamp, in equal shares* _____ .
alternate residuary beneficiary

How to Enter Beneficiaries' Names

Many people worry that precise birth certificate names must be used in living trusts to identify their beneficiaries, or their gifts won't be legally binding. Fortunately, this isn't true. You simply need to give the name that clearly identifies a beneficiary, so that your successor trustee understands to whom the gift is to be made. You don't have to worry about using a person's "legal" name, such as the full name on a birth certificate. Nor do you need to list the beneficiary's address or Social Security number.

If you name an institution (charitable or not) to inherit property from your trust, enter its complete name. It may be commonly known by a shortened version, which could cause confusion if there are similarly named organizations. Call to ask if you're unsure. (An institution that stands to inherit some of your money will be more than happy to help you.) Also, be sure to specify if you want a specific branch or part of a national organization to receive your gift—for example, a local chapter of the Sierra Club.

Identifying Property Left to Beneficiaries

There are three basic approaches to identifying property in a beneficiary clause:

- Use exactly the same words you used on your property schedule. For example, if you listed "Money Market Account #60-32 2240001 at International Money Inc., Boston, Massachusetts" on your schedule, use exactly the same words in the beneficiary clause.
- Group items left to a certain beneficiary. If you listed and specifically identified a number of similar items on a schedule (for example, five bank accounts, ten valuable paintings, four automobiles) and you wish to leave all items in a particular group to the same beneficiary, it's sufficient to say "all bank accounts listed on Schedule A" or "all paintings listed on Schedule A."
- Be more specific in the body of your trust than in your trust schedule. For example, suppose on Schedule A you listed "all books

in possession of the grantor" to indicate that ownership of all your books is transferred to your living trust. However, you don't wish to leave all these books to one beneficiary. When making gifts, you could state:

> Beth Ruveen shall be given all books by F. Scott Fitzgerald in the possession of the grantor.
>
> John Advale shall be given all books in French in the possession of the grantor.
>
> Jim Horton shall be given all books in the possession of the grantor, except those left or given by this trust document to Beth Ruveen and John Advale.

COUPLES

Shared property. On Form 2, each spouse can give away only that spouse's half-interest in shared property, not all of it. So, when naming a beneficiary or beneficiaries for property listed on Schedule A of a shared living trust, it must be clear that each spouse is giving away only his or her share of the co-owned property. To accomplish this, when you leave a gift from property on Schedule A, add an identifying phrase to the beneficiary clause. Here are two examples; the language you must add is underlined:

If property left to one beneficiary:

> _Karen Zombanski_ shall be given _all Lonnie Zombanski's_
> beneficiary
>
> _interest in the house listed on Schedule A_ .
> property identified

If property left to more than one beneficiary:

> _Charles Berry_ shall be given _50%_ , and
> beneficiary
>
> _Le Petit Richard_ and _B. Diddly_ each shall
> beneficiary   beneficiary
>
> be given _25% of all Jackson Marquez's interest in_
>
> _the stock account at Greco Financial Management,_
>
> _NYC, #177-4N-2044, as listed on Schedule A._
> property identified

Naming Children or Young Adults as Beneficiaries

You name a child or a young adult as a beneficiary exactly as you do an adult beneficiary, entering the child's name and identifying the trust property left to that child.

Later in the trust document, you can arrange for an adult to manage property left to a young beneficiary. (See Step 10.)

Leaving All Trust Property to One Beneficiary or Group of Beneficiaries

If you are using Form 1 or 2 and you want to leave all of your trust property to one person or to be shared by several, you can use just one beneficiary clause. Here are some examples:

For a shared trust, all property to your spouse:

> John Andrews shall be given all grantor Mary Andrews's interest in the property listed on Schedule A and Schedule B.

For an individual trust, all property equally to children:

> Steve Cronin, Elizabeth Cronin, and Roarke Cronin shall be given all property listed on Schedule A in equal shares.

Leaving Property to Several Beneficiaries to Share

You may want to leave an item of trust property to be shared among several beneficiaries. This is fine, as long as you use language that clearly identifies what share each beneficiary is to receive. This is best done by using percentages. If you use a shared trust (Form 2), be sure you are clear that you're giving away only your own interest in any property you share with your spouse. (Shared gifts are discussed in detail in Chapter 7.)

EXAMPLE: From a stock account transferred to his shared living trust (Form 2), Jim Denniston makes the following gifts:

> Melinda Denniston shall be given 20% of Jim Denniston's interest in the trust's brokerage account #660134-N, Citibank.
>
> Mike Denniston shall be given 30% of Jim Denniston's interest in the trust's brokerage account #660134-N, Citibank.
>
> Roger Denniston shall be given 5% of Jim Denniston's interest in the trust's brokerage account #660134-N, Citibank.
>
> Margo Denniston shall be given 35% of Jim Denniston's interest in the trust's brokerage account #660134-N, Citibank.
>
> Cerrita Gibbs shall be given 10% of Jim Denniston's interest in the trust's brokerage account #660134-N, Citibank.

Naming Beneficiaries of Proceeds From a Life Insurance Policy

If you have named your living trust as the beneficiary or alternate beneficiary of a life insurance policy, you can simply name, within the trust, a beneficiary, or beneficiaries, for any insurance proceeds payable to the trust. The usual reason for doing this is that the life insurance beneficiaries are minors. (See "Child's Trusts" in Chapter 8.) In your trust, you arrange for an adult to manage property, including insurance proceeds that minors or young adults may inherit. (See Step 10.) Remember, you don't need to list the policy on a trust schedule, because the trust never owns the policy; it is simply the beneficiary of it.

EXAMPLE:

> The grantor's children, Zack Philson and Zelda Philson, shall be given, in equal shares, all life insurance proceeds on the grantor's life paid to the trust.

Explanations and Commentary Accompanying a Gift

There are times, particularly in family situations, when explaining the reasons for your gifts can help avoid hurt feelings or family fights. If you wish, you can provide a brief commentary when making a gift. There are two ways to do it—in the trust document itself, or in a separate letter.

In the trust document. You'll need extra space for your comments. If you're using an electronic version of the form to make your rough draft, just include your note where you enter the gift. If you're using a hard copy of the form for your rough draft, write out your comments on a separate piece of paper with a note about where they should be inserted in the trust document. When you prepare your trust, you can integrate your comments into the trust form.

EXAMPLE:

> The grantor's business associate, Mildred Parker, who worked honestly and competently over the years, shall be given $40,000 from the Money Market Fund #166-SJ-4111, Parnassus Mutual Funds, San Francisco, California.
>
> The grantor's best friend, Hank Salmon, whom the grantor enjoyed fishing with for so many years, shall be given the cabin and boathouse on Lake Serene, and the boat and outboard motor in the boathouse.
>
> Theodore Stein shall be given 40% of Alfred Stein's interest in the house at 465 Merchant Street, Miami, Florida.
>
> Sandra Stein Rosen shall be given 40% of Alfred Stein's interest in the house at 465 Merchant Street, Miami, Florida.
>
> Howard Stein shall be given 20% of Alfred Stein's interest in the house at 465 Merchant Street, Miami, Florida.
>
> I love all my children deeply and equally. I give 20% to Howard because he received substantial family funds to go through medical school, so it's fair that my other two children receive more of my property now.
>
> Matt Jackson shall be given the bank account #41-6621-9403 at First Maple Bank.
>
> I love all my children deeply and equally. I leave more of my property to Matt than my other children because Matt is physically disadvantaged and is likely to need special care and attendants throughout his life.

Notice that in your explanations, you can refer to yourself in the first person, as "I," not "the grantor." It just sounds too awkward to express deep feelings as "the grantor." Besides, this type of wording isn't making a gift, but explaining it, so it's hard to imagine that any trouble could possibly arise from referring to yourself as "I" when speaking of your love for your kids.

In an accompanying letter. Another approach is to write a letter stating your views and feelings and attach it to your living trust document. Many people prefer this approach because it allows personal sentiments to be kept private. The living trust will have to be shown to people in various institutions, from banks to title companies to brokerage offices to county records offices. Many people don't want their personal feelings exposed to strangers in the business world. A letter can simply be removed from the trust document when showing the trust to any outsider. Also, if you have a lot to say, a letter is generally better than trying to express all your sentiments in the trust document itself.

Your letter isn't a legal part of your trust document, and it has no legal effect. It is prudent for you to state in your letter that you understand this, to eliminate any possibility someone could claim you intended the letter to somehow modify the terms of your trust.

When you use a separate letter, the length and scope of your remarks are limited only by your imagination, short of libel. (If you write something so malicious (and false) that you libel someone, your estate could be liable for damages.) Some writers have expressed, at length and in their own chosen words, their love for a mate, children, or friend. By contrast, Benjamin Franklin's will left his son William, who was sympathetic to England during our Revolution, only some land in Nova Scotia and stated, "The fact he acted against me in the late war, which is of public notoriety, will account for my leaving him no more of an estate that he endeavored to deprive me of."

Imposing a Survivorship Period

When you leave property to a primary beneficiary, you can specify that if the beneficiary doesn't survive you by some specified period of time, the gift will go to the alternate beneficiary, if you name one, or the residuary beneficiary if you don't name an alternate. The pros and cons of survivorship periods are discussed in Chapter 7.

If you want to add a survivorship period, simply insert a specific time period before naming the alternate beneficiary. To avoid creating unnecessary delays for your estate, make the survivorship period relatively short—less than 45 days.

EXAMPLE:

> _____ Hester Dinsdale _____ shall be given _____ Herbert Grant's _____
> <small>beneficiary</small>
>
> _____ interest in the antique doll collection located at _____
> <small>property identified</small>
>
> _____ 161 Hawthorn Lane, Gabels, Massachusetts _____ .
>
> If _Hester Dinsdale_ doesn't survive _Herbert Grant_
> <small>beneficiary</small> <small>husband's name</small>
>
> _by 30 days_ , that property shall be given to
>
> _____ Pearl Dinsdale _____ .
> <small>alternate beneficiary</small>

Naming Alternate Beneficiaries

As discussed, you are not required to name an alternate beneficiary for a gift. Some people don't wish to contemplate the chance of an inheritor, usually someone younger, dying before they do. But most people name an alternate beneficiary for each gift to a primary beneficiary. After all, there is always the chance that the primary beneficiary may not survive you, and you won't be able to amend your trust in time to leave the gift to someone else.

If you want to name alternate beneficiaries for a shared gift, be sure you read the discussion of this subject in Chapter 7.

With Form 1 or Form 2, if you don't name an alternate, the property that beneficiary would have received will be distributed to the person or institution you name as your "residuary beneficiary." (See Step 8, below.)

You can name more than one person or institution as alternate beneficiaries. These beneficiaries will share the property equally, unless you specify otherwise.

EXAMPLE: Sherry names her husband as beneficiary of her interest in their house, which they have transferred to their shared living trust. As alternate beneficiaries, she names their three children, Sean, Colleen, and Tim, to share equally.

Sherry's husband dies just before she does, leaving his half of the house to Sherry. Under the terms of the trust document, it stays in the living trust. At Sherry's death, because her husband (the primary beneficiary) is no longer alive, the house goes to the three children. All three own equal shares in all of it.

For shared gifts, it's easiest to name the other surviving beneficiaries to receive a deceased beneficiary's share. You can accomplish this by using or adapting the following language, which may require some minor changes in the printed portion of a beneficiary clause:

> _____ Gwen Riordan, Richard Riordan, and Martha _____
> <small>beneficiary</small>
>
> _Riordan Ling_ shall be given _____ Jack Riordan's _____
> <small>property identified</small>
>
> _interest in the house at 41 Sussex Road, Needles_ ,
>
> _Arizona, in equal shares_ .
>
> If _any of these beneficiaries_ does not survive
> <small>beneficiary</small>
>
> _Jack Riordan_ , ~~that property shall be given to~~
> <small>husband's name</small>
>
> _the deceased beneficiary's interest shall be_
> <small>alternate beneficiary</small>
>
> _shared equally by the surviving beneficiaries_ .

You can also name different alternates for each beneficiary of a shared gift. For example, an older person who leaves a shared gift to his children may list each child's children (or spouse) as alternate beneficiaries for that child's share of the gift.

Gwen Riordan, Richard Riordan, and Martha
beneficiary

Riordan Ling shall be given ___all Jack Riordan's___
property identified

interest in the house at 41 Sussex Road, Needles,

Arizona .

If _Gwen Riordan_ does not survive _Jack Riordan_ ,
husband's name

~~that property shall be given to~~ _her children, Mike_

Riordan James and Tracy Riordan James, shall

be given the interest in the property she would

have received .

If _Richard Riordan_ does not survive _Jack Riordan_ ,
husband's name

that ~~property shall be given to~~ _Richard's child,_

Sean Riordan, shall be given the interest in the

property he would have received .

If _Martha Riordan Ling_ does not survive _Jack_
husband's name

Riordan , ~~that property shall be given~~ to _her_

husband, Patrick Ling, shall be given the

interest in the property she would have received .

Step 8 : Name Your Residuary Beneficiary (Forms 1 and 2)

If you are preparing a trust for one person (Form 1) or a shared living trust (Form 2), the next step is to name your residuary beneficiary or beneficiaries.

You must name one or more residuary beneficiaries for your living trust where you see the 8 .

The residuary beneficiary of your living trust is the person or organization who will receive:

- any trust property designated for primary and alternate beneficiaries who die before you do
- any trust property that you didn't leave to a named beneficiary (this could include property you transferred to the trust later but didn't name a beneficiary for)

- any property you leave to your living trust through a pour-over will (because property left through a pour-over will doesn't avoid probate, there's usually no reason to use one; see Chapter 15), and
- any property that you actually transferred to your living trust but didn't list in the trust document.

Sometimes the residuary beneficiary of a living trust doesn't inherit anything from the trust, because all trust property is left to primary beneficiaries, with alternates. In this situation, naming a residuary beneficiary can be just a backup measure, to guard against the extremely small chance that both a primary and alternate trust beneficiary do not survive you.

You may, however, deliberately leave the residuary beneficiary trust property. For example, you can:

- Choose not to name specific beneficiaries for most trust property. Everything not left to a specific beneficiary will go to your residuary beneficiary. It's common, for example, for a grantor to leave much of his estate to his children as residuary beneficiaries.
- Add property to the trust later without amending your trust document to name a specific beneficiary to receive it after your death.
- Use a pour-over will to leave property to your living trust without naming a specific beneficiary in the trust document to receive property that passes through the will. (Wills are discussed in Chapter 15.)

More than one residuary beneficiary. If you name more than one residuary beneficiary (or alternate residuary beneficiary), you need to state, in the clause, what portion or percentage each residuary beneficiary will receive. It's common, especially if one's children are the residuary beneficiaries, to state that they each receive an equal share.

EXAMPLE:

> The residuary beneficiaries ... shall be Rachel Weinstock and Alan Weinstock, each to receive 50% of all trust property not specifically and validly disposed of by earlier gifts ....

Of course, you can also specify that residuary beneficiaries receive unequal shares. In that case, you must specify what percentage of the property each residuary beneficiary will receive.

EXAMPLE: Zane Jilconty names three siblings—Lucy, Jill, and Warren—as his residuary beneficiaries. For several reasons, he wants to leave them unequal amounts. So he provides, in his residuary clause, that his residuaries are:

> Lucy Jilconty, 50% of the residuary property; Jill Jilconty Jackson, 30% of the residuary property; and Warren Jilconty, 20% of the residuary property.

Alternate residuary beneficiaries. You should also name an alternate residuary beneficiary, or beneficiaries, to be sure you have one final backup to receive trust property if all other beneficiaries, including your residuary beneficiary, predecease you and you can't amend your trust in time. (True, this is a remote possibility, but remote possibilities are lawyers' stock-in-trade, and even we at Nolo can't bring ourselves to completely jettison concern for such unlikely contingencies.)

Step ⑨ : Provide for Payment of Debts and Taxes

There are two ways to handle payment of debts and taxes after your death:

- leave it up to the successor trustee, or
- designate that certain trust assets be used.

For many people, payment of debts and taxes is not a serious concern. Their estates are well under the minimum estate tax threshold, so they don't expect that federal taxes will be due, and their debts are relatively minor—perhaps a few personal bills, credit card charges, household utilities, and any unpaid bills from the last illness or funeral/burial costs.

SEE AN EXPERT

See a lawyer if you have complex debt or tax problems. If your estate is likely to face difficult debt or tax problems, see an attorney to discuss how to handle this. A good lawyer can help you draft specific provisions for payment of these obligations. Similarly, if much of the value of your estate will be transferred by methods other than your living trust, do not rely on the debt and tax payment options presented here, which do not apportion payment between trust and nontrust assets.

Leave the Decision to the Trustee

You do not have to decide what assets will be used to pay your debts and taxes. Many people prefer to leave this decision to their successor trustee, who will know what the real financial situation is when these debts must be paid. You can, at best, make only a reasonable guess now. If you direct that a specific asset or assets be used to pay any debts or estate taxes, it can cause problems later on. If you've also left the asset to a specific beneficiary, the provision for payment of debts and taxes takes priority, so that beneficiary may receive little or nothing from your gift. Also, if the property you identified isn't sufficient to pay all your debts and taxes, your successor trustee will still have to decide how to pay any balance due.

If allowing the trustee to make the decision makes sense to you, for an individual trust, where you see the ⑨ , delete all language after the first sentence of this section, as shown in the example below.

With a shared living trust (Form 2), each spouse can choose how that spouse's debts are to be paid. If both spouses want their successor trustee to decide this, there's a little more crossing out to do. Make deletions like those shown below for "Wife's Debts and Taxes," Section VIII C (1), and "Husband's Debts and Taxes," Section VIII C (2). Then delete all of the next provision, "If Specified Property Insufficient," Section VIII C (3).

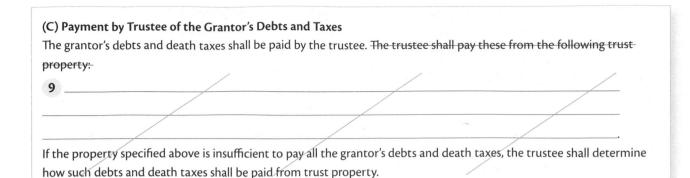

(C) Payment by Trustee of the Grantor's Debts and Taxes

The grantor's debts and death taxes shall be paid by the trustee. ~~The trustee shall pay these from the following trust property:~~

9 _____

_____

_____ .

If the property specified above is insufficient to pay all the grantor's debts and death taxes, the trustee shall determine how such debts and death taxes shall be paid from trust property.

Designate Specific Assets

If you decide you want to make specific provisions for payment of your debts and taxes from trust property, write in the specific items you want used to pay them in the blank where you see the **9** on the trust forms. And do your best to be sure these assets will actually be sufficient to pay all your debts and taxes.

EXAMPLE:

> The grantor's debts and death taxes shall be paid by the trustee from the following trust property:
> - First, from the bank account #99-8062144, Wells Fargo Bank, Berkeley, California.
> - Second, from stock account #82-304, Charles Schwab, 100 Post Street, San Francisco, CA 94108.

Remember that any property you specify to pay your debts and taxes must be owned by your trust. That means you must list it on a property schedule and transfer title into the trustee's name. (That process is explained in Chapter 10.)

 COUPLES
In a shared living trust, each spouse can specify the property to be used to pay that spouse's debts and death taxes.

> **EXAMPLE:** Sid and Ellen Wall want each one's debts and taxes paid from a shared stock account. In their shared living trust, they provide:

1. Wife's Debts and Taxes
Ellen Wall's debts and death taxes shall be paid by the trustee from the following trust property: her interest in stock account #54-3309, Charles Schwab, 100 Post Street, San Francisco, CA 94108.

2. Husband's Debts and Taxes
Sid Wall's debts and death taxes shall be paid by the trustee from the following trust property: his interest in stock account #54-3309, Charles Schwab, 100 Post Street, San Francisco, CA 94108.

Step 10 : Provide Property Management for Young Beneficiaries (Optional)

Next, you can provide property management for any young beneficiaries whom you've named to receive trust property. You can use either a child's trust or the UTMA for each beneficiary. You can use a child's trust for one beneficiary and the UTMA for another, but you cannot set up a child's trust and the UTMA for the same beneficiary—you must choose one method for each beneficiary.

Create Children's Trusts (Optional) 10A

In the blank with the 10A on the trust forms, list each person (minor or young adult) you want to name as beneficiary of a child's trust. This may include minors and young adults you've named as alternate beneficiaries.

Be sure not to list as child's trust beneficiaries any persons you want to make gifts to using the Uniform Transfers to Minors Act (UTMA). You'll do that in Step 10B. You cannot leave a gift to a minor by both the UTMA and a child's trust.

Children as Beneficiaries of Life Insurance

As discussed in Chapter 8, you can make minor children beneficiaries of life insurance policies in three steps:

1. Register the policy beneficiary in the name of the trustee(s).
2. In your trust, name the minor children as beneficiaries of the policy.
3. In your trust, create a child's trust or an UTMA custodianship for each minor child who will receive proceeds from the policy.

For each trust beneficiary you list where you see the **10A**, you also state the age at which you want that beneficiary to receive trust property. If you die before the beneficiary reaches the age you specify, the beneficiary's property will be retained in a child's trust until the age is reached. (See Chapter 8.) If you don't specify an age, each listed beneficiary will receive the trust property outright at the age of 35.

Create Custodianships Under the Uniform Transfers to Minors Act (Optional) **10B**

If you want to make a gift to a child using your state's Uniform Transfers to Minors Act (UTMA), complete the custodianship clause where you see a **10B**. The form contains three blank clauses for individual beneficiaries, but you can add as many additional clauses as you want.

To complete the UTMA clause, begin by listing the state where you live. (You can use the UTMA in any state except South Carolina.) Then, fill in the beneficiary's name, the custodian's name, and the age the beneficiary will receive the property outright. You can also use an UTMA clause to leave gifts to any minors, such as grandchildren, if they live in a state that has an UTMA law.

The age a child will receive the gift outright depends on state law. Check the chart in Chapter 8 which lists each state's termination age. In some states, you are

given a limited choice of when the custodianship ends. For example, you can choose any age from 18 to 21 in Maine, and 18 to 25 in California. But most states allow you no choice. The gift must end at the age set by the state. In those states, all you need do is fill in the age from the list in Chapter 8.

In California, where you can choose an age between 18 and 25:

> All property _Ned Clark_ becomes entitled to under this trust document shall be given to _Mary Clark_ as custodian for _Ned Clark_ under the _California_ Uniform Transfers to Minors Act until _Ned Clark_ reaches age _24_.

In New Hampshire, where a custodianship must end at age 21:

> All property _Luisa Brookside_ shall become entitled to under this document shall be given to _Nancy Curtis_ as custodian for _Luisa Brookside_ under the _New Hampshire_ Uniform Transfers to Minors Act until _Luisa Brookside_ reaches age _21_.

If You Do Not Create a Child's Trust or Make Gifts Using the Uniform Transfers to Minors Act

If you do not create a child's trust or make any gifts under the Uniform Transfers to Minors Act, simply delete the blank section(s) before your final trust is typed. These clauses are at the end of the trust form so that you do not have to renumber other trust clauses if you delete both of them.

If you create children's trusts but do not make gifts under the Uniform Transfers to Minors Act, simply delete that later clause. Again, no renumbering of clauses is required.

However, if you do not create any children's trusts but do make gifts under the Uniform Transfers to Minors Act, you must delete the child's trust clause and renumber the Uniform Transfers clause. To do this, simply change the clause number for gifts under the Uniform Transfers to Minors Act:

- From "X" to "IX" in Form 1, and
- From "XI" to "X" in Form 2.

Prepare Your Final Trust Document

When you have completely filled in the draft of your trust form, proofread it carefully. Check to be sure you have:

- included all property you want to leave through the trust
- clearly and accurately identified all property (double-check account and serial numbers, for example)
- included all beneficiaries to whom you want to leave property
- spelled beneficiaries' (including alternate and residuary beneficiaries) names correctly and consistently, and
- made adequate arrangements for management of trust property that young beneficiaries might inherit.

When preparing the final trust, you want a document that looks as much like a conventional lawyer's living trust as possible. **So in your final version, be sure you have deleted:**

- the top caption of the form, such as "Form 2, Shared Living Trust." You can leave the heading of the trust schedules as printed. For example, if you use a Schedule C, keep "Schedule C, Husband's Separate Property Placed in Trust," as the header of that page.
- instructions
- circled or bracketed numbers, and
- any printed material on the form that doesn't apply to you, including:
  - blank beneficiary clauses, if you don't have as many beneficiaries as the forms provide space for
  - the alternate beneficiary provision of a beneficiary clause, if you decided not to name alternates for a specific gift
  - all material relating to trusts for minor beneficiaries, if you didn't create any, and
  - all material relating to the Uniform Transfers to Minors Act, if you didn't make any gifts using it.

Delete all material you want to eliminate before the final trust document is typed or printed.

Form

The **1** _____ Living Trust
        your name

Draft

The **1** _____ _Denis Clifford_ _____ Living Trust
              your name

Final

The Denis Clifford Living Trust

If you made a draft using a hard copy form from Appendix B, once you're satisfied that your trust form is fully completed, type the final document from your draft, including all trust schedules. Be sure the pages of the final document are consecutively numbered correctly. You may have to change the numbering from that on the form. For instance, if you add material (such as commentary about gifts) or have quite a number of primary beneficiaries—say 16—you'll have to renumber the pages of your final document. Similarly, if you delete material (such as the sections on children's trusts or gifts under the Uniform Transfers to Minors Act), you'll need to renumber the pages of your final document.

If you used the downloadable forms, make sure page numbers print out with your document, use at least a 12-point font (so that it's easier to read), and print your final document single-sided. Proofread the final trust document carefully and make corrections, if needed.

The final version should be typed or printed out on good quality 8½" x 11" paper.

> **TIP**
> **Double-check the numbering of the sections.** As you review your trust document, make sure the sections —and references to sections—are numbered correctly. Because you may have deleted or added some optional clauses, it's quite possible that you will have to renumber several sections.

Consider Having Your Work Checked by a Lawyer

After you are sure your final trust document is clear and correct, consider whether or not you want to look for a lawyer who can review your work. This can sound like a good idea that shouldn't cost much, but the reality is that it is often difficult to find a lawyer willing to do the job; most want a full fee for preparing a trust from scratch and won't accept review work. (Read more about finding a lawyer in Chapter 16.)

Before setting off to try to find a lawyer, take stock of whether you are really likely to benefit by employing one. If your desires are clear and straightforward, and you've followed the forms and instructions in this book, your trust should work just fine. On the other hand, if you have an estate large enough to be liable for estate taxes, or have other complex property or beneficiary concerns, this book has surely referred you to a lawyer already.

Sign Your Living Trust in Front of a Notary

It is essential that you sign and date your trust document and have your signature notarized by a notary public in the state where you live, even if you work in another state. Normally, no witnesses watch you sign a living trust. Because of this, it's always possible that after your death someone could claim that the signature wasn't genuine. As you won't be around to verify it then, you should do it now. The best way to remove any question of whether or not the signature on the document is authentic is to sign it in front of a notary.

The signature line on the trust form is preceded by a provision entitled "Certification by Grantor(s)." Here you state that you've read the trust document and approve of it. This is a bit of legalese, included to make your trust look more like ones with which most financial institutions are familiar.

When you go to the notary, say that you need a "certificate of acknowledgment" for your living trust. The notary's form may have a slightly different title, but it should include the term "acknowledgment." Be prepared to provide a photo ID, give a thumbprint, sign the notary's log with your current address, and pay a small fee—usually less than $10 per signature. However, notary laws vary by state, and it is your notary's job to know and follow the notary rules. At the least, the notary will watch you sign your living trust, check your ID, fill out and stamp the certificate, and attach it to your document.

Hopefully, finding a notary shouldn't be a problem; many advertise online and in the yellow pages. Or check with your bank, which may provide notarization as a service to customers. Real estate offices and title companies may also have notaries on site.

No Lawyer Required

There is no legal requirement that a lawyer must review or approve your living trust before it can be notarized. Anyone, including a notary, who tells you that a lawyer must be involved is wrong.

CAUTION

Special Florida requirements. In Florida, you must sign your living trust in front of two witnesses. Since the notary counts as one, you must have at least one other. Use the special Florida Witness Statement, Form 3.

COUPLES

Both spouses must sign a shared trust, and both spouses must appear together before a notary.

CAUTION

Don't stop now. Even after your trust document is signed and notarized, you're not done. You must transfer the property you listed in the trust schedules into the name of the trust. Do it as soon as possible. Chapter 10 shows you how.

CAUTION

Don't rely on a bank guarantee for your signature. Some banks provide guarantees for customers' signatures on bank and other important documents. Some readers have asked whether they can use a bank guarantee for their living trust, in place of notarization. The answer is no. After your death, it's vital that your living trust be accepted by many institutions, from title companies to county land records offices to stockbrokers. These institutions are not used to seeing living trust signatures validated by a bank guarantee. If any institution refuses to accept your living trust for this reason, there is little or nothing your successor trustee will be able to do about it. Getting a bank guarantee may, for some people, be easier than locating a notary. Unfortunately, this convenience is irrelevant. You must have your signature notarized.

Transferring Property to Your Trust

After you sign your living trust document, you have a valid living trust. But the trust is of absolutely no use to you until the property you listed in the trust document (on the property schedules) is actually transferred into the trust. Lawyers call this "funding" the trust.

Transferring your property to your living trust is crucial, and takes some time and paperwork, but it's not difficult. You should be able to do it yourself, without a lawyer.

We're Counting on You: Make Sure You Do It Right

Many lawyers who prepare living trusts insist on doing all the property transfer work themselves, because they claim their clients cannot be trusted to do this work themselves. In other words, lawyers get paid hundreds of dollars per hour to do paperwork and won't allow their clients to do it.

Both this book and Nolo rest on the belief that people can be trusted to understand basic legal forms and do the work required to make the forms work. It is absolutely essential that you do the work necessary to formally transfer your property to your trust. If you don't, your trust will not work and you may be proving that those lawyers who say people just can't be trusted to do basic tasks correctly are, sadly, sometimes correct. So, study this chapter carefully and be absolutely sure you've properly transferred all trust property into the trust's name.

Paperwork

Each item of property listed on your trust schedule(s) must be transferred to the trust. How much paperwork is required depends on whether or not the property has a document of title—a formal ownership paper—such as a real estate deed, car registration, securities account ownership registration form, or boat registration.

Property Without a Document of Title

Property without a document of title includes most furniture, clothing, books, appliances, and other household goods, as well as some more valuable items, like jewelry, artworks, furs, promissory notes, loans owed to you, precious metals, electronic and computer equipment, and most farm equipment and livestock.

In most states, to transfer property without a title document, you don't need to do anything but prepare your trust document and list the property on a trust schedule. However, many lawyers use an "assignment of property" to provide additional written proof that these items of property have been transferred. Certainly it can't hurt.

To prepare a written Assignment of Property for your trust, use Form 4 or 5. Form 4 is an assignment form for a one-person trust. It is also for a member of a couple who assigns separately owned property to a shared trust. Form 5 is for a couple to assign shared ownership property to a shared trust.

> **CAUTION**
> **New York residents must prepare a notice of assignment for property without documents of title.** New York law requires you to prepare a separate Notice of Assignment for property without documents of title transferred to your trust. (N.Y. Estates, Powers and Trusts Law § 7-1.18.) Simply listing such property on a trust schedule is not sufficient. If there's no Notice of Assignment, the property is not validly placed in the trust. However, the notice can simply repeat the listing of such property as used in a trust schedule. (Use Form 4 or 5.)

Property With a Document of Title

For items that have a title document that shows ownership, you will have to prepare new documents to establish that the trust owns the property. This chapter shows you how to accomplish this.

Technically, you transfer your property to yourself, as trustee of your living trust. You'll see how this works when you come to actually preparing title transfer documents below.

Some types of property without a title document may seem to require formal transfer because they are owned in paper form—such as promissory notes or deeds of trust. You can use an assignment form to make absolutely clear that this type of property is transferred to the trust. (Use Form 4 or 5.)

Finally, trademarks, patents, and copyrights have special transfer forms and are discussed below.

CAUTION

Don't delay. Formally transferring property to your trust is so vital that I'll give you one more warning, at the risk of redundancy. Failing to transfer property to the trust is the most serious mistake people can make when creating a living trust. If you don't get around to preparing, signing, and filing (where required) these new documents, your trust document will have no effect on what happens to any of your property after your death. Instead, that property will go to the residuary beneficiary named in your backup will. (See Chapter 15.) If you don't have a will, that property will go to certain close relatives, according to state law. Either way, it will probably go through probate.

Transferring Joint Tenancy Property If You Live in a Common Law State or Are Not Married

If you are a couple and live in a common law state—that is, any state except Arizona, California, Idaho, Louisiana, Nevada, New Mexico, Texas, Washington, or Wisconsin (and Alaska, South Dakota, or Tennessee, if agreed to in writing by both spouses)—transfers of property held in "joint tenancy" or "tenancy by the entirety" often require one more step than do transfers of other shared property. Also, if you are an unmarried couple in any state, you must go through the additional step described here to transfer joint tenancy property into a shared trust. If your deed or title document lists you as "tenants-in-common owners" (or lists ownership as "tenants in common"), you can safely go ahead and prepare a deed or title document transferring the property from you to the trust. But if you are listed as "joint tenants" or as holding the property "in joint tenancy" or "tenancy by the entirety," you'll likely have to do more work. Also, if your deed simply lists your names and makes no mention of what type of ownership you two share, you need to either take this extra step or check with a local lawyer regarding real estate ownership rules for your state. In some states, any deed to a husband and wife by itself creates a tenancy in the entirety, even if the document does not specifically state that.

Normally, before you transfer joint tenancy property to your trust, you'll need to prepare and execute an additional deed or title document transferring that property from you as "joint tenants" (or tenants by the entirety) to you as "tenants in common, in equal shares." This breaks the joint tenancy. Then you prepare a second deed or document of title transferring the property from you as "tenants in common" into the trust.

Why is this rigmarole necessary? Because some lawyers argue that joint tenancy property transferred to a living trust in common law states (somehow) retains its character as joint tenancy property, even if the trust declares otherwise. Worse, the IRS could argue the same. You do not want any risk of having joint tenancy property in your trust. Joint tenancy property must go to the surviving joint tenant. This may be what you want; indeed, if it is, consider leaving the property in joint tenancy rather than putting it in your trust. (See Chapter 14.) But if you want to leave some of that property to someone other than the other joint tenant(s), or you want to name alternate beneficiaries for your share of the property, you should be sure no one can assert, after you die, that the trust property is, in legal reality, still joint tenancy property.

To be absolutely safe, prepare the extra deed or document of title wherever your present ones list you as owning the property as "joint tenants" or as "tenants by the entirety," or simply lists your two names.

Technical Ownership

To transfer ownership of property with a document of title to your living trust, list the new owner(s) as your name, or names, followed by "as trustee(s) for the [*your name(s)*] Trust." It's common to include the date the trust was signed and notarized; however, including the date is optional, not mandatory.

> **EXAMPLE 1:** Denis Clifford creates a living trust and transfers real estate to it. On a new real estate deed, he lists the new owner as "Denis Clifford, as trustee of the Denis Clifford Living Trust."

> **EXAMPLE 2:** Denise and Fred Gulekston create a shared living trust and transfer their home, a money market account, and a stockbrokerage account to the trust. On each title document, they name the new owners as "Denise and Fred Gulekston, as trustees of the Denise and Fred Gulekston Living Trust."

Including the date your living trust was signed and notarized isn't necessary, but it may make your documents appear more lawyer-like, and, therefore, perhaps more acceptable to banks, title companies, and other financial institutions. It also avoids confusion over subsequent trusts with the same name, if there are any.

Another form of dating a living trust is to include the letters "UTD" (for Under Trust Dated) and then give the date. For example, "Denis Clifford, as trustee of the Denis Clifford Living Trust, UTD July 10, 20xx."

Formally, the property is owned by the trustee(s), not the trust itself. (There's one exception, which affects real estate in Colorado. See "Real Estate," below.)

Property You Acquire Later

If, after your trust has been created, you acquire property you want to hold in trust, you can simply take ownership in the trustee's name directly. There's no reason to buy the property in your personal name and then transfer it to you as trustee.

> **EXAMPLE:** Mr. and Mrs. Siqueiros buy a new house. They take title in their individual names, listing the new owners as "Juan and Luisa Siqueiros, as trustees of The Juan and Luisa Siqueiros Living Trust, dated September 20, 20xx." The couple then amends Schedule A of their living trust to list their new home as a trust asset.

Problems With Financial Institutions

I've received a few reports, from readers of other Nolo books and from lawyers, that some banks, mutual funds, or other financial institutions have balked at reregistering trust property in the trustee's name. People have been told, "You can't do that. Only our trust department does that," or "You need a federal tax ID number."

If this happens to you, simply insist that it is absolutely legal, and essential, for you to reregister your property in the trustee's name, and that this can be done without a new taxpayer ID. If you have to, go higher up in the institution's bureaucracy until you find someone who understands the law.

Certifications of Trust

A certification of trust, sometimes called an "abstract of trust," is a kind of shorthand version of the trust document. You may find one useful when actually transferring property to your trust. County records offices, banks, or other institutions may require proof that the trust exists. The purpose of a certification of trust is to establish that the trust exists, without revealing the heart of it—that is, what property is in it and who will inherit. Some people do not want to reveal this core information to institutions that require proof of the trust's existence, so they submit a certification of trust rather than a copy of the entire trust.

Almost all states have statutes that set out the requirements for a certification of trust. (See the chart, below.) Some states also provide a specific form in their statutes. If yours does, it is prudent to use that form so that your certification looks familiar to the institutions that will see it. If your state does not provide a form, you can make your own using photocopies of the pages that show the required sections of the trust. Only three states, Connecticut, Hawaii, and New York, do not have statutes on Certifications of Trust. However, Certifications are used and accepted in all three states.

Typically, certifications show:

- that the trust was created (the first page of the trust document will do)
- who the original trustees are
- the date the trust was created (the date the trust document was signed and notarized)

- what the trustees' powers are (this can be quite a bit of verbiage), and
- the signature of the grantor(s).

The example on the next page is based on a certification of trust for California.

TIP

Finding your state's requirements. To read your state's requirements for trust certifications, you can either Google the statute listed in the chart or find it through your state's website. Nolo provides a list of state resources at www.nolo.com/legal-research/state-law.html.

State Statute Sections on Certification of Trust

State	Statute	State	Statute
Alabama	Ala. Code § 19-3B-1013	Nebraska	Neb. Rev. Stat. § 30-38, 102-106
Alaska	Alaska Stat. § 13.36.079	Nevada	Nev. Rev. Stat. Ann. § 164.410
Arizona	Ariz. Rev Stat. Ann. § 14-11013	New Hampshire	N.H. Rev. Stat. Ann. § 564-A:7
Arkansas	Ark. Code Ann. § 28-73-1013	New Jersey	N.J. Stat. Ann, § 3B:31-81
California	Cal. Prob. Code § 18100.5	New Mexico	N.M. Stat. Ann. § 46A-10-1013
Colorado	Colo. Rev. Stat § 11-105-111	North Carolina	N.C. Gen. Stat. § 36C-10-1013
Delaware	Del. Code Ann. tit. 12, § 3591	North Dakota	N.D. Cent. Code § 59-18-13
Dist. of Columbia	D.C. Code Ann. § 19-1310.13	Ohio	Ohio Rev. Code Ann. § 5301.01
Florida	Fla. Stat. Ann, § 736.1017	Oklahoma	Okla. Stat. Ann. tit. 60, § 175.6
Georgia	Ga. Code Ann. § 53-12-280	Oregon	Or. Rev. Stat. Ann. § 130.860
Idaho	Idaho Code § 68-115	Pennsylvania	20 Pa. Cons. Ann. § 7790.3
Illinois	Ill. Comp. Stat. 306 ILCS § 5/8.5	Rhode Island	R.I. Gen. Laws § 34-4-27
Indiana	Ind. Code Ann. § 30-4-4-5	South Carolina	S.C. Code Ann. § 62-7-1013
Iowa	Iowa Code § 633.4604	South Dakota	S.D. Codified Laws § 55-4-42
Kansas	Kan. Stat. Ann. § 58a-1013	Tennessee	Tenn. Code Ann. § 35-15-1013
Kentucky	Ky. Rev. Stat. Ann. 386B § 10-120	Texas	Tex. Prop. Code Ann. § 114.086
Maine	Me. Rev. Stat. Ann. tit. 18-B § 1013	Utah	Utah Code Ann. § 75-7-1013
Maryland	Md. Code Ann. § 14-5-910	Vermont	Vt. Stat. Ann. tit. 14A § 1013
Massachusetts	Mass. Gen. Laws ch. 203E § 1013	Virginia	Va. Code Ann. § 55-550.13
Michigan	Mich. Comp. Laws § 565.432	Washington	Wash. Rev. Code Ann. § 11.98.075
Minnesota	Minn. Stat. Ann. § 501B.56	West Virginia	W.Va. Code § 36-1-4a
Mississippi	Miss. Code Ann. § 91-9-7	Wisconsin	Wis. Stat. § 701.1013
Missouri	Mo. Rev. Stat. § 456.10-1013	Wyoming	Wyo. Stat. Ann. § 4-10-1014
Montana	Mont. Code Ann. § 372-38-1013		

Certification of The Elijah Hammond Living Trust

[California Probate Code, Section 18100.5]

Elijah Hammond, being of legal age, declares under penalty of perjury:

1. Declarant certifies the existence of the following described trust and states that he is the current trustee.

    Name of Trust: The Elijah Hammond Living Trust

    Date of Trust: February 23, 2021

    Grantor: Elijah Hammond

    Original Trustee: Elijah Hammond

    Trust Social Security Number: XXX-XX-4330

2. Declarant states that the Trust is in full force and effect and has not been revoked, terminated, or otherwise amended in any manner which would cause the representations in this Certification to be incorrect. The name of the only person who has any power to revoke the Trust is Elijah Hammond.

3. Declarant states the following named trustee is fully empowered to act for said Trust and is properly exercising his authority under said Trust in negotiating for, contracting for, and executing the Trust document, and that no trustee other than the following named trustee is necessary under the Trust to execute said document: Elijah Hammond.

Trustee authorized to sign: Elijah Hammond

Date of document: February 23, 2021

4. Declarant states that to the best of his knowledge, there are no claims, challenges of any kind, or causes of action alleged, contesting or questioning the validity of the Trust or the trustee's authority to act for the Trust.

5. Declarant states that the trustee powers clause of the Trust is as set forth below:

. . . .

VIII. Trustee's Powers and Duties

(A) Powers Under State Law

To carry out the provisions of The Elijah Hammond Living Trust, the trustee shall have all authority and powers allowed or conferred on a trustee under California law, subject to the trustee's fiduciary duty to the grantor and the beneficiaries.

(B) Specified Powers

The trustee's powers include, but are not limited to:

1. The power to sell trust property, and to borrow money and to encumber property, specifically including trust real estate, by mortgage, deed of trust, or other method.

2. The power to manage trust real estate as if the trustee were the absolute owner of it, including the power to lease (even if the lease term may extend beyond the period of any trust) or grant options to lease the property, to make repairs or alterations, and to insure against loss.

3. The power to sell or grant options for the sale or exchange of any trust property, including stocks, bonds, debentures, and any other form of security or security account, at public or private sale for cash or on credit.

4. The power to invest trust property in property of any kind, including but not limited to bonds, debentures, notes, mortgages, stocks, stock options, stock futures, and buying on margin.

5. The power to receive additional property from any source and add to any trust created by this Declaration of Trust.

6. The power to employ and pay reasonable fees to accountants, lawyers, or investment experts for information or advice relating to the trust.

7. The power to deposit and hold trust funds in both interest-bearing and non-interest-bearing accounts.

8. The power to deposit funds in financial accounts insured or uninsured by the FDIC.

9. The power to enter into electronic fund transfer or safe deposit arrangements with financial institutions.

10. The power to continue any business of either grantor.

11. The power to institute or defend legal actions concerning the trust or the grantors' affairs

12. The power to execute any documents necessary to administer any trust created in this Declaration of Trust

13. The power to diversify investments, including authority to decide that some or all of the trust property need not produce income.

. . . .

This Declaration is prepared and executed pursuant to California Probate Code Section 18100.5.

Signed under penalty of perjury, this _____3_____ day of, _____November_____ 2021

Elijah Hammond
Elijah Hammond, Grantor and Trustee

[Attached: Notary Certificate]

Real Estate

The term "real estate" includes land, houses, condominiums, cooperatives, many time-shares, and any other interest in what lawyers call "real property." To transfer title of a piece of real estate to a living trust, you prepare and sign a deed listing the trustee or trustees of the trust as the new owner. You can fill out the new deed yourself; it's not difficult. Then you sign the deed in front of a notary public and record a copy of it with the county land records office, usually a county recorder. You don't have to prepare a second document transferring your mortgage; that liability follows the asset, the real estate. Nor do you need to notify the mortgage holder (the bank) of the transfer. (See Chapter 3.)

Colorado Real Estate

If you want to transfer Colorado real estate to your living trust, transfer title into the name of the trust itself, not the trustee. Although Colorado law does not mandate that real estate be held in the trust's name, a state statute encourages it, and it is becoming the expected way to proceed. (Colo. Rev. Stat. § 38-30-108.5.) Additionally, the Colorado statute requires that the trustee of the living trust prepare a "statement of authority" complying with Colo. Rev. Stat. § 38-30-172 and file that statement in the county recorder's office where the real estate is located.

Co-op apartments. If you own a co-op apartment, you can't simply use a deed to transfer your shares in the co-op. You will have to check the co-op corporation's rules to see if the transfer is allowed. Some co-ops resist such transfers because they are afraid a living trust isn't a proper shareholder in the corporation. You can probably overcome any resistance you encounter by reminding the powers that be that, for all practical purposes, you and the trust are the same—you have the same tax identification number, for example.

Mobile or manufactured homes. Whether or not a mobile home is treated as real estate depends upon the law of the state where it is located, and, in some states, whether it is permanently affixed to land or not. You'll have to check with the state agency that handles mobile home registrations to learn how to transfer title to your trust.

Time-shares. A time-share is an ownership interest in a vacation property. Each owner has the right to exclusive use of the property for set time periods. Ownership can be held by real estate deed, lease, or contract, depending on your state's law. If a deed is used, the time-share must be transferred to your living trust by a deed. If ownership is by lease or contract, you can use a simple assignment form.

Preparing the Deed

First, locate your existing deed. Then get a warranty deed form in common use in the state where the real estate is located. The technical requirements for real estate deed forms vary from state to state, so it is essential that you get one from the appropriate state.

Finding Deed Forms and Instructions

Here are some ideas for finding a warranty deed form for your state:

- **Search online.** Do an online search for the name of your state and "warranty deed."
- **Try an office supply store.** Some office supply stores may still sell blank deed forms. Just make sure you go to one in your state, and then double-check online to make sure it's the right form.
- **Go to a law library.** If you live near a law library; look for books on "real property" that have deed forms you can photocopy. Let a reference librarian help you find what you need.
- **Ask a title company.** A local title company may be willing to provide a form for you, especially if you've used that company before. You might even ask them if they would be willing to help you fill it out (for a fee).

In most states, it's best to use a "warranty" deed, which promises full and clear ownership. However, in Virginia, you'll need to use a "deed of gift" or "gift deed."

Although warranty deed forms vary somewhat, they all require the same basic information:

- **The recording information, at the top left of the document.**
- **The date.**
- **The current owners' names.** If you are the sole owner, or if you and someone else co-own the property and you are transferring just your share, only your name goes here. If you are transferring only a portion of ownership, you can specify what portion (for example, "⅓ ownership of …" or simply state "all his/her interest in …"). If you and your spouse own the property together and are transferring it to a shared marital trust, type in both of your names. Use exactly the same form of your name as is used on the deed that transferred the property to you and you used in your living trust document.

  Depending on the form, you may have to type in the correct ending of some printed words, like "part…." If you are a couple, you add "ies" to make this "parties." If you are a single person, you add a "y" to make it "party."
- **The new owner's name.** Fill in the trustee's name or trustees' names, and add the date of notarization of the trust if you wish. (See "Technical Ownership," above.) Remember that for Colorado real estate, the new owner is the trust, not the trustee.
- **The "legal description" of the property.** This is usually something like, "From a point 12 degrees South of… Map 4, Book 6," etc. Copy the description exactly as it appears on the previous deed. Depending on the form you use, you may need to cross out inappropriate printed language, such as words stating the transfer is "forever," or that the property is also transferred to the second party's (here, the trust's) "assigns, etc."

If Your Name Has Changed

When you sign a new deed (as transferor) to transfer your property to your living trust, use the name you used (as the transferee) on your previous deed, even if you have changed your name since then. In other words, the name on your old deed and the name on your new deed should match so that it won't be flagged for a flaw by a title company. When you sign your new deed as the trustee, you can use your new name.

EXAMPLE: After she bought her house, Mary Johnson changed her name to Mary Greenbaum. When she makes a new deed to transfer her house into her living trust, she uses the name "Mary Johnson" as the transferor, and the name "Mary Greenbaum, as the Trustee of the Mary Greenbaum Living Trust" as the name of the transferee.

After everything is filled in, sign and date the deed in front of a notary public for the state in which the property is located. Everyone listed as a current owner who is transferring interest in the property into the trust must sign the deed.

Recording the Deed

After the deed is signed and notarized, you must record it—that is, put a copy of the notarized deed on file in the county office that keeps local property records. Depending on the state, the land records office is called the county recorder's office, land registry office, or county clerk's office.

Just take the original, signed deed to the land records office. (You can probably mail it in, if you wish. Call the land records office to find out the correct procedure.) For a small fee, a clerk will make a copy and put it in the public records. You'll get your original back, stamped with a reference number to show where the copy can be found in the public records.

Out-of-State Real Estate

If you own real estate located in another state, you face a few problems transferring that property to your trust:

- Tracking down the deed form for that state, and getting a blank deed. Often the easiest way to get the correct deed is to call a title company in the state where the real estate is located.
- Making sure your notarization of the deed is acceptable in the other state. Generally, deeds can be notarized in the state you live in, even for out-of-state real estate.
- Learning whether any other paperwork is required for a valid transfer. One example of this is California's Preliminary Change of Title Report, discussed in "California Property Taxes," below.
- Properly recording the deed.

SEE AN EXPERT

Transferring out-of-state real estate. Transferring out-of-state real estate located in the United States can be a real hassle. If it becomes one for you, you might decide to hire a lawyer to do just this one task.

Transfer Taxes

Very rarely, if ever, will you have to pay a state or local transfer tax when you transfer real estate to a revocable living trust. Most real estate transfer taxes are based on the sale price of the property and do not apply when no money changes hands. Further, many states specifically exempt transfers where the real owners don't change—as is the case when you transfer property to a revocable living trust you control.

To be safe, before you record your deed, get information on any possible transfer tax from the county tax assessor, county recorder, or state tax officials.

Additional Forms May Be Required for Recording

Before you record your new deed, check with your county recording office to see if any additional forms must be filed with the deed. (If they are, you can easily obtain them by downloading them from the county recorder's website.) For instance, every real estate deed recorded in California must be accompanied by a "Preliminary Change of Ownership Report," so the county can determine if there will be a property tax reappraisal on the transferred real estate. (Under California law, there's no reappraisal for a transfer of real estate to one's living trust.)

CAUTION

Check with your county recorder. Before you record your deed, check with your county recorder's office to see if there are any local requirements that must be included on that deed. For instance, some California county recorder's offices now require that a specific statute be cited and summarized on the deed form to establish that a deed transferring property to a living trust is exempt from transfer tax. For example: "The undersigned grantors declare that the transfer is to a living trust for the benefit of the grantors and is not pursuant to a sale and is exempt from the documentary transfer tax pursuant to California Revenue and Taxation Code Section 11911."

Due-on-Sale Mortgage Clauses

Many mortgages contain a clause that allows the bank to call ("accelerate") the loan—that is, demand that you pay the whole thing off immediately—if you transfer the mortgaged property. Fortunately, in most instances lenders are forbidden by federal law to invoke a due-on-sale clause when property is transferred to a living trust. The lender can't call the loan if the borrower is a trust beneficiary and the transfer is "unrelated to occupancy" of the premises. (Garn-St. Germain Act, 12 U.S.C. §§ 1464, 1701.) Also, it's doubtful that the transfer of any real estate to your trust is the type of transfer that would legally permit a bank to call a loan. (See Chapter 3.)

Insurance

Your insurance policies should not be changed simply because your home has been placed in your living trust. You do not need to notify your insurance company (or any title company) of the transfer of real estate property. (Why disturb a bureaucracy if you don't have to?)

Transferring Deeds of Trust

One type of real estate asset is called a "deed of trust." It is similar to a mortgage. If you lend money to someone, you may receive a deed of trust, making real estate collateral for a loan—that is, if the borrower defaults, you can foreclose on the real estate to collect what's owed you. Because a deed of trust is an interest in real estate, it should be recorded.

To transfer a deed of trust to your living trust, you can prepare a "Notice of Assignment" transferring it from you to your trust. You then record that document. Use Form 4 or 5.

Real Estate Outside the United States

There is no reason to transfer foreign real estate to a U.S. living trust. That property wouldn't go through U.S. probate anyway, and U.S. courts don't have authority to order transfer of real estate in another country. Each country has its own rules and laws regarding real estate. (When I lived in Ireland, I had to visit a lawyer—a "solicitor"—and sign a fancy legal document to rent an apartment.)

 SEE AN EXPERT

Transferring foreign real estate. If you own property in another country, consider hiring someone in that other country to learn what you need to do. After all, if you own real estate in a foreign country, that's fortunate, so spending a little money to learn how to transfer that property after your death isn't a disaster.

Bank Accounts and Safe Deposit Boxes

It should be simple to reregister ownership of a bank account in your name(s) as trustee(s) of your living trust or open a new account in the trustee's name. Just ask the bank what paperwork you need to submit.

The bank will be concerned with the authority granted to the trustees to act on behalf of the trust. Depending on the kind of account, the bank may want to know whether the trustees have the power to borrow money, put funds in a non-interest-bearing account, or engage in electronic transfers. (The trust forms in this book include all these powers.)

To verify your authority, the bank may want to see a copy of your trust document or a certification of trust, or it may have you fill out its own form.

If you want to transfer title to a safe deposit box to your trust, you'll have to reregister its ownership, too. The bank will have a form for you to fill out.

Estate planning note. Instead of transferring a bank account to a living trust, you may want to turn the account into a pay-on-death account. It's another, even easier, way to avoid probate of the money in the account. (See Chapter 14.)

Securities

How you transfer stocks, bonds, mutual funds, and other securities to your living trust depends on how you want to hold them.

Brokerage Accounts

If, like most people, you hold your stocks, bonds, or other securities in a brokerage account, you have two choices:

- Name the trust as beneficiary or alternate beneficiary of the accounts.
- Transfer ownership of your accounts into the trust. (Technically, transfer ownership of the accounts to your name as trustee.)

With either method, you are likely to have to give each financial institution a copy of your trust or a certification of trust. Use whichever method works best for you. However, note that various retirement accounts, including IRAs and 401Ks, cannot be legally transferred into trust ownership.

> **EXAMPLE 1: A married couple with children and grandchildren.** Both spouses named the other spouse as the beneficiary for their financial accounts. The couple also wants to provide that after both spouses die, all remaining funds in those financial accounts will go to each child and grandchild in defined percentages. To do this, they name their trust as the alternate beneficiary for their financial accounts. In their trust documents, they name each child and grandchild as a beneficiary of funds the trust receives from the financial accounts and define the percentage of the funds each beneficiary is given. (And they make sure that the percentages add up to 100%.)

> **EXAMPLE 2: A single woman.** Simone has two financial accounts—a small IRA and a substantial stock/investment account. Simone hopes to live long enough to deplete all or almost all of her IRA, so she does not consider that IRA a major source for her estate-planning gifts. She names her favorite niece as the beneficiary of that account. She wants to leave many gifts to family, friends, and charities from her investment account. She decides to transfer that account into trust ownership. Then in the trust document she defines each beneficiary of the investment account and what percentage of the total value of the account each beneficiary receives.

To name your trust as a beneficiary of a financial account or to transfer a financial account to trust ownership, start by asking your broker for instructions. The brokerage company may have a straightforward form that you can fill out, giving information about the trustees and their authority.

When changing an account's ownership, tell the institution that you want the account to keep the same account number as when it was in your name. If they don't want to, insist (politely). If they still refuse, you've got a technical problem, because the account number listed in your trust document isn't the same as the new number of that account in the trustee's name. You'd have to revise a trust schedule to get the new account number in it. So, you can see why you want to insist the account keep your original number.

If the brokerage company doesn't have its own form, you will probably need to send the broker:

- a copy of the trust document or certification of trust, and
- a letter instructing the holder to transfer the brokerage account to the trustee's name or open a new account in the trustee's name.

After you've submitted your request, get written confirmation that the account's ownership has in fact been put in the trustee's name.

Stock Certificates

If you have the actual stock certificates or bonds in your possession—most people don't—you must get new certificates issued, showing the trustee as owner. Ask your broker for help. If the broker is unwilling or unable to help, write to the "transfer agent" of the corporation that issued the stock. You can get the address from your broker or the investor relations office of the corporation. The transfer agent will give you simple instructions.

You will probably have to send in:
- your certificates or bonds
- a form called a "stock or bond power," which you must fill out and sign
- a copy of the trust document or a certification of trust, and
- a letter requesting that the certificates be reissued in the trustee's name.

The stock or bond power may be printed on the back of the certificates; if not, you can probably find a copy online or at an office supply store.

Government Bonds

You can now only buy series EE U. S. government bonds online; no formal bond certificates are issued. You can buy EE bonds in your name as trustee of your living trust. To transfer EE bonds you already own in your own name to yourself as trustee, you need to complete Treasury form PDF 1851E and mail it to the U.S. Treasury. You can get the form through your stockbroker, the local Federal Reserve Bank, or possibly a local bank. You can also find the form online—just search for "treasury department FS Form 1851E."

If you own treasury bonds in a "Legacy Treasury Direct Account," you transfer those bonds to your trust by using Form 5178.

Mutual Fund Accounts

Mutual funds should be reregistered in the name of the trustee of your living trust by communicating with the company and meeting its requirements. You'll probably just need to send a letter of instructions (or a form the company provides) and a copy of the trust document.

Stock Options

You can transfer publicly traded stock options by using a Notice of Assignment (Form 4 or 5). Private, employee stock options often cannot be transferred to a living trust. (See Chapter 5.)

Retirement Accounts

Do not transfer your retirement accounts to your living trust. Some major types of retirement accounts, including IRAs, SEP IRAs, and 401(k)s, cannot legally be transferred to a living trust. For a discussion of naming your living trust as the beneficiary of your retirement accounts, see "Listing the Property to Be Put in Your Living Trust" and "Property You Should Not Put in Your Living Trust" in Chapter 5.

Vehicles, Boats, and Planes

Most people don't transfer vehicles such as cars or trailers to a living trust, for reasons discussed in Chapter 5. (A mobile home may be considered real estate rather than a vehicle. See "Real Estate," above.)

If you want to put a vehicle in trust, you must fill out a change of ownership document and have title to the vehicle reissued in the trustee's name. The title certificate to your vehicle may contain instructions. If you have questions, call your state's motor vehicles department.

Transferring a large boat to your living trust requires you to reregister title with the Coast Guard. The paperwork is handled by the U.S. Coast Guard's National Vessel Documentation Center (800-799-8362). The form needed to transfer a boat into a trust is contained in the "Exchange Packet," available without charge. You also need to complete Form CG-1258 ("Application for Initial Issue, Exchange, or Replacement of Certificate of Documentation") and Form CG-1340 (a "Bill of Sale"). Then you pay the appropriate fee. The forms can be obtained online; just Google "U.S. coast guard forms."

To transfer larger, motorized boats registered with a state agency, you must prepare a new state registration form, listing the trust—that is, you as trustee—as the new owner. Transferring small boats, such as rowboats or canoes, can be done simply by listing them on a trust schedule, and, if you wish, by preparing a Notice of Assignment for them.

If you own an airplane, you must contact the FAA to obtain a new certificate of registration in the trustee's name.

Business Interests

How you transfer small business interests to your living trust depends on the way the business is owned.

Trademarks and Service Marks

If you have a registered trademark or service mark, you must reregister ownership in the name of the trustee of the living trust. For sample forms, see *Trademark: Legal Care for Your Business & Product Name*, by Stephen Fishman (Nolo).

Sole Proprietorships

An unincorporated business that you own by yourself is the easiest to transfer to a trust. First, you list the business, by name, as an item of property on a trust schedule—for example, "De Tach Restaurant." That transfers the name and whatever customer goodwill that goes with it, to your living trust.

Because you own the business assets in your own name (a sole proprietorship, unlike a corporation, is not an independent entity that can own property), you transfer them to your living trust like you would any other valuable property. For many businesses, this simply means listing those business assets on the appropriate trust schedule—for example, "… all property and assets used in the grantor's business, Jim Dimes Hardware." Because there is no ownership document for the business, nothing further is required.

Solely Owned Corporations

If you own all the stock of a corporation, you shouldn't have any problem transferring it to your living trust. Follow these steps:

1. Fill out the stock transfer section on the back of the stock certificate.
2. Mark the certificate "canceled" and place it in your corporate records book.
3. Reissue a new certificate in the name of the trustee of the living trust.
4. Show the cancellation of the old certificate and the issuance of the new certificate on the stock ledger pages in your corporate records book.

Closely Held Corporations and Limited Liability Companies

Normally, you can transfer your shares in a closely held corporation or interest in a limited liability company (LLC) to your living trust by following corporate bylaws or an LLC operating agreement and having the ownership document reissued in the name of the trustee of the trust. But first, check the corporation's bylaws and articles of incorporation, as well as any separate shareholders' agreements or the LLC operating agreement, to see if there are any restrictions on such transfers. If an agreement limits or forbids transfers, it will have to be changed before you can put your shares in your living trust.

Partnership Interests

To transfer your partnership interest to your living trust, you must notify your business partners and modify the partnership agreement to show that your partnership interest is now owned by the trustee of your living trust. If there is a partnership certificate, it must be changed to substitute the trustee as owner of your share.

RESOURCE
Revising a partnership agreement. You can revise your partnership agreement by using *Form a Partnership*, by Denis Clifford and Ralph Warner (Nolo).

Limited Partnerships

Limited partnerships are a form of investment, governed by securities laws. Contact the partnership's general partner to find out what paperwork is necessary to transfer your interest to a living trust.

Copyrights

If you want to transfer your interest in a copyright to your living trust, list the copyright on a trust schedule. Then sign and file, with the U.S. Copyright Office, a document transferring all your rights in the copyright to the trustee of the living trust. Sample transfer forms are in *The Copyright Handbook,* by Stephen Fishman (Nolo).

Patents

If you own a patent and want to transfer it to your living trust, you should prepare a document called an "assignment" and record it with the U.S. Patent and Trademark Office in Washington, D.C. There is a small fee for recording. Assignment forms and instructions are in *Patent It Yourself,* by David Pressman (Nolo).

 RESOURCE
Learn more about patents. Other Nolo patent resources include *Nolo's Patents for Beginners,* by David Pressman and Richard Stim, and *Patent Pending in 24 Hours,* by Richard Stim and David Pressman.

Royalties

Your rights to receive royalties—from sales of a book, copies of photos, residuals for TV ads, whatever—can be transferred to your trust, with technical ownership held by the trustee. It's best to transfer any royalty rights by preparing an Assignment of Property (Form 4 or 5), although legally, just listing these rights on a trust schedule would suffice. But with an assignment form, you can clearly specify, in a separate, distinct document, exactly what royalty rights are transferred to the trust.

It is sensible to give a copy of the assignment form to whatever company pays you the royalty rights. Let them know, of course, that they are to keep making payments to you while you live. It can help get these payments to your beneficiaries without great hassles if you give the company some warning that your royalty rights will be transferred by your successor trustee out of your living trust when you die.

Copying, Storing, and Registering Your Trust Document

After you've completed your living trust and signed all documents necessary to transfer property to the trust, you're almost done. There are just a couple of minor tasks left to accomplish.

Making Copies

You will probably need some copies of your completed trust document. Some lawyers advise stamping or writing the word "COPY" on each duplicate, so none can ever be mistaken for an original. While you can certainly do this, it seems a bit overcautious to me. Photocopies of your original trust are different from the original—your signature is not in ink on the copy, nor is the notary stamp original. But then again, these days, original signatures can be difficult to determine, so if you want maximum security, go ahead and write or stamp "COPY" on each copy, or even on each page of each copy.

You may well need copies to transfer certain types of property—stocks, for example—to your trust. (See Chapter 10.) If a broker, a bank, or another institution wants to see your trust document, use a photocopy of the original.

You may want to give a copy of your trust document to your successor trustee so that person knows what is in your trust well in advance of actually serving as trustee. Keep the original where your successor trustee can readily find it.

Finally, you should instruct your successor trustee to give copies after your death to any custodian you named for trust property inherited by a young beneficiary.

There's no requirement that you give copies to any beneficiaries. Indeed, there can be drawbacks to this. If you later revoke or amend the trust but don't collect all the old copies, there will be outdated copies of your trust document floating around. Someone who is given less (or nothing) in the new document may cause trouble later on. Also, the property in the trust may substantially change later if the trustee must dip into or even deplete the trust because of a grantor's illness or other unexpected expenses. Why set up expectations that may not be fulfilled even with the best of intentions?

On the other hand, if you doubt the trust property will change much, and if there are only a few beneficiaries and you trust them all—as is true for many families—why not let your beneficiaries know now what they'll receive? What's wrong with revealing your generosity?

In addition, some states require that, when a successor trustee takes over, the successor trustee provide information about the trust to all beneficiaries. Even when this is not legally required, it's wise policy. (See Chapter 13.)

> **CAUTION**
> **Sign only one trust document.** Do not sign more than one copy of your living trust form. This is because each trust document you actually sign becomes, legally, a distinct trust document (even if it isn't notarized). If you revoke or change one original, that does not revoke or change other originals. Clearly, you don't want any duplicate original trust documents floating around.

Storing the Trust Document

Store your living trust document where you keep other important papers, such as your financial records, will, or durable power of attorney.

Many people keep their living trust and other estate planning documents in a drawer in a home desk or file cabinet. It is vital that your successor trustee have ready access to your trust document and an unlocked drawer provides that access. They do contain some sensitive information, but generally speaking there is little risk that a thief would steal your trust and other estate planning documents.

However, if you want to be extra careful about storing your documents, a fireproof lockbox in your home or office can be fine, as long as your successor trustee knows where the box is and how to open it. You could even put your documents in a bank safe deposit box, but make sure that your successor trustee is authorized to open that box after your death.

Again, make sure your successor trustee (or spouse, if you made a shared trust) knows where your original trust document is and can get hold of it soon after your death or incapacity. The new trustee will need it to manage or distribute trust property. (The new trustee's responsibilities are discussed in Chapter 13.)

Registering the Trust

In a handful of states, the law requires the trustee to register a living trust. These states are:

Alaska	Idaho	Missouri
Colorado*	Maine*	Nebraska**
Florida**	Michigan	North Dakota
Hawaii		

* Registration not required until grantor's death.
** Registration is optional.

However, these laws address situations in which beneficiaries sue trustees. Such a scenario could only occur after the original trustees have died, because beneficiaries have no rights to living trust property while the original trustees are alive. So, because there is no possibility of trust beneficiaries suing you over trust property before you die, there is no practical reason to register a living trust. That said, if you want to register a living trust in these states, you can.

If you register your trust, it is possible for others to have access to certain information about the trust. But only minimal information need be made public through registration—the name of the grantor, the date of the trust—not the key terms of the trust, such as the property in it, and who are the beneficiaries.

Registration of a living trust doesn't give the court any power over the administration of the trust, unless there's a dispute. Registration serves to give the court jurisdiction over any disputes involving the trust—for example, if after your death a beneficiary wants to object to the way your successor trustee distributed the trust property. But if you don't register your trust, the result is the same: The court still has jurisdiction if a disgruntled relative or creditor files suit.

To register a revocable living trust, the original trustee(s) must file a statement with the court where the trustee resides or keeps trust records. The statement must include at least the following:

- the name(s) of the grantor(s)
- the name(s) of the original trustee(s)
- an acknowledgment of the trusteeship (that is, a written acceptance by the trustees of their role), and
- the date of the trust document.

A trust can be registered in only one state at a time.

Living With Your Living Trust

This chapter discusses what you need to know after you have established your living trust, including how to change your trust document if your circumstances change.

By now, you know that as a day-to-day, practical matter, it makes no difference that your property is now owned by your revocable living trust. You have no special paperwork to prepare, tax forms to file, or other duties to perform as the trustee of your own revocable living trust. Nor do you have any legal responsibilities to any of the beneficiaries you named in the trust document. They have no rights over any trust property while you are alive.

Some lawyers urge you to have your trust reviewed and updated by a lawyer every year. There's no need for this. Indeed, there's no need for you to review your trust yourself every year. Review your trust if something major has changed, or you want to make a major change. But for many, probably most, people who create living trusts, there's very little or no change that affects their trusts from the time they create them to the time they go into effect at their deaths.

Adding Property to Your Living Trust

The living trust forms in this book specifically give you the right to add property to your trust. If you acquire valuable items of property after you create your living trust, you should promptly add them to the trust so that they won't have to go through probate at your death.

There are four steps to adding property to your trust:

Step 1. Type a revised Property Schedule A, B, or C of your trust document, adding the new property. (If you made an individual trust, you have only one schedule, Schedule A. If you and your spouse made a shared living trust, Schedule A lists your co-owned property, Schedule B lists the wife's separate property, if any, and Schedule C lists the husband's separate property, if any.)

Step 2. Remove the old schedule from your trust document and attach the new one.

Step 3. If the property you're adding has a document of title, you need to transfer the title into the name or names of the trustee(s). (See Chapter 10.) Of course, if you acquire titled property in the name of the trust, you won't need to retitle it.

EXAMPLE: Rose and Michael prepare a shared trust. Later on, they buy a new house, and they want it to be in their living trust. So, on the deed, they take title in the name of "Rose Morris and Michael Morris, trustees of the Rose Morris and Michael Morris Living Trust, dated January 13, 20xx." They then type a revised Schedule A (which lists shared property) of their trust document and replace the old Schedule A.

If the property does not have a document of title, ignore this step—simply listing that property on a trust schedule is all you need to do. But if you made an Assignment of Property for non-titled trust assets, then add the new property to that list and attach the revised assignment to your trust.

Step 4. Amend the trust document if you need to name a beneficiary for the new property. You won't need to amend the trust document if you've left all your trust property to one person or if you want the property to go to your residuary beneficiary.

EXAMPLE: Mercedes adds a new money market account to her living trust. She wants to leave this account to her brother, Neil, who is not her residuary beneficiary. Mercedes must prepare an amendment of her trust, listing Neil as the beneficiary for this new property.

Selling or Giving Away Trust Property

You have complete control over the property you have transferred to the living trust. If you want to sell or give away any of it, go ahead, using your authority as trustee. If you sell or give away trust property that has no document of title, you simply need to delete that property from the appropriate trust schedule. Remove that schedule from the trust document, prepare a new schedule that omits the sold or given-away property, and attach the new schedule to the trust document. If, however, the sold or given-away property has a document of title, you need to prepare a new one that transfers the title out of the name of the trustee.

> **EXAMPLE:** Martin transfers ownership of his house to his living trust, but later decides to sell it. He transfers the house to the buyer by signing the new deed as "Martin Owens, trustee of the Martin Owens Living Trust dated June 18, 20xx."

If you and your spouse made a shared living trust, either trustee (spouse) has authority over shared-ownership trust property. That means that either spouse can sell or give away any of the shared trust property. However, one spouse cannot control what was the separate property of the other spouse before it was transferred to the trust. Also, even for shared property, both spouses will probably have to consent to transfer real estate out of the living trust. Especially in community property states, buyers and title insurance companies usually insist on both spouses' signatures on transfer documents.

If for any reason you want to take property out of the trust but keep ownership of it, you can transfer the property back to yourself. So if Martin, in the previous example, wanted to take his house out of his living trust but keep ownership in his own name, he would make the deed out from "The Martin Owens Living Trust dated June 18, 20xx, Martin Owens, trustee" to "Martin Owens." He would sign the deed "Martin Owens, trustee of the Martin Owens Living Trust dated June 18, 20xx."

Unless this change will be for a brief period (for example, only for the time necessary to obtain refinancing of your home loan), you should modify the property schedule of your trust document to reflect the change. If you don't, the schedules will still show that the property is owned by the trust. Legally, the trust no longer owns it, and the discrepancy could be confusing to the people who carry out your wishes after your death.

> **EXAMPLE:** Wendy and Brian, a married couple, made a shared living trust several years ago. Wendy transferred a valuable antique dresser, which she inherited from her grandfather before she was married, to the living trust. It's listed on Schedule B of the trust document. The trust document provides that the dresser will go to her son at her death. But she's changed her mind and decided while she's alive to give the dresser to her daughter.
>
> After Wendy gives the dresser to her daughter, she prepares two documents. First, she prepares a new Schedule B, deleting the dresser from the list of property, and replacing the old Schedule B attached to her trust document. Second, she prepares a trust amendment, stating that the paragraph that left the dresser to her son is no longer in effect.

When to Amend Your Living Trust Document

One of the most attractive features of a revocable living trust is its flexibility: You can change its terms, or end it altogether, at any time. This section discusses several events that should be red flags alerting you that you may need to amend your living trust.

In most circumstances, you will want to amend your living trust document, not revoke it. At first glance, it might seem easier to revoke it and start again, as is usually done with a will. But if you revoke your living trust and create another one, you must transfer all the trust property out of the old living trust and into the new one. This means preparing new documents of title and all the other paperwork required to transfer property to your original trust. ("Revoking Your Living Trust," below, discusses when it is advisable to revoke your living trust and make another.)

As explained above, you may need to amend your trust document if you sell or give away property from your trust. Here are some other events that normally require amendment of a trust.

You Marry or Have a Child

If you get married or have a child, you'll almost certainly want to amend your trust document to provide for your new spouse or offspring. And remember that your spouse or minor child may be entitled, under state law, to a certain portion of your property. (See Chapter 7.)

You Move to Another State

Although your living trust is still valid if you move to another state, you may want to change your living trust in response to your new state's laws. Here are several aspects of your trust, and overall estate plan, that may be affected by a move to a new state.

Registering Your Trust

Your new state may authorize you to register your living trust document with a state agency or court. (See "Registering the Trust," in Chapter 11.)

Marital Property Laws: Who Owns What

If you are married and move from a common law state to California, Idaho, or Washington, property you acquired during marriage may become "quasi-community property," and so owned by both spouses, however it was originally owned. Wisconsin has a similar rule. See "Marital Property Laws" in Chapter 5. You'll need to review your property disposition to make sure it complies with your new state's laws.

Property Management for Young Beneficiaries

Your state's law determines the choices you have when it comes to arranging for property management for young trust beneficiaries. In all states, you can create a child's trust for any beneficiary who might inherit trust property before age 35. In all states except South Carolina you can use the Uniform Transfers to Minors Act to appoint an adult custodian to manage property you leave the child until that child becomes an adult. The age at which the child receives the property outright can vary from state to state, between the ages of 18 to 25. (See Chapter 8.)

If you made a gift using your old state's version of the Uniform Transfers to Minors Act (UTMA) and you move to a state that has a different UTMA age for turning over the property to the minor, you may need to amend your trust to update the age for the child to receive the gift. Or if you move to South Carolina, you'll need to replace the UTMA provisions with a child's trust or with a custodianship under the South Carolina Uniform Gifts to Minors Act. (See Chapter 8.)

Rights of a Surviving Spouse to Inherit

Different states entitle surviving spouses to different shares of a deceased spouse's estate. If you prepare a shared living trust and you plan to leave at least one-half of your total estate to your spouse, you don't have to worry about this. But if you want to leave your spouse less than one-half, and you're concerned that your spouse might challenge your estate plan and demand the "statutory share" of your property after your death, you'll need to know what your new state's laws allow. (See "Disinheritance" in Chapter 7.)

State Inheritance Tax and Estate Tax

If you move to a new state, that state's laws, including its law on inheritance tax and estate tax, will govern all your property, except for out-of-state real estate. (See Chapter 14.)

You Change Your Name

If you legally change your name, for whatever reason —marriage, divorce, desire for a new identity—you should amend your trust to use your new name.

> **EXAMPLE:** Helen obtains a divorce and resumes using her maiden name, Hickman, instead of her married name of Delouch. She amends her living trust, renaming it the Helen Hickman Living Trust. This amendment must be notarized. If Helen previously had a shared trust with her now-ex-spouse, she would need to prepare a new trust for one person.

> CAUTION
>
> **Changing the name of your trust.** If you change the name of your trust, you also need to change the title to all property with documents of title in your trust. This is particularly true for real estate. While this requires some paperwork, it isn't a serious hassle.

> **EXAMPLE:** Helen Hickman had previously transferred real estate to her trust when she used the name Helen Delouch. Helen prepares and records a new deed, transferring the property to herself as "Helen Hickman, trustee of the Helen Hickman Living Trust," from "Helen Delouch, trustee of the Helen Delouch Living Trust."

Your Spouse Dies

With a shared living trust, when one spouse dies, the other will probably inherit some, if not all, of the deceased spouse's trust property. The surviving spouse may want to amend the remaining living trust to name beneficiaries for that property.

A Major Beneficiary Dies

If you left much or all of your trust property to one person, and that person dies before you do, you may well want to amend your trust document. If you named an alternate beneficiary for the deceased beneficiary, there's not an urgent need; the alternate will inherit the property. But it still makes sense to amend the trust so that you can name another alternate beneficiary, who will receive the property if the former alternate (now first in line) dies before you do.

> **EXAMPLE:** Maria and Carlos make a shared living trust together. Maria leaves all her trust property to Carlos, but he dies before she does. Because she named her daughter Teresa as alternate beneficiary for her husband, she has already planned for the possibility of Carlos's death. But it still makes sense for her to amend her trust to name Teresa as the beneficiary and then to name an alternate beneficiary for Teresa.

Remember that your trust document has another backup device built into it—the residuary beneficiary. If both the primary and alternate beneficiary die before you do, the residuary beneficiary will inherit the trust property.

You Want to Change Ownership of Trust Property

Sometimes couples decide, for various reasons, to change shared property into property owned separately by one spouse or the other. Or a spouse may decide to change separate property into shared ownership property. The legal term for this is "transmutation of property."

If, after you've placed property in a trust, you want to make this type of change, you'll need to:

- Prepare the appropriate transfer documents for a change of ownership. If real estate is involved, new deeds reflecting the changed ownership must be prepared. If it's property without documents of title, you need what's called a "reverse assignment." A reverse assignment is simply a document transferring property from the trust (technically, you as trustees back to yourself as a couple). There's no standard legal form for a reverse assignment. Any notice you prepare that's clear will do.
- Revise the appropriate trust schedules, so the changed property is deleted from the old schedule and placed on the correct one.

> **EXAMPLE:** Soon after they get married, Felicity and Russell Jones create a shared living trust. They live in a home in New Jersey that is Felicity's separate property, and is listed as such on Schedule B of their trust. After several happy years together, Felicity decides she wants to place the house in shared ownership with Russell. So she lists the house on Schedule A, the shared property schedule of their trust, removing it from Schedule B. As trustee, Felicity executes a deed transferring the house to herself, as her separate property. She then executes a second deed, identifying the property as co-owned equally between her and her husband. The house is now owned by the couple as trustees of their trust.
>
> Since each spouse owns half the house, they'll need to revise their beneficiary provisions, unless both spouses simply leave all of their property to the other spouse.

Who Can Amend a Living Trust Document

Who can amend the terms of a living trust document depends on the kind of trust you created.

If you created an individual living trust, you (the grantor) can amend any of its provisions at any time, as long as you are mentally competent.

If you created a shared trust, while both spouses are alive, both must agree to any changes in the provisions of the trust documents—for example, to change a beneficiary, successor trustee, or the management set up for a young beneficiary.

After one spouse dies, a shared living trust is split into two trusts. The deceased spouse's trust can no longer be amended. The surviving spouse can, of course, amend the remaining revocable trust.

A trust document created from a form in this book cannot be amended by someone acting on a grantor's behalf. Granting someone else the power to amend your trust is inherently dangerous. You've gone to considerable trouble to set up your estate plan and living trust. Normally, those plans shouldn't change if you become incapacitated. Therefore, the trust forms in this book do not authorize amendment by others if you become incapacitated.

If you do want to allow your successor trustee to be able to amend your living trust if you become incapacitated, you need to do two things:

- **Expressly authorize amendments in your living trust.** To accomplish this, you would add a new provision to the trustee powers clause of your trust. The wording of this new provision would vary, depending on the type of trust. For a one-person trust, you'd need something like:

> If the original trustee of this trust becomes incapacitated, the acting successor trustee shall have authority to amend this trust.

For a couple's trust, you might use something like the following:

> If one spouse becomes incapacitated, the other spouse can amend this trust. If both spouses become incapacitated, the successor trustee can amend this trust.

SEE AN EXPERT

Do not add these provisions yourself. The above provisions are only examples, not actual clauses for your trust. If you want to allow your successor to be able to amend your trust, see a lawyer. You could impose a variety of different limits on the power to amend.

- **Prepare a durable power of attorney for finances.** In this type of power of attorney, you name a person to handle your financial matters if you are incapacitated and cannot handle them yourself. This person is called your "attorney-in-fact" or your "agent." To avoid conflicts, you should name the same person to be both your attorney-in-fact under a durable power of attorney and your successor trustee under your living trust. And to make your intention absolutely clear, in your power of attorney you should expressly authorize your attorney-in-fact to amend your living trust. (See "Planning for Incapacity," in Chapter 14, for more information about durable powers of attorney.)

Making Changes to Your Trust

After some time, you may need to make some changes to the terms of your trust document. If you need to make only a few simple changes, you can make a trust amendment and attach it to your existing trust document. However, if you have many changes to make, or if your changes are complicated, it will be better to make a new trust or to make a trust restatement.

Simple Trust Amendments

You can use a trust amendment to change a beneficiary, successor trustee, custodian, or to change nearly any other provision. Simply complete this book's Form 6 or 7, sign it, have the form notarized, and then attach it to your original trust document. If you have an individual trust, use Form 6; if you have a shared living trust, use Form 7.

You can subsequently refer to your trust by the date of the amendment. For example:

> The Jane and Werner Kopf Trust, as amended September 3, 20xx.

A sample draft amendment of a shared living trust, ready for final typing, is shown below.

~~Form 7: Amendment to Shared Living Trust~~

Amendment to Living Trust

This Amendment to The **①** _____ *Jim and Toni Nance* _____

your names (or name of trust, if different)

Living Trust dated _____ *July 1* _____ , 20__ *xx* , is made this _____ *30th* _____ day of_____ *November* _____ ,

date Declaration of Trust signed

20__ *xx* , by _____ *Toni Nance and Jim Nance* _____ ,

your names

_____ the grantors and trustees of the trust. Under the power of amendment

reserved to the grantors by Section II, Paragraph (F), of the Declaration of Trust, the grantors amend the trust as

follows:

1. The following is deleted from the Declaration of Trust:

   in Section IV, Paragraph A(1), Eileen Nance Jones shall be given all Jim Nance's interest in the Wyche Co. stock

   _____ .

2. The following is added to the Declaration of Trust:

   in Section IV, Paragraph A(1), Aaron Nance shall be given all Jim Nance's interest in the Wyche Co. stock

   _____ .

[Repeat as needed]

In all other respects, the Declaration of Trust as executed on _____ *July 1* _____ , 20 *xx*

date

by the grantors is affirmed.

Executed at _____ *Fairview* _____ , _____ *Ohio* _____ , on

city   state

_____ *November 30* _____ , 20__ *xx* .

date

_____

Grantor and Trustee

_____

Grantor and Trustee

EXAMPLE: Jim and Toni created their shared trust three years ago. Jim named his sister Eileen as a specific beneficiary for some stock in the Wyche Co. that Jim transferred to the trust. He named no alternate beneficiary. But since then, Jim and his sister have had a falling out. He wants to amend the trust document to leave the stock to his brother Aaron.

All Jim and Toni need to do is use Form 7 to prepare a trust amendment. The amendment deletes the paragraph in the Declaration of Trust that left the stock to Eileen. It also adds a paragraph leaving the stock to Aaron and stating that if Aaron doesn't survive him, that it should go to Jim's nephew David.

Their draft trust amendment form (before typing, with appropriate cross-outs in the form) is shown above.

Similarly, you can amend your trust document if you change your mind about whom you want to serve as:

- **Successor trustee.** The person who handles the trust, and any children's trusts, after your death or after the surviving spouse's death if a shared trust was created.

CAUTION

Do not change the original trustees of your living trust. You (and your spouse, if you made a shared living trust) must be the original trustees of your living trust. If you aren't, the tax treatment of the trust changes. (See Chapter 6.)

- **Alternate successor trustee.** The person who takes over as trustee if your first choice can't serve.
- **Custodian of a child's property.** The person who manages a young beneficiary's property under the terms of the Uniform Transfers to Minors Act, if it's available in your state.
- **Alternate custodian.** The person who serves as custodian if your first choice can't serve.

EXAMPLE: Geoffrey creates a living trust and names his brother as successor trustee. His brother moves to Europe two years later, so Geoffrey prepares a trust amendment to his trust document, naming his friend Brad as successor trustee instead.

Subsequent Amendments

If you've already amended your trust once, how do you do it again? It's vital that any later amendment clearly state which document(s) you are amending. So refer to both your original trust and all prior amendments. For example, say Cindy Dallis wants to amend her trust for the second time. The caption of her new amendment reads:

> This Second Amendment to the Cindy Dallis Living Trust dated January 23, 20xx, and the First Amendment to the Cindy Dallis Living Trust dated August 2, 20xx, is made this 18th day of February, 20xx.

Then, using Form 6, you set out whatever provisions you want to add to your trust. If any provisions are changed or deleted, identify them. Finally, reaffirm the original declaration of trust and the prior amendment, like this:

> In all other aspects, the Declaration of Trust dated January 23, 20xx, and the First Amendment to that trust dated August 2, 20xx, are reaffirmed.

It is fine to delete all of a prior amendment by a subsequent amendment. For example, Anthony has already amended his trust once and now he wants to use a second amendment to delete that first amendment and make new changes. So the second amendment begins like this:

> **Second Amendment to the Anthony Billings Living Trust dated January 24, 2011**
>
> All of The First Amendment to the Anthony Billings Living Trust, dated November 11, 2014, is revoked in its entirety.
> (The second amendment goes on to provide all other changes, revisions, additions, and deletions to the trust.)

Making two or more amendments to your trust can become complicated, especially when in a subsequent amendment you want to delete part or all of an earlier amendment. It's crucial that your amendments be coherent and that the successor trustee, your beneficiaries, and any financial institution holding trust assets can understand them. While there are no specific rules explaining how you make your documents coherent and understandable, I can offer some pointers:

- Quote the precise words of each section, provision, or term of the trust you are deleting by an amendment.
- State the precise language of every change or addition to the trust document.
- End each amendment by stating that "In all other aspects, I/We restate and reaffirm the [*name of your trust*] and all nondeleted provisions of the trust amendment dated [*date of amendment*]."

If you are careful and clear, this can work well. However, if there is any possibility that subsequent amendments will create confusion, use a trust restatement instead.

Trust Restatements

If you need to make complicated or numerous changes to your trust, it's best to use a "restatement of trust." In a restatement of trust, you essentially rewrite your existing trust to reflect the changes you want to make. The document keeps the same name, but you add a restatement subtitle, like this:

> The Denis Clifford Living Trust, dated Oct. 11, 2001, Revised and Restated, January 3, 20XX.

This solution has a great advantage over making an entirely new trust, namely: You don't have to retitle all of your property documents, because the trust keeps the same name. Like the original living

trust, as well as any certifications, amendments, and revocations, a restatement of trust must be signed, dated, and notarized.

There is no standard form for a restatement of trust. A restatement needs to be geared to your individual needs and desires. You need to carefully draft a restatement to include any new provisions or changes you want to make in your trust and to delete any provisions you no longer want.

Be specific. Restatements must be absolutely complete, coherent, and understandable to your successor trustee, your beneficiaries, and any financial institution holding trust assets. While it is not legally necessary that an attorney draft a restatement, it will almost certainly be worth the time and money to get help from an experienced estate planning lawyer.

CAUTION

If you have registered your trust. If you live in a state where you can register your trust with a government agency, and have chosen to do so, you should file a copy of any amendment, revocation, or restatement with that agency. (See "Registering the Trust" in Chapter 11 for a list of states that authorize registration of living trusts.)

Revoking Your Living Trust

You can revoke your living trust at any time, but you probably won't want to. After all, the reasons you established a trust won't go away, and revoking a living trust (unlike revoking a will) requires some work. The revoked trust ceases to exist and cannot own property. That means you must transfer ownership of all the trust property out of the living trust, back into your own name (or names), or into the name of a new living trust.

Who Can Revoke a Living Trust

Who can revoke your living trust depends on the kind of trust you created.

Individual Living Trust

If you create an individual living trust, you (the grantor) can revoke it at any time. The trust document does not allow the trust to be revoked by someone acting on your behalf (your attorney-in-fact, for example) unless you have specifically granted that authority in another document. (See "Who Can Amend a Living Trust Document," above.)

Shared Living Trust

Either spouse can revoke a shared living trust, wiping out all terms of the trust. The trust property is returned to each spouse according to how they owned it before transferring it to the trust.

> **EXAMPLE:** Yvonne and André make a shared living trust. Each transfers separately owned property to the trust. They also transfer their house, which they own together equally, as tenants in common, to the trust. Later Yvonne, anticipating a divorce, transfers the trust property she owned back to herself, and the property her husband owned back to him. The co-owned house goes back to both of them, who own it as tenants in common as before. She then revokes the trust.

The reason either spouse can revoke a shared trust, but it takes both to amend one, is that revocation simply returns both spouses to the status quo. By contrast, in the event of divorce or bitter conflict, it's risky to allow one spouse to amend a trust that governs both spouses' property.

When to Revoke Your Living Trust

If you're like most people, amending your living trust will take care of your changing circumstances over the years, and you will never need to revoke your trust. But here are two situations in which you might need to revoke a living trust and start over.

You Want to Make Extensive Revisions

If you want to make very extensive revisions to the terms of the trust document, you should consider revoking it and starting fresh with a new trust document. If you don't, you risk creating inconsistencies and confusion.

You Get Divorced

If you divorce, you should revoke your living trust, and you and your ex-spouse should make new, separate ones. In a few states, the provisions of your living trust that affect your spouse are automatically revoked by divorce, but you should definitely not rely solely on these laws. They might change. Your own revocation will not.

How to Revoke Your Living Trust

To revoke your living trust, you must do two things:

Step 1. Use this book's Form 8 to prepare a simple document called a Revocation of Living Trust. If you use the form in the back of the book, retype the form using a computer or typewriter. If you use the downloadable form, make sure to delete any extraneous text, like the instructions. Sign the revocation in front of a notary. Then store the revocation in a safe place, with your other vital papers.

Step 2. Transfer ownership of trust property from the trust back to yourself. Basically, you must reverse the process you followed when you transferred ownership of the property to the trust's name. (See Chapter 10.) You can make the transfer because of your authority as trustee of the trust.

For example, if you placed your home in your living trust, you must prepare and record a deed transferring that house from yourself as trustee of your trust back to yourself individually. If you do not transfer trust property back to yourself after you have revoked your living trust, you could wind up with a mess.

After a Grantor Dies

The benefits of a revocable living trust do not come until after a grantor's death, when trust property is transferred to beneficiaries without probate. The all-important responsibility of handling that transfer falls to your surviving spouse if you made a shared living trust, or to your successor trustee if you made an individual living trust.

To transfer property outside of probate, the successor trustee or surviving spouse does not have to file any reports with, or be supervised by, any government agencies or court.

This chapter provides a summary of the job of the successor trustee. It does not provide specific instructions or definitive details about what is required, but rather offers an overview of the job to give you a sense of what your successor trustee will be expected to do.

Who Serves as Trustee After the Grantor's Death

With a shared living trust, the surviving spouse serves as sole trustee after one spouse's death. With an individual trust, or when the surviving spouse dies, the successor trustee is in charge.

Who Serves as Trustee After Grantor's Death?

Individual Living Trust
1. Successor trustee(s)
2. Alternate successor trustee(s)

Shared Living Trust
1. Surviving spouse
2. Successor trustee(s)
3. Alternate successor trustee(s)

More Than One Successor Trustee

If more than one person is named in the trust document as successor trustee, they all serve together.

Whether each must formally agree on any action taken with regard to the living trust property or they can act independently depends on the terms of the trust document.

If one of the trustees cannot serve, the others remain as trustees. The person named as alternate successor trustee does not take over unless all the people named as successor trustees cannot serve.

SEE AN EXPERT

The assistance of a lawyer is normally required. It is quite difficult for a successor trustee or a surviving spouse of a shared trust to do all this work unaided. Most successor trustees work with a lawyer to get the work done. While that lawyer will charge fees, those fees will be much less than probate lawyers' fees would have been, and the work should take only weeks at most, not months or years. *The Trustee's Legal Companion* (Nolo), by Liza Hanks and Carol Elias provides good explanations of what trust administration involves and what a successor trustee must do.

If a Trustee Resigns

A trustee can resign at any time using a resignation statement like the one shown below. The ex-trustee should prepare the notice, sign the notice in front of a notary public, and then deliver the notice to the person who is next in line to serve as trustee.

Notice of Resignation

I, Lucia Freni, current trustee of The Robert Ambruzzi Living Trust dated March 3, 20xx, resign my position as trustee, effective immediately.

Date: November 19, 20xx

Lucia Freni

[Notarization]

Appointing a New Trustee

Under the terms of Nolo living trusts, any trustee, including the last acting trustee, can appoint someone else to take over if no one named in the trust document can serve.

Normally, it would be the last, or alternate, successor trustee who names someone else to act as trustee if the need arises. The appointment must be in writing, signed, and notarized. The trustee making the appointment can prepare a simple document like the one shown below.

Appointment of Trustee

I, Lucia Freni, Trustee of The Robert Ambruzzi Living Trust dated March 3, 20xx, appoint Clarence Ryan as trustee, effective immediately. This appointment is made under the authority granted in the Declaration of Trust.

Date: November 19, 20xx

Lucia Freni
_____

[*Notarization*]

Trust Administration After Death of a Grantor

After the grantor of a living trust dies, there are several things that must be done, either by the successor trustee or the surviving trustee of a shared trust. This process is generally called "trust administration." The details vary depending on the laws and legal practices of the state of death, but generally, the trustee must:

1. Obtain several certified copies of the death certificate.

2. Prepare and record documents that establish the authority of the current trustee. For example, in California, the executor may have to file an Affidavit of Death of Trustee, a Preliminary Change of Ownership Report, and a Death of Real Property Owner.

3. Transfer trust property from the deceased grantor to beneficiaries of the trust.

4. For any trust real estate owned by the grantor, an appraisal must be obtained of the market value of that property as of the date of the grantor's death. Usually, a statement of that value by a real estate agent will suffice. The reason an appraisal is needed is because the real estate will receive a "stepped-up basis" to its market value at death. (See "Will Property in My Living Trust Get a 'Stepped-Up' Tax Basis When I Die?" in Chapter 3.)

5. Notify each trust beneficiary of the trust's existence and other pertinent information about the trust. State laws in almost all states require this, and it is a good idea even if not required.

However, in reality, this requirement is often ignored when there are just a few trust beneficiaries who are also family members. However, because the trustee can be exposed to liability by a disgruntled beneficiary who didn't receive proper notice of the trust, a prudent trustee sends out the notices.

6. For all securities or stock accounts owned by the grantor, acquire a statement from each financial institution holding an account of the value of the account as of the date of death (to document the stepped-up basis of the account for any subsequent capital gains tax assessed against sales of the securities or stocks).

7. If the deceased grantor had a retirement account, check to see if she or he took the required minimum distribution in the year of death.

8. File federal and state income tax returns for the year of the decedent's death (as well as any unfiled returns for previous years).

9. Notify the Social Security Administration and all companies that issued credit cards to the deceased grantor that the grantor has died.

10. If the deceased grantor was a married or partnered, the surviving spouse may need to make:
    - a new will
    - a new durable power of attorney for finances
    - a new durable power of attorney for health care and living will, or
    - possibly, changes to the surviving spouse's living trust.

Removing a Trustee

Very rarely, a beneficiary becomes seriously unhappy with the way a trustee handles trust property. For example, the beneficiary of a child's trust might complain that the trustee isn't spending enough of the trust property's income on the beneficiary's education. If the dispute can't be worked out, the beneficiary can file a lawsuit to try to force the removal of the trustee.

The Trustee's Duties

Every trustee must take two steps immediately after assuming responsibility for your living trust: The trustee must 1) execute and record a document establishing that the trustee can act for the trust and 2) must obtain at least a rough estimate of the value of major trust assets.

Beyond these basics, a trustee's job depends on whether your state imposes specific requirements on trustees and on whether you made an individual living trust or a shared living trust.

> **SEE AN EXPERT**
>
> **The trustee may want expert help with tax returns.** In the rare event that the value of the grantor's estate is over the estate tax threshold, a federal estate tax return must be filed. Also, a federal estate tax return must be filed if the surviving spouse may subsequently claim "portability." See Chapter 14. The successor trustee (as well as the executor of the deceased's will) is responsible for filing this document. It is a complicated tax form, and an expert lawyer or tax accountant should be hired to do the work. Similarly, if a state inheritance or estate tax return must be filed, the successor trustee or executor must handle that.

All Trustees

All successor trustees should take the following steps after assuming responsibility for a living trust.

Preparing an Affidavit of Successor Trustee

The trustee may need proof of authority to act for the trust, particularly for transactions involving real estate, since there are no court proceedings to officially give the trustee authority. The accepted convention in many states is to record a document called "Affidavit of Assumption of Duties by Successor Trustee" at the county land records office. (In some states, this document may also be defined by other words, such as "Acknowledgment of Trusteeship" or "Affidavit of Death of Trustee.") There is no standard for this document because its contents vary by state, but it should always include:

- the name of the trust
- the date the trust document was signed, and
- the name of the person becoming successor trustee.

A certified copy of the grantor's death certificate should be attached. Certified copies can be obtained from your county or state's vital records department.

See the sample of a California Affidavit of Death of Trustee prepared for the surviving spouse of a shared living trust.

Appraising the Value of Significant Trust Assets

The successor trustee should obtain written statements of the market value of major trust assets as of the date of the grantor's death. (The IRS also permits the trustee to value all the assets as of six months after death. This is an all-or-nothing proposition. The trustee cannot value some assets as of the date of death and others as of six months thereafter.)

Defining the market value of major trust assets can be important for two reasons. First, if the trust (the deceased's property) could be liable for estate or inheritance taxes, accurate values for trust assets are crucial. Second, even if the trust property will not be subject to estate or inheritance taxes, the beneficiaries must have proof of the value of trust property at the grantor's death in order to determine later profit or loss if that property is subsequently sold. All property of the deceased, including all living trust property, is entitled to a stepped-up basis under current estate tax laws (see Chapter 3). If the market value of living trust property is not obtained promptly after the grantor dies, it may be difficult or impossible to obtain reliable evaluations later. This may mean that the IRS will not allow any stepped-up basis when calculating profit, or loss, from any subsequent sale of the property.

Recording Requested by

And when recorded
mail statements to:
Elizabeth Foster
2324 Thomson Street
Celestial, CA 94XXX

Affidavit of Death of Trustee

Elizabeth Foster, of legal age, first being duly sworn, declares:

That Thomas Foster, the decedent named in the attached copy of the Certificate of Death attached hereto, is the same person as Thomas Foster, who was a grantor and cotrustee of the Thomas Foster and Elizabeth Foster Living Trust (hereinafter, "the trust"), created by declaration of trust on Oct. 23, 20XX.

That at his death said decedent Thomas Foster in his capacity as cotrustee of the trust, held title to the property located at 2324 Thomson Street, Celestial, CA 94XXX, and more particularly described in the Legal Description below, pursuant to that certain quit claim deed executed on Dec. 5, 2009, from Elizabeth Foster and Thomas Foster as trustees of the Trust, and recorded that deed as Instrument No. 2012348618 on Oct. 23, 20XX, in the Official Records of the Divine County Recorder, State of California.

Legal Description: [*transcribed verbatim from deed*]

That pursuant to the terms of the trust, the undersigned, Elizabeth Foster, became the sole trustee of the trust upon the death of Thomas Foster.

That pursuant to the terms of the trust, Elizabeth Foster, as trustee, has the power to sell, convey, exchange, lease, encumber, or transfer in any way all or a portion of the real property held in the trust.

Executed on March 14, 20XX, at Celestial, California.

I declare under penalty of perjury that the foregoing is true and correct.

_____

Elizabeth Foster

[Attached: Notary Certification]

EXAMPLE: Marcello has a living trust with property worth $900,000. The most valuable item in his trust is a sculpture he bought more than 30 years ago for $10,000. When he dies, it is appraised at $550,000. That figure is the inheritors' tax basis. (The basis is stepped up to the market value at death.) If they sell the sculpture a week later for $550,000, they have no taxable profit.

But if no appraisal had been done, the IRS could argue that the inheritors' basis was Marcello's original purchase price of $10,000. So if they sold the sculpture for $550,000, their taxable profit would be $540,000.

The lesson is clear: For any asset that's increased significantly in value since the grantor bought it, determine the market value of that property at the grantor's death.

Some valuations are easy to obtain. Stock and bond prices are, obviously, printed daily during the week. Other valuations may require more work. Real estate needs an appraisal, unless the property is promptly sold. In practice, a broker should be able to make a sensible estimate. Other valuable property, such as jewelry, collectibles, or artworks, requires appraisal by an expert in the field.

Providing Basic Information to Trust Beneficiaries

A successor trustee has a basic, if not always clearly defined, duty to provide essential trust information to trust beneficiaries. Doing so is also wise trustee policy—it's not hard to do and can eliminate conflicts or even lawsuits that could arise if a trustee works in secret.

Pay Debts of the Trust Creator

If the trust creator had any debts, the successor trustee must pay them from trust property, unless the creator provided some other means for payment of those debts.

State-Specific Duties

A number of states impose specific duties on the successor trustee. Usually, these duties involve a notice that must be given the trust beneficiaries. Upon taking over management of a living trust, the successor trustee should check state law to determine precisely what duties, if any, the state imposes.

 RESOURCE

The successor trustee's specific legal duties. *The Executor's Guide: Settling a Loved One's Estate or Trust*, by Mary Randolph (Nolo), and *The Trustee's Legal Companion*, by Liza Hanks and Carol Elias Zolla (Nolo), list every state's rules regarding a successor trustee's duties. If a state imposes specific duties, the citation to that state's statute is provided.

Trust-Specific Duties

A successor trustee's job depends primarily on whether you made an individual trust or a shared trust.

Individual Trust

When the grantor, who is also the trustee, dies, the successor trustee named in the trust document takes over as trustee. The new trustee is responsible for distributing the trust property to the beneficiaries named by the grantor in the trust document.

EXAMPLE: Jamie is Elliot's successor trustee. Elliot's trust leaves his house to his children, Clarence and Grace. Elliot dies. Jamie, as trustee, deeds the house from the trust to Clarence and Grace, who can do with it what they wish— live in it, rent it, or sell it. Jamie does not sell the house and divide the proceeds between the beneficiaries; that's not his decision to make.

Normally, the trust continues to exist only as long as it takes the successor trustee to distribute trust property to the beneficiaries. In many cases, a living trust can be wound up within a few weeks after a grantor's death. No formal termination document is required. Once the trust property has been distributed, the trust ends.

The successor trustee must manage trust property only during the (hopefully short) period between the death of the original trust grantor and the actual distribution of property, or title to property, to the trust beneficiaries. Pragmatically, it is not part of the successor trustee's job to sell any trust property. Technically, the successor trustee does have the power to sell trust property, as does any trustee. However, the authority to sell trust property is actually granted to the trustee for two reasons: (1) so that the original grantor(s) can sell trust property any time she, he, or they want; (2) so that a successor trustee managing the trust for an incapacitated grantor can sell trust property if that becomes necessary. When distributing trust property to the beneficiaries, the successor trustee should manage that property as little as possible. It is for the beneficiaries, not the successor trustee, to decide what will be done with trust property—whether it will be sold or held, mortgaged or rented, etc.

The successor trustee is also in charge of managing any property left to a young beneficiary in a child's trust. A child's trust will exist until the beneficiary reaches the age specified in the trust document, so if there's such a trust, the successor trustee may have years of work ahead. (See Chapter 8.)

If trust property inherited by a young beneficiary is to be managed by a custodian under the Uniform Transfers to Minors Act, instead of in a child's trust, the person named as custodian will receive that property and be responsible for it. The successor trustee may also have been named as the custodian for a young beneficiary's property.

The Successor Trustee's Duties: Individual Trust

- Distribute trust property to beneficiaries named in the trust document.
- Manage trust property left in a child's trust, if any.
- File federal estate and state inheritance tax returns, if necessary. This is also the responsibility of the executor of the estate, if there was a will. (See "Preparing and Filing Tax Returns," below.)

Shared Living Trust

When a spouse dies, a shared living trust technically splits into two separate trusts:

- Trust 1 contains the deceased spouse's share of trust property, excluding any trust property left to the surviving spouse. The terms of Trust 1 cannot be changed; it cannot be revoked.
- Trust 2 contains the surviving spouse's trust property, including any of the deceased spouse's share of the trust property that is left to the surviving spouse. The surviving spouse remains free to amend the terms of Trust 2, or even revoke it.

The survivor is sole trustee of Trust 1, Trust 2, and any child's trusts set up for the deceased spouse's young beneficiaries.

EXAMPLE: Debra and Timothy Zeltzer create a shared living trust. When Timothy dies, Debra can refer to her trust as "The Debra and Timothy Zeltzer Trust, Trust 2," and to her husband's trust, now irrevocable, as "The Debra and Timothy Zeltzer Trust, Trust 1."

Revising or Revoking Trust 2

Revising or revoking the surviving spouse's continuing Trust 2—the trust that now contains the surviving spouse's trust property—is not common because normally after one spouse dies, the surviving spouse wants to keep the same trust beneficiaries and successor trustees as named in the original trust. This is what Trust 2 does. However, the surviving spouse may revise or revoke Trust 2 if desired. (Section V(D)(2) of the Shared Living Trust specifically gives that right to the surviving spouse.)

If a surviving spouse decides to revise or revoke Trust 2, that should be done with the aid of a lawyer. This work is part of the "trust administration" discussed above. Do not try to adapt Form 8, Revocation of Living Trust, for this purpose. Use Form 8 only when both grantors are alive.

It's the surviving spouse's job to distribute the property from Trust 1 to the beneficiaries the deceased spouse named in the trust document. If, as is common, much of the trust property is left to the surviving spouse, that spouse will have little to do. The trust property the surviving spouse inherits is already in the revocable trust (Trust 2), and remains there. The trust document provides that trust property left to the survivor does not go to the surviving spouse in a personal capacity but instead stays in the trust as part of the property in Trust 2. If it did not contain such a provision, the property would have to be transferred from the living trust to the spouse and then, if the surviving spouse wanted it to avoid probate, back to the surviving spouse's living trust again.

When all the property in Trust 1 has been distributed to the beneficiaries, that trust ceases to exist. No formal termination document is required.

Trust 2 contains only the surviving spouse's property and remains revocable. The surviving spouse is free to change it.

Generally, the surviving spouse "creates" Trust 1 and Trust 2 for the purposes of property distribution only. The surviving spouse does not need to create formal new living trusts. The surviving spouse must simply figure out what property was owned by the deceased spouse, and what property was owned by the surviving spouse. Then the deceased spouse's property is distributed as the living trust directs.

The trust document provides that all property of the surviving spouse, including all trust property left to the surviving spouse by the deceased spouse, stays in the original living trust. The surviving spouse simply continues on with that trust, which remains revocable until the surviving spouse's death.

> **EXAMPLE:** Edith and Jacques create a shared living trust. They transfer their house, which they own together, into the trust, and name each other as beneficiaries. Edith names her son as alternate beneficiary.

> When Jacques dies, Edith inherits his half-interest in the house. Because of the way the trust document is worded, she doesn't have to change the trust document to name a beneficiary for the half-interest in the house that she inherited from her husband, nor does she have to prepare a new deed for the house. Both halves of the house will go to her son at her death. She may, however, want to amend the trust to make her son the primary beneficiary and name someone else to be alternate beneficiary.

When the second spouse dies, the successor trustee named in the trust document takes over as trustee. The process of winding up the living trust is the same as that for an individual trust.

> **EXAMPLE:** Harry and Maude, a married couple, set up a shared living trust to avoid probate. They appoint Maude's cousin Emily as successor trustee, to take over as trustee after they have both died. They transfer ownership of much of their co-owned property—their house, savings accounts, and stocks—to the trust. Maude also puts some of her family heirlooms, which are her separate property, in the living trust.

> In the trust document, Maude leaves her heirlooms to her younger sister. She leaves her half of the trust property she and Harry own together to Harry.

> When Maude dies, Harry becomes the sole trustee. Following the terms of the trust document, he distributes Maude's heirlooms (from Trust 1) to her sister, without probate. Maude's half of the property they had owned together stays in the trust (in Trust 2); no transfer is necessary. After Maude's death, Harry decides to amend the trust document to name his nephew, Burt, as successor trustee instead of Maude's cousin Emily. When Harry dies, Burt will become trustee and distribute the property in Trust 2 to Harry's beneficiaries. When all the property is given to Harry's beneficiaries, the trust ends.

Transferring Property to Beneficiaries

The procedure for transferring trust property depends on who the beneficiaries are:

- Property of a shared living trust left by a deceased spouse to the surviving spouse remains in the trust, and no action is required.
- Trust property left to adult beneficiaries must be actually transferred to them.
- Property left to a young beneficiary in a child's trust stays in that trust until the child reaches the age to receive the trust property outright.
- Property left to a custodian under the Uniform Transfers to Minors Act must be given to the custodian named in the trust document.

To obtain the trust property, the trustee usually needs a copy of the grantor's death certificate (both grantors' death certificates, if both are dead and the trust property was originally co-owned) and a copy of the trust document. (The trustee should be prepared to show the original trust document in case anyone doubts the copy's authenticity.) Frequently, an Affidavit of Assumption of Duties by Successor Trustee will also be needed. And finally, in some cases, the trustee will need to prepare some other paperwork, such as a specific form of a brokerage company or a new deed for real estate.

Normally, the successor trustee transfers the trust property to the beneficiaries relatively soon after the trust creator dies. To accomplish this, the successor trustee does not need to obtain a federal taxpayer ID. However, if the successor trustee's responsibilities include ongoing trust financial transactions, a taxpayer ID is required, and a trust income tax return must subsequently be filed. For example, if the trust document requires that a house be retained in trust and rented for months or years, a taxpayer ID will be needed to report rental income and expenses.

Specific requirements for transferring property vary slightly from place to place, and the trustee may have to make inquiries at banks, stockbrokerages, and other institutions about current procedures, but here are the general rules. A trustee who runs into difficulties has the authority to get help—from a lawyer, an accountant, or another expert—and pay for it from trust assets.

RESOURCE

Help for California residents. *How to Probate an Estate in California,* by Julia Nissley and Lisa Fialco (Nolo), contains forms and instructions for transferring the property of a deceased person, including living trust property.

Terminology. This section refers to whoever takes over as trustee after a grantor's death as the "trustee." To remind you, if you made an individual trust, the trustee is the person you named as successor trustee. If you made a shared living trust, the trustee is the surviving spouse or, after both spouses have died, the successor trustee.

Property Without Title Documents

For trust property that doesn't have a title document —furniture, for example—the task of the trustee is quite simple. The trustee must promptly distribute the property to the beneficiaries named in the trust document. If the trustee thinks it's a good idea, it's appropriate to have the recipient sign a receipt. But in many family situations, where all trust each other, this formality isn't necessary.

Some trusts leave all personal property without title to one beneficiary or divide property between just a few beneficiaries. By contrast, other trusts leave numerous specific gifts of personal property to many different beneficiaries. The successor trustee must gather each specific item of property and get that item to the named beneficiary.

Bank Accounts

It should be simple for the trustee to transfer the funds in a bank or savings and loan account already held in the name of the living trust to the beneficiary. Financial institutions are familiar with living trusts and how they work, and the bank probably has the trust document (or a bank form with information about the trust) already on file.

The trustee will need to show the bank or savings and loan:

- a certified copy of the trust grantor's death certificate
- a copy of the living trust document, if the bank doesn't already have one (again, being prepared to show the original trust document, if demanded), and
- proof of the trustee's identity, perhaps including an Affidavit of Assumption of Duties by Successor Trustee.

Real Estate

If real estate is left to specific beneficiaries, the trustee needs to prepare and sign a deed transferring ownership of real estate from the trust to those beneficiaries. The trustee signs the deed as trustee.

EXAMPLE: Jane Adanski, Trustee of The Robert Whilhite Living Trust, dated October 25, 20xx.

The signed and notarized deed should also be filed (recorded) with the county land records office. In most places, recording costs no more than a few dollars per page. It's unlikely, but depending on local and state law, there may be a transfer tax to pay. (Deeds, recording, and transfer taxes are discussed in "Real Estate" in Chapter 10.)

EXAMPLE: The deed to Evelyn Crocker's house shows that it is owned by Evelyn Crocker, as trustee of her living trust. The living trust document states that Evelyn's daughter, Amanda, is to inherit the house when Evelyn dies. Amanda is also the successor trustee of the trust.

After Evelyn's death, Amanda prepares and signs a new deed, transferring ownership of the house from the trust to herself. She signs the deed in her capacity as trustee of the trust, and records the deed in the county land records office, along with an Affidavit of Assumption of Duties by Successor Trustee.

A title company, before it will issue title insurance to the new owners, will probably want a copy of the trust document and a certified copy of the death certificate of the trust grantor.

Some trusts direct the grantor to sell real estate and divide profits between various specified beneficiaries. In these cases, the successor trustee is responsible for arranging for the sale of the house, signing the deed of sale, and then distributing the net profits of the sale to the beneficiaries.

Stocks and Bonds

How to transfer stocks or bonds from a trust to the beneficiary depends on whether they were held in a brokerage account or separately. (For information about transferring stock in closely held corporations, see "Small Business Interests," below.)

Brokerage Accounts

The trustee should contact the broker and ask for instructions. The brokerage company will almost surely already have either a copy of the living trust document or a form that includes relevant information about the trust. (These are necessary to transfer the account to the living trust in the first place.)

If not, the trustee will probably need to send the broker:

- a copy of the trust document or an "abstract of trust" (the first, last, and other relevant pages of the trust document, showing the notarized signature—see Chapter 10 for a sample abstract of trust), and
- a letter instructing the holder to transfer the brokerage account to the beneficiary's name.

Stock Certificates

If the deceased grantor kept possession of the stock certificates or bonds—most people don't—the trustee must get new certificates issued, showing the beneficiary as the new owner.

The trustee will have to send the securities' transfer agent several documents. It's a good idea to write the transfer agent and ask exactly what is needed. Usually, the name and address of the transfer agent appear on the face of the stock or bond certificate. But because transfer agents change occasionally, the first thing the trustee should do is write or call (or check with a stockbrokerage firm) to verify the name and address of the current transfer agent.

The trustee will probably have to send in:

- a certified copy of the grantor's death certificate
- the certificates or bonds
- a document called a "stock or bond power," which the trustee must fill out and sign, with the signature guaranteed by an officer of a bank or brokerage firm (the stock or bond power may be printed on the back of the certificates; if not, office supply stores carry them)
- a copy of the trust document or an abstract of trust if the transfer agent did not receive one when the securities were transferred into the trust
- an Affidavit of Domicile (a form available from banks and stockbrokers) signed by the trustee, showing what the trust grantor's state of residence was, and
- a letter of instructions requesting that the certificates be reissued in the beneficiary's name.

Also, the trustee may be required to have his or her signature "guaranteed" by a stockbroker. If neither the trustee nor the deceased grantor have, or had, a stock account with a brokerage company, this too may cause trouble. The trustee will have to locate a broker—maybe one who handles a friend's account—to guarantee the trustee's signature.

The trustee may be required to produce certified copies of the living trust, although the transfer agent may not be sure what agency certifies documents. Your best bet here is to file the original document with your local county records office and have them certify copies for you.

Government Securities

To transfer government securities—Treasury bills or U.S. bonds, for example—the trustee should ask the broker to contact the issuing government agency, or contact the government directly.

Mutual Funds or Money Market Accounts

For mutual funds or money market accounts owned in the trust's name, the trustee should ask the company what it requires to reregister ownership of the account in the beneficiary's name. Generally, the trustee must send the company proof of identity, a copy of the grantor's death certificate, a letter of instructions (or a form that the company provides), and a copy of the trust document.

Small Business Interests

How a trustee transfers small business interests owned by a living trust depends on the way the business was organized.

RESOURCE

Transferring trademarks. A registered trademark or service mark of a small business must be reregistered in the name of the beneficiary. See *Trademark: Legal Care for Your Business & Product Name,* by Stephen Fishman (Nolo).

Sole Proprietorships

The trustee must transfer business assets to the beneficiary as would be done for any other trust property. The name of the business itself, if owned by the living trust, does not have a title document, so the trustee doesn't need to do anything to transfer it to the beneficiary.

Solely Owned Corporations

Corporation officers must prepare the appropriate corporate records to show that ownership has been transferred to the beneficiary. The specifics depend on the incorporation papers and company bylaws. Often a resolution by the board of directors is required.

Additional paperwork may include such documents as Notice of Special Meeting of Board of Directors and Waiver of Notice of Time Requirements to Hold Special Meeting of Board of Directors. Then the trustee must have the stock certificates reissued in the beneficiary's name.

Closely Held Corporations and Limited Liability Companies

The stock certificates or ownership interest owned by the trust will have to be reissued in the beneficiary's name. The trustee should contact the officers of the corporation or LLC; the other shareholders or owners may have the right, under the corporation's bylaws or a shareholders' agreement, to buy back the shares or interest. For LLC information, see *Form Your Own Limited Liability Company,* by Anthony Mancuso (Nolo).

Partnership Interests

The trustee should contact the deceased grantor's partners, who may have the right to buy out the grantor's share. If the beneficiary wants to enter into the partnership, the partnership agreement must be changed to add the beneficiary. See *Form a Partnership: The Complete Legal Guide,* by Denis Clifford and Ralph Warner (Nolo).

Copyrights

To transfer an interest in a copyright to a beneficiary, the trustee should sign and file, with the U.S. Copyright Office in Washington, D.C., a document transferring all the trust's rights in the copyright to the beneficiary. Sample transfer forms are in *The Copyright Handbook: What Every Writer Needs to Know,* by Stephen Fishman (Nolo).

Patents

To transfer a patent from a living trust, the trustee should prepare a document called an "assignment" and record it with the U.S. Patent and Trademark Office in Washington, D.C. There is a small fee for recording. Sample assignment forms and instructions are in *Patent It Yourself,* by David Pressman (Nolo).

Other Property With Title Documents

If an item of trust property has a title document that shows ownership in the name of the trust, the trustee must prepare and sign a new title document transferring ownership to the beneficiary. Usually, the trustee will need a copy of the trust document and of the trust grantor's death certificate if the property is in someone else's possession.

If a vehicle was owned by the trust, the trustee should contact the state department of motor vehicles to get the forms required to transfer it to the beneficiary.

Preparing and Filing Tax Returns

Depending on the circumstances, the successor trustee may have to file several tax returns:

- federal estate tax return for the deceased grantor, if the value of the estate is over the estate tax threshold for year of death
- state inheritance tax or estate tax return for the deceased grantor, if state law requires it, and
- final federal income tax return (and state return, if there's a state income tax) for the deceased grantor.

Legally, filing these returns is the responsibility both of the successor trustee and of the executor named in the deceased grantor's will. The same person usually serves as both executor and successor trustee.

Generally, the state and federal income tax returns are due April 15 of the year following the grantor's death. The federal estate tax return is due nine months after the grantor's death.

The trustee is entitled, by the terms of the trust document, to pay for professional help out of the trust assets. And that help may well be necessary, because tax matters—particularly estate tax matters—can get quite tricky.

 RESOURCE

Help with tax returns. The successor trustee can get helpful instructions from the Internal Revenue Service at irs.gov.

Administering a Child's Trust

If, in the trust document, the deceased grantor set up a child's trust, the trustee will have to manage that property if the beneficiary isn't old enough to receive it outright. A child's trust comes into being only if, at the grantor's death, the beneficiary has not yet reached the age the grantor specified.

> **EXAMPLE:** Carl sets up a living trust and names his two young children as beneficiaries. He specifies that if either child is younger than 30 when he dies, the property that child is to inherit from the trust should be kept in a separate child's trust.
>
> When Carl dies, one child is 30; the other is 25. The 30-year-old receives her trust property with no strings attached. But a child's trust is created for the 25-year-old. The successor trustee is responsible for managing the property and turning it over to the child when he turns 30.

The trustee's duties when managing a child's trust are explained in Chapter 8.

Administering a Custodianship

Someone who is appointed in the trust document to be the custodian of trust property inherited by a young beneficiary has roughly the same management responsibilities as the trustee of a child's trust. (See Chapter 8.) The specifics of the custodian's duties are set out in the Uniform Transfers to Minors Act, as adopted by the particular state's legislature.

A Living Trust as Part of Your Estate Plan

A revocable living trust can accomplish the goal of leaving property to loved ones while avoiding probate. But a living trust is not, by itself, a complete estate plan. For example, in most states, parents of young children can't use a living trust to appoint a personal guardian to care for their minor children. To do this, you need a will. A living trust also can't take care of property you buy or inherit shortly before you die and don't get around to transferring to the trust.

This chapter provides an overview of estate planning methods that you may want to explore in addition to a living trust. Basically, estate planning includes:

- deciding who will inherit your property when you die
- deciding who will take care of your children and their finances if you die while they are young
- setting up procedures and devices to minimize probate fees at your death
- if your estate is large, planning to reduce federal estate taxes and state death taxes, if your state has them, and
- arranging for someone to make financial and health care decisions for you in case at some time you can no longer do so yourself.

Using a Backup Will

Even though you create a living trust, you also need a simple backup will. Like a living trust, a will is a document in which you specify what is to be done with your property when you die.

Having a will is important for several reasons:

- A will is an essential backup device for property that you don't get around to transferring to your living trust.
- In a will you can name someone to be the personal guardian of your minor child, in case you and the child's other parent die while the child is still younger than 18. In most states, you can't do that in a living trust. (A few states' laws can be construed to permit appointing a child's personal guardian in a living trust, but it's prudent to be conventional and appoint the guardian in a will.)

- If you want to disinherit your spouse or a child, you must make your wishes clear in a will. (State law may restrict your freedom to disinherit a spouse; see Chapter 7.)
- If you receive an unexpected windfall—like a surprise inheritance or lottery winnings—your will ensures that when you die, your windfall (or what remains of it) goes to someone you have chosen.

Chapter 15 instructs you how to prepare your backup will using Form 9 or 10.

Other Probate-Avoidance Methods

A living trust is not the only way to transfer some kinds of assets without probate, and it's not the best in all circumstances. For example, it's usually cumbersome to have your personal checking account held in the name of your living trust, because businesses may be reluctant to accept your checks.

Fortunately, you can mix and match probate-avoidance techniques. Just put whatever property you want in your living trust, and choose other transfer methods—ones that also avoid probate—for the rest of your property.

You might, for example, want to put your checking account into joint tenancy with your spouse; at your death, your spouse would automatically take sole ownership of the account. Some helpful probate-avoidance methods are summarized below.

Pay-On-Death Financial Accounts

Setting up a pay-on-death account is an easy way to transfer cash at your death, quickly and without probate. All you do is designate, on a form provided by a financial institution, one or more persons you want to receive the money when you die.

Pay-on-death accounts are used primarily for bank accounts, including savings, checking, or certificate of deposit accounts. You can also register ownership of certain kinds of government securities, including bonds, Treasury bills, and Treasury notes, in a way that lets you name a beneficiary to receive them at your death.

Other Nolo Estate Planning Resources

Plan Your Estate, by Denis Clifford, covers all the estate planning methods briefly discussed in this chapter and more. It contains extensive discussion about probate-avoidance methods and estate tax reduction techniques, from gift giving to generation-skipping trusts, including estate and gift taxes, and ongoing trusts.

Estate Planning Basics, by Denis Clifford, provides concise, straightforward, and easy-to-read explanations of the major components of estate planning.

Quicken WillMaker & Trust (software) helps you prepare a comprehensive will, living trust, health care directive, durable power of attorney for finances, a final arrangements letter, and many other useful legal forms.

Nolo's Online Forms. Nolo offers several estate planning forms that you can create online and download to your computer. All forms provide Nolo's time-tested documents, helpful legal information, and thorough signing instructions. Go to www.nolo.com for more information.

Nolo's Free Articles & FAQs. At Nolo.com, you can read thousands of articles that explain important legal issues in plain English. Find information about estate planning at www.nolo.com/legal-encyclopedia/wills-trusts-estates.

Quick & Legal Will Book, by Denis Clifford, enables you to prepare a basic will easily and effectively.

8 Ways to Avoid Probate, by Mary Randolph, provides in-depth explanations of all major probate-avoidance methods.

Saving the Family Cottage, by Stuart Hollander, Rose Hollander, and David Fry, explains how to handle succession planning for a vacation home in your estate plan, covering issues that can arise with shared ownership—from choosing the right legal entity for that home to renting it.

Special Needs Trusts, by Kevin Urbatsch and Michele Fuller-Urbatsch, explains how special needs trusts work to protect government benefits for a person with a disability. It also provides the forms and instructions needed to make a simple special needs trust.

How to Probate an Estate in California, by Julia Nissley and Lisa Fialco, explains how to handle a simple California probate without an attorney.

The Executor's Guide, by Mary Randolph, offers a thorough self-help explanation of what an executor/trustee must do after a will writer or trust grantor dies. The book covers handling the legal and financial matters that arise after a death.

The Trustee's Legal Companion, by Liza Hanks and Carol Elias Zolla, presents a thorough explanation of all that is or may be involved in serving as a trustee of a living trust, including state-by-state charts of all relevant laws.

Get It Together, by Melanie Cullen and Shae Irving, shows you how to organize and file important paperwork, so that you and your survivors can quickly locate vital documents and records.

Long-Term Care: How to Plan & Pay for It, by Joseph Matthews, discusses how to finance and choose long-term care.

Social Security, Medicare & Government Pensions, by Joseph Matthews, is an excellent resource about rights and benefits of older Americans.

EXAMPLE: Terry opens a savings account in her name, and names Lynn Harris as the pay-on-death (P.O.D.) beneficiary. When Terry dies, whatever money is in the account will go to Lynn.

During your life, the beneficiary has absolutely no right to the money in the account. You can withdraw some or all of the money, close the account, or change the beneficiary, at any time. When you die, the beneficiary can claim the money simply by showing the bank the death certificate and personal identification.

CAUTION

Bank accounts may be frozen. Like other bank accounts, a pay-on-death account may be temporarily frozen at your death if your state levies inheritance taxes. The state will release the money to your beneficiaries when shown that your estate has sufficient funds to pay the taxes. If you live in a state that imposes inheritance taxes, you might want to check with your bank to learn if your accounts, including any pay-on-death accounts, may be frozen after you die. If so, it's sensible to warn your inheritors that they could face this hassle.

Most banks have forms for setting up this kind of account, and they don't charge more for keeping your money this way. Before you open a pay-on-death account, ask your bank if there are any special state law requirements about notifying the beneficiary. In a few states, a pay-on-death provision isn't effective unless you have notified the beneficiary that you've set up the account. Your bank should be able to fill you in on your state's rules.

Transfer-On-Death Registration for Stocks and Bonds

In every state but Texas, you can register securities (individual stocks or bonds or accounts, including mutual funds) in a transfer-on-death form. You simply designate a beneficiary or beneficiaries to receive the securities outside of probate. Your brokerage company should have a form for opening this kind of account.

Individual Retirement Accounts

Retirement accounts such as IRAs, Roth IRAs, SEP-IRAs, and 401(k) and 403(b) plans weren't designed to be probate-avoidance devices, but if you have any money left in such accounts when you die, they can function that way. All you have to do is name a beneficiary to receive the funds still in your pension plan or retirement account at your death, and the funds will not go through probate. If you are considering making your living trust the beneficiary of your retirement account, see the discussion in "Naming Your Living Trust as Beneficiary of Your Retirement Account" in Chapter 5.

Except for a Roth IRA, after age 72, federal law requires you to withdraw at least a certain amount of money every year from your individual retirement account or face a monetary penalty. (If your 70th birthday was before July 1, 2019, required withdrawals kicked in when you turned 70½.) The withdrawal amount is refigured every year, based on your current life expectancy and that of your beneficiary.

Life Insurance

As insurance agents will be delighted to explain, life insurance is a good way to provide surviving family members with quick cash for debts, living expenses, and, for very large estates, estate taxes. And because you name the beneficiary in the policy itself, not in your will, life insurance proceeds don't go through probate.

The only circumstance in which life insurance proceeds are subject to probate is if the beneficiary named in the policy is your estate. That's done occasionally if the estate will need immediate cash to pay debts and taxes. Still, it's almost always a better idea to name your spouse, children, or another beneficiary who can take the money free of probate and use it to pay debts and taxes.

Although the proceeds of a life insurance policy don't go through probate, they are included in your estate for federal estate tax purposes. If you think your estate will be liable for federal estate taxes, you can reduce the tax bill by giving away the policy to the beneficiary, another person, or an irrevocable life insurance trust (discussed later in this chapter).

Life Insurance to Provide for Your Children

If you have young children but not much money, consider buying a moderate amount of term life insurance, which would provide cash to support your children if you died while they were still young. Because term life insurance pays benefits only if you die during the covered period (often five or ten years), it's far cheaper than other types of life insurance. You can stop renewing the insurance when, by the end of the current term, the children will be on their own or your estate would be large enough to support them until they are.

Common Probate-Avoidance Methods

Method	Advantages	Disadvantages
Revocable living trust	Flexible, private. Easy to create. You keep control over property during your life.	Some paperwork involved. May need an attorney if yours is a complicated estate.
Pay-on-death financial accounts	Easy to create using a form provided by the bank or brokerage company.	Limited to bank accounts and securities.
Naming beneficiary of pension plan or retirement account	Easy to do. Beneficiary inherits all funds in the account at your death.	None, unless particular program imposes limits.
Life insurance	Good way to provide quick cash for beneficiaries or to pay estate taxes. Proceeds don't go through probate.	If family members won't need much immediate cash, expense of policy may not be justified.
Joint tenancy with right of survivorship	Easy to create.	If you already own property, you may not want to add another owner who could sell his or her share. (For larger estates, there are negative gift tax consequences, too.) Can be a problem if a co-owner becomes incapacitated. No probate avoidance if all joint owners die at once. In Alaska, restricted to husband and wife.
Tenancy by the entirety	Easy to create.	Available in only about half the states; limited to married couples (or in a few states, to registered same-sex couples). Can be a problem if one spouse becomes incapacitated.
Community property with right of survivorship	All the benefits of community property ownership plus probate avoidance when one spouse dies.	Available only to married couples in Alaska, Arizona, California, Idaho, Nevada, and Wisconsin. (In California, registered domestic partners may also own property this way.)
Gifts of property made while you're alive	Reduces amount of property in your estate, which avoids both probate and estate taxes.	You lose control over property given away. Large gifts use up part of your federal gift/estate tax exemption. Insurance policies must be given away at least three years before death, or proceeds are included in your taxable estate.
State laws that allow simplified probate proceedings	Exempts certain property from formal probate.	Applies only to small estates.
Transfer-on-death designation for motor vehicles	Easy to do. All you do is name, on your registration form, someone to inherit your vehicle.	Available only in Arizona, Arkansas, California, Colorado, Connecticut, Delaware, Illinois, Indiana, Kansas, Maryland, Minnesota, Missouri, Nebraska, Nevada, Ohio, Oklahoma, Texas, Vermont, and Virginia, but other states are considering it.
Transfer-on-death registration for securities	Easy to do. All you do is name, on the registration form, someone to inherit the securities at your death.	Not available in Texas.
Transfer-on-death real estate deeds	Easy to do. You prepare, sign, notarize, and file the deed form.	Available only in Alaska, Arizona, Arkansas, California, Colorado, District of Columbia, Hawaii, Illinois, Indiana, Kansas, Maine, Minnesota, Mississippi, Missouri, Montana, Nebraska, Nevada, New Mexico, North Dakota, Ohio, Oklahoma, Oregon, South Dakota, Texas, Utah, Virginia, Washington, West Virginia, Wisconsin, and Wyoming.

Joint Tenancy

Joint tenancy is one of the more commonly used probate-avoidance devices. It's an efficient and practical way to transfer some kinds of property in some situations, but for most kinds of property, a living trust is usually a better choice. In many states, married couples can use a special type of joint tenancy called "tenancy by the entirety," described below.

How Joint Tenancy Works

Joint tenancy is a way two or more people can hold title to property they own together. It is available in almost all states. All joint tenants must, by law, own equal shares of the property, except unequal shares are allowed in Connecticut and Vermont.

For estate planning purposes, the most important characteristic of joint tenancy is that when one joint owner (called a joint tenant) dies, the surviving joint owners automatically get complete ownership of the property. This is called the "right of survivorship." The property doesn't go through probate court—there is only some simple paperwork to fill out to transfer the property into the name of the surviving owner.

> **EXAMPLE:** Evelyn and her daughter own a car in joint tenancy. When Evelyn dies, her half-interest in the car will go to her daughter without probate. Her daughter will need only to fill out a simple form to transfer ownership of the car into her own name.

Joint tenancy certainly has the virtue of simplicity. To create a joint tenancy, all the co-owners need to do is pay attention to the way they are listed on the document that shows ownership of property, such as a deed to real estate, a car's title slip, or a card establishing a bank account. In the great majority of states, by calling themselves "joint tenants with the right of survivorship," the owners create a joint tenancy. In a few states, additional specific words are necessary. If you want to set up a joint tenancy and aren't sure how to word a title document, ask a real estate lawyer or someone at a land title company.

A joint tenant cannot leave his or her share to anyone other than the surviving joint tenants. So even if Evelyn, in the preceding example, left a will giving her half-interest in the car to her son instead of her daughter, the daughter would still get the car.

This rule isn't as ironclad as it may sound. A joint tenant can, while still alive, break the joint tenancy by transferring his or her interest in the property to someone else (or, in most states, to him- or herself, but not as a "joint tenant"). The new owner isn't a joint tenant with the other original owners.

Joint Bank Accounts

If you and someone else want to set up a joint tenancy account together so that the survivor will get all the funds, normally you can do it in a few minutes at the bank. Your bank should be able to tell you about any requirements. In a few states, you may need to comply with certain specific formalities.

> **EXAMPLE:** David, Jan, and Loren own property together in joint tenancy. David sells his one-third interest to Paul. Paul is not a joint tenant with Jan and Loren; he is a "tenant in common," free to leave his property to whomever he wants. Jan and Loren, however, are still joint tenants with respect to their two-thirds of the property; when one of them dies, the other will own the two-thirds.

When to Consider Joint Tenancy

Joint tenancy often works well when couples (married or not) acquire real estate or other valuable property together. If they take title in joint tenancy, probate is avoided when the first owner dies.

But there are advantages to transferring the property to your living trust, even if you already own it in joint tenancy. First, a living trust, unlike joint tenancy, allows you to name an alternate beneficiary—someone who will inherit the property if the first beneficiary (your spouse) doesn't survive you. If you own property in joint tenancy, and you and your spouse die at the same time, the property will go to the residuary beneficiary named in your will—but it will have to go through probate first.

Second, if you transfer joint tenancy property to a living trust, you will avoid probate both when the first spouse dies and when the second spouse dies. With joint tenancy, probate is avoided only when the first spouse dies. The second spouse, who owns the property alone after the first spouse's death, must take some other measure—such as transferring it to a living trust—to avoid probate.

> ⊘ **CAUTION**
>
> **Transferring joint tenancy property in common law states.** As discussed in Chapter 10, if you live in a common law state, when transferring joint tenancy property to a living trust you need first to transfer the property into "tenancy in common, in equal shares" by preparing a new deed, and then transfer the property to your trust.

Restrictions on Joint Tenancy

A few states limit joint tenancy. Here are the rules you should know:

- Alaska prohibits joint tenancy except between a wife and husband, who may own property as tenants by the entirety. (See "Tenancy by the Entirety," below.)
- In Oregon and Tennessee, a transfer to a husband and wife creates a tenancy by the entirety, not a joint tenancy.
- Wisconsin does not allow joint tenancy between spouses (after January 1, 1986). Any attempted joint tenancy between spouses is treated as community property with right of survivorship. (See "Common Probate-Avoidance Methods," above.)

When to Think Twice About Joint Tenancy

Joint tenancy is usually a poor estate planning device when an older person, seeking only to avoid probate, puts solely owned property into joint tenancy with someone else. Doing this creates several potential problems that don't occur with a living trust.

You can't change your mind. If you make someone else a co-owner, in joint tenancy, of property that you now own yourself, you give up half ownership of the property. The new owner has rights that you can't take back. For example, the new owner can sell or mortgage his or her share. And even if the other joint tenant's half isn't mortgaged, it could still be lost to creditors.

> **EXAMPLE:** Maureen, a widow, signs a deed that puts her house into joint tenancy with her son to avoid probate at her death. Later, the son's business fails, and he is sued by creditors. His half-interest in the house may be taken by the creditors to pay the court judgment, which means that the house might be sold. Maureen would get the value of her half in cash; her son's half of the proceeds would go to pay the creditors.

By contrast, if you put property in a revocable living trust, you don't give up any ownership now. You are always free to change your mind about who you want to get the property at your death.

There's no way to handle the incapacity of one joint tenant. If one joint tenant becomes incapacitated and cannot make decisions, the other owners must get legal authority to sell or mortgage the property. That may mean going to court to get someone (called a "conservator," in most states) appointed to manage the incapacitated person's affairs. (This problem can be dealt with if the joint tenant has signed a document called a Durable Power of Attorney for Finances, which gives someone authority to manage joint tenant's affairs if the joint tenant cannot.)

With a living trust, if you (the grantor) become incapacitated, the successor trustee (or the other spouse, if it's a shared trust) takes over and has full authority to manage the trust property. No court proceedings are necessary.

Gift taxes may be assessed. If you create a joint tenancy by making another person a co-owner, federal gift tax may be assessed on the transfer. This probably isn't a reason not to transfer property; making a gift can be a sound estate planning strategy. But be aware that if gifts to one person (except your spouse) exceed $15,000 per year, you must file a gift tax return with the IRS. (See below.) There's one exception: If two or more people open a bank account in joint tenancy, but one person puts all or most of the money in, no gift tax is assessed against that person. A taxable gift may be made, however, when a joint tenant who has contributed little or nothing to the account withdraws money from it.

Surviving spouse misses an income tax break. If you make your spouse a joint tenant with you on property you own separately, the surviving spouse could miss out on a potentially big income tax break later, when the property is sold.

When it comes to property owned in joint tenancy, the Internal Revenue Service rule is that a surviving spouse gets a stepped-up tax basis only for the half of the property owned by the deceased spouse. The tax basis is the amount from which taxable profit is figured when property is sold. You may not face this problem if you live in a community property state. If property held in joint tenancy property is actually community property, it will still qualify for a stepped-up tax basis if the surviving spouse can show the IRS that it was in fact community property. But it's up to you to prove it; when one spouse dies, the IRS presumes that property held in joint tenancy is not community property. When the property is later sold, this means higher tax if the property has gone up in value after the joint tenancy was created but before the first spouse died.

If you leave your solely owned property to your spouse through your living trust, however, the entire property gets a stepped-up tax basis.

Tenancy by the Entirety

"Tenancy by the entirety" is a form of property ownership that is similar to joint tenancy, but is limited to married couples (and in some states, same-sex couples registered with the state). It is available only in the states listed below.

States That Allow Tenancy by the Entirety		
Alaska[1]	Maryland	Oklahoma
Arkansas	Massachusetts	Oregon[1,2]
Delaware	Michigan	Pennsylvania
District of Columbia[2]	Mississippi	Rhode Island[1,2]
Florida	Missouri	Tennessee
Hawaii[2]	New Jersey[2]	Vermont[2]
Illinois[1,2]	New York[1]	Virginia
Indiana[1]	North Carolina[1]	Wyoming
Kentucky[1]	Ohio[3]	

1 For real estate only.

2 Also available to registered domestic partners (D.C., OR), civil unions (IL, HI, NJ, RI, VT), or reciprocal beneficiaries (HI).

3 For real estate only, and only if created before April 4, 1985.

Tenancy by the entirety has almost the same advantages and disadvantages of joint tenancy and is most useful in the same kind of situation—that is, a couple acquires property together. When one spouse dies, the surviving spouse inherits the property. The property doesn't go through probate.

If property is held in tenancy by the entirety, neither spouse can transfer his or her half of the property alone, either while alive or by will or trust. A living spouse must get the other spouse's consent to transfer the property; at death, it must go to the surviving spouse. (This is different from joint tenancy; joint tenants are free to transfer their individual shares to someone else during life.)

> **EXAMPLE:** Fred and Ethel hold title to their apartment building in tenancy by the entirety. If Fred wanted to sell or give away his half-interest in the building, he could not do so without Ethel's signature on the deed.

A special aspect of tenancy by the entirety is that creditors of one spouse cannot attach that spouse's interest in the tenancy in the entirety property. Several states have enacted laws explicitly allowing tenancy by the entirety that is transferred to a living trust to retain that protection from creditors. Those states are: Delaware, Hawaii, Illinois, Indiana,

Maryland, Missouri, Virginia, and Wyoming. The details of these state laws vary, so if protection from creditors for tenancy by the entirety property transferred to a living trust is important to you, you'll need to check out the specifics of your state's law.

Options in Community Property States

In some states, married couples and some registered domestic partners have additional community property tools with which they can avoid probate.

Married couples in most community property states can hold title to their community property "with right of survivorship"—meaning that when one spouse dies, the other automatically owns all the property.

This arrangement offers all the benefits of community property ownership, plus the important advantage that the property doesn't go through probate when one spouse dies. Instead, the surviving spouse owns it automatically.

In most community property states—as well as Alaska, South Dakota, and Tennessee—married couples can sign a written agreement to declare all or some of their property to be community property, and then leave it to the survivor, without probate, when one spouse dies. The agreement functions much like a will—with the important difference that the property doesn't have to go through probate when the first spouse dies.

You can learn more about community property with right of survivorship and community property agreements in the "Wills, Trusts & Probate" section of Nolo.com.

Transfer-On-Death Deeds

In Alaska, Arizona, Arkansas, California, Colorado, District of Columbia, Hawaii, Illinois, Indiana, Kansas, Maine, Minnesota, Mississippi, Missouri, Montana, Nebraska, Nevada, New Mexico, North Dakota, Ohio, Oklahoma, Oregon, South Dakota, Texas, Utah, Virginia, Washington, West Virginia, Wisconsin, and Wyoming, you can leave real estate using a special kind of deed that is effective only at death. The deed document should be clearly titled "transfer-on-death" or "T.O.D." The deed must clearly state that the transfer to the beneficiary you name is not to take effect until your death. Like any deed, a T.O.D. deed must be properly signed, notarized, and then recorded with the property records office in the county where the real estate is located.

Transfer-On-Death Registration for Vehicles

Arizona, Arkansas, California, Colorado, Connecticut, Delaware, Illinois, Indiana, Kansas, Maryland, Minnesota, Missouri, Nebraska, Nevada, Ohio, Oklahoma, Texas, Vermont, and Virginia offer car owners the sensible option of naming a beneficiary, right on the certificate of title or title application, to inherit a vehicle. If you do this, the beneficiary you name has no rights to the car as long as you are alive. You are free to sell or give away the car, or name someone else as the beneficiary.

To name a transfer-on-death beneficiary, all you do is apply for a registration in "beneficiary form." The new certificate lists the name of the beneficiary, who will automatically own the vehicle after your death. You can find more information on the website of your state's motor vehicles department.

Gifts

If you give away property while you're alive, there will be less property in your estate to go through probate when you die. But if probate avoidance is your goal, usually it's better to use one of the other methods discussed above, which let you keep control over your property while you're alive, than it is to give away everything before you die.

Making tax-exempt gifts every year, however, may be a good strategy if you expect your estate to owe federal estate tax after your death and you want to reduce the eventual tax bite. (See below.)

Probate Shortcuts for Small Estates

Many states have begun, albeit slowly, to dismantle some of the more onerous aspects of probate. Who benefits? As you might guess, one big category comprises people who don't leave much of monetary value—and whose probate cases therefore aren't worth much to lawyers.

Because of the way the laws are written, however, not only small estates can benefit. Many larger estates—worth hundreds of thousands of dollars—legally qualify as "small estates," eligible for special transfer procedures that speed property to inheritors.

Listed below are the kinds of shortcuts available for small estates.

Claiming property with affidavits—no court required. If the total value of all the assets you leave behind is less than a certain amount, the people who inherit your personal property—that's anything except real estate—may be able to skip probate entirely. The exact amount varies tremendously. The highest limit is $200,000 in Wyoming.

If the estate qualifies, an inheritor can prepare a short document stating that the inheritor is entitled to a certain item of property under a will or state law. This paper, signed under oath, is called an affidavit. When the person or institution holding the property—for example, a bank where the deceased person had an account—receives the affidavit and a copy of the death certificate, it releases the money or other property.

Leaving property to the surviving spouse—no court required. In some states, if a surviving spouse inherits less than a certain amount of property, no probate is necessary.

Simplified court procedures. Another option for small estates (again, as defined by state law) is a quicker, simpler version of probate. The probate court is still involved, but it exerts far less control over the settling of the estate. In many states, these procedures are straightforward enough to handle without a lawyer, so they save money as well as time.

Most people leave property that is worth more than can be passed through these probate shortcuts. In many states, if the value of your entire estate exceeds the maximum set by law for simplified procedures, you cannot use the procedures to pass any property.

> **EXAMPLE:** At her death, Jane has an estate worth $300,000. Her major asset is her home, worth $200,000, which she passes to her daughter through a living trust. She also passes $80,000 worth of other property through other probate-avoidance devices. That leaves $20,000 worth of property. In Jane's state, the maximum total estate (including all property transferred by all methods) for streamlined probate procedures is $25,000. So Jane's heirs can't use the simplified procedures for the last $20,000 because Jane's total estate exceeds the limit.

In some states, however, even if your total estate is too large, you can still make use of simplified procedures if the amount that actually goes through probate is under the limit. For example, in California, property worth less than $166,250 transferred by will is exempt from normal probate, no matter how large the total estate. So if Jane lived in California, the $20,000 worth of property left through Jane's will could be transferred out of court or through simplified court procedures.

RESOURCE

How to find out about your state's probate shortcuts. Some states have all the shortcuts discussed above; others have just one. You can learn the details of your state's law in *8 Ways to Avoid Probate* or *The Executor's Guide*, both by Mary Randolph (Nolo). See also, "Probate Shortcuts in Your State" at www.nolo.com.

Federal Gift and Estate Taxes

Under the current rules, very few people need to be concerned with estate or gift taxes because only wealthy estates are subject to these taxes. According to the Tax Policy Center, only 1,900 estates will pay estate tax for 2020. This means that the federal estate tax affects less than 0.1% of all estates.

Federal Estate Taxes

The vast majority of estates will not owe estate taxes because:

- In 2021, the personal estate tax exemption is $11.7 million. This allows the estates of people who die in 2021 to transfer up to $11.7 million dollars free of federal estate tax. This amount rises each year with inflation.

- A surviving spouse can use any unused portion of the deceased spouse's federal estate tax exemption. This is called "portability." For example, a husband dies in 2021, when the exemption is $11.7 million. He leaves all his estate, worth $4,000,000, to his spouse. This gift is exempt from estate tax because of the marital deduction. When his wife dies she can add all $11.7 million of her husband's unused personal exemption to her own exemption. So, the wife can leave property worth up to $23.4 million free of estate tax. To be eligible for portability, a surviving spouse must file a federal estate tax return after the death of the first spouse, even if that spouse did not owe any estate taxes.

- The marital deduction exempts from tax all property, no matter how large the dollar value, left by a deceased spouse to a surviving spouse. But if the surviving spouse is not a citizen of the United States, the marital deduction does not apply.

- The charitable exemption authorizes all property given or left to tax-exempt charities to pass tax-free.

RESOURCE

Federal estate taxes. A comprehensive explanation of federal estate taxes is contained in *Plan Your Estate*, by Denis Clifford (Nolo).

A federal estate tax return must be filed if the gross value of the estate exceeds the exempt amount for the year of death. Estate taxes will be due if the net estate exceeds the amount of all applicable exemptions. The assets in the estate are valued as of the date of death or, as an optional alternative, six months later if it produces a lesser estate value. An exception is that any asset distributed to beneficiaries or sold at an earlier date must be valued when it is distributed or sold. Tax must be paid within nine months of death.

Federal Gift Taxes

The federal government also taxes substantial gifts made during life. Congress reasoned that if only property left at death were taxed, people would give away as much property as they could during their lives. Gift tax rates are the same as estate tax rates, to eliminate any tax incentive to gift making.

Federal law provides an annual exemption from gift tax. As of 2021, you can give up to $15,000 per person per year without owing gift tax. This gift tax exemption is indexed yearly to the cost of living. As the cost of living rises (assuming it does), the gift tax will also rise, in increments of $1,000. In other words, cost-of-living increases must cumulatively raise the current exemption by something more than $1,000 before the gift tax exemption will be raised to $16,000.

Additionally, there is a lifetime gift tax exemption. The gift tax exemption is combined with the estate tax exemption. So, if you use up $1 million of your gift tax exemption before your death, your personal estate tax exemption will be reduced by $1 million.

If gift tax is assessed, no tax is actually paid on gifts until your death, when your combined gift and estate tax liability is calculated.

Other gifts are exempt regardless of amount, including:

- gifts between spouses who are U.S. citizens
- gifts to directly pay someone else's medical bills or school tuition, and
- gifts to tax-exempt charitable organizations.

Special Rules for Noncitizen Spouses

The unlimited marital deduction for property one spouse leaves (or gives while living) to another applies only if the recipient spouse is a citizen of the United States. It doesn't matter that a noncitizen spouse was married to a U.S. citizen or is a legal resident. While both are alive, a spouse can, however, give the other, noncitizen, spouse up to $159,000 per year free of gift tax (in 2021).

The personal estate tax exemption, however, remains available no matter who inherits the property. A citizen can leave a noncitizen spouse property tax-free under this exemption.

> **SEE AN EXPERT**
> **Special trusts for noncitizen spouses.** Property left by one spouse to a noncitizen spouse in what's called a "Qualified Domestic Trust" is allowed the marital deduction. To create one of these trusts, you'll need to see a lawyer. Indeed, if you're married to a noncitizen and have an estate worth more than the exempt amount, see a lawyer for estate tax planning.

Reducing Estate Tax

If your property is likely to be subject to estate tax, there are a few additional options you can consider. For the very rich, tax avoidance schemes can become extraordinarily twisted. Here we'll briefly look at some more common options.

Gifts

If you don't need all your income and property to live on, making tax-exempt gifts from your trust, or indeed from any of your assets, while you're alive can be a good way to reduce eventual federal estate taxes.

As of 2021, every person can give $15,000 to any one person per year, so a couple can give $30,000 per year to any one person.

> **EXAMPLE:** Allen and Julia give each of their two daughters $30,000 every year for four years. They have transferred a total of $240,000 without becoming liable for gift tax.

> **CAUTION**
> **Gifts made within three years of death.** The gift tax exemption is not allowed for a few types of gifts made in the last three years of someone's life. The gift itself is valid, but for estate tax purposes, the value of the gift is included in the giver's estate. Most importantly, a gift of a life insurance policy is not entitled to the gift tax exemption if made within three years before death.

How to choose property to give away. It's usually wise to give away property that you think will go up in value substantially before your death. That way, you may avoid gift tax now—if the gift is worth less than the gift tax exemption—and you may avoid estate tax later, because the increased value of the property won't be included in your estate when you die. Also, if the recipient is in a lower tax bracket, you may want to give away income-generating property, so that the income will be taxed at the recipient's lower tax rates. However, any income of more than $2,100 per year received by a child 18 years or younger (or younger than 24 if a full-time dependent student) from any gift (whether from parents or anyone else) is taxed at the parents' rate.

You may not, however, want to give away property that has already appreciated greatly in value. Usually, it's wiser to hold onto it until death to take advantage of the stepped-up tax basis rules discussed above.

Gifts of life insurance. Life insurance policies you own on your own life and give away at least three years before your death are excellent gifts, from an estate planning view. Your gift tax liability is determined by the current value of the policy, which is far less than the amount the policy will pay off at death. For many policies, the present value will be less than the $15,000 annual gift tax threshold, which means that no gift tax will be assessed.

To give away a life insurance policy, you must comply with some fairly technical IRS rules, which should be available from your insurance company. The process of actually transferring ownership is simple. Insurance companies have forms you can use to make the transfer. You must make an irrevocable gift of the policy. If you keep the right to revoke the gift and get the policy back, the proceeds will be taxed as part of your estate.

Tax-Saving Trusts and Devices

Here are some important trusts and devices which could achieve estate tax savings:

- **Property left to spouse.** A married person with an estate worth more than the amount that can be shielded from estate tax may leave the overage outright to the surviving spouse. No tax is due when the first spouse dies, because all property left to a surviving spouse is exempt.

- **QTIP trusts** (for married couples only). A QTIP trust postpones payment of estate taxes that otherwise are due when the first spouse dies. A QTIP trust can be desirable for a spouse with property over the estate tax threshold who wants:
  - to leave all of his or her property to the other spouse with no payment of taxes until that surviving spouse dies, and
  - to name final beneficiaries of the trust property (that is, doesn't want to leave the property outright to the other spouse).

  One drawback of a QTIP trust is that the federal estate taxes eventually paid on the property of the first spouse to die are assessed against what the property is worth when the surviving spouse dies, not what the property was worth when the first spouse died. Usually, that means higher taxes.

  EXAMPLE: Mary Edna, a widow with three grown children, marries Roberto. Her estate has a net value of $13 million. Roberto has little property beyond his monthly Social Security check. Mary Edna wants Roberto to be able to continue to live in both her houses if she predeceases him. After his death, she wants all her property to go to her children.

  If Mary Edna creates a trust, that gives Roberto a life estate. Her entire $13 million estate will be subject to tax when she dies. Concerned that this could necessitate the sale of one of her houses, Edna creates a QTIP trust. No estate taxes will be assessed against her property until Roberto dies. However, if the worth of the property has risen to $16 million when Roberto dies, estate taxes will be based on this value.

- **Generation-skipping trusts.** One of the legal devices traditionally used by the very wealthy to minimize estate taxes has been to leave the bulk of their property in trust for their grandchildren, with the income (but not the principal) from the trusts available to their children. This strategy avoids death taxes several times. Without a trust, taxes would typically be paid when the first grandparent died, then again when the second grandparent died, and then when each of their children died.

  Current law imposes a tax on all "generation-skipping transfers" in excess of the amount of the personal estate tax exemption. A generation-skipping trust worth more than the exempt amount is subject to tax on the overage. This tax is assessed against the trust property when the middle (income) generation dies.

  EXAMPLE: Paul dies, leaving a generation-skipping trust for his daughter and her children. When his daughter dies, the trust property is worth $2 million more than the personal exemption for that year. Tax must then be paid on $2 million of the trust property.

  Generation-skipping trusts are very complicated. These trusts are designed to have effect for at least two generations after the grantor's life, normally over 50 years, and many contingencies should be considered. Also, there are IRS requirements regarding the age of the trustee and when estate taxes will be assessed.

- **Disclaimers.** A disclaimer means that someone who has been left a gift declines to accept it. The gift is then given to an alternate beneficiary originally named by the gift giver. A beneficiary who disclaims a gift generally does so to make the overall estate tax picture better. Of course, this usually means that the disclaiming person doesn't need the gift to live on. Any beneficiary has the legal right to disclaim a gift, but often that right is expressly stated in estate planning documents.

- **Life insurance trusts.** An irrevocable life insurance trust is a legal entity you create for the purpose of owning life insurance you previously owned. It becomes operational during your lifetime. An irrevocable trust, like a corporation or any other trust, is a legal entity, distinct from any human being.

  Transferring ownership of your life insurance policy to a new owner—the trust—can reduce federal estate taxes by removing the proceeds of the policy from your taxable estate. Why create a life insurance trust, rather than simply transferring a life insurance policy to someone else? One reason is that there may be no one you want to give your policy to. In other words, you want to get the proceeds out of your taxable estate, but you don't want the risks of having an insurance policy on your life owned by someone else. For example, the trust could specify that the policy must be kept in effect while you live, eliminating the risk that a new owner of the policy could decide to cash it in.

  Strict federal requirements govern life insurance trusts. To gain the estate tax savings:
  - The life insurance trust must be irrevocable. If you keep the right to revoke the trust, you will be considered the owner of the policy, and the proceeds will be considered part of your estate upon death.
  - You cannot be the trustee. You must name either an "independent" adult (that is, someone not under your legal control) or an institution to serve as trustee.
  - You must establish the trust at least three years before your death. If the trust has not existed for at least three years when you die, the trust is disregarded for estate tax purposes, and the proceeds are included in your taxable estate.

- **Charitable remainder trusts.** With a charitable remainder trust, you make an irrevocable gift of property to a tax-exempt charity while you're alive. You are entitled to receive certain income from the property as well as continue to use and control it while you're alive, with significant income tax breaks. When you die, the property, of course, must go to the charity—and, therefore, no estate tax can be due.

SEE AN EXPERT

Don't try this on your own. If you want to create any of these kinds of trusts or devices, see an experienced estate planning lawyer.

RESOURCE

More about saving on taxes. *Plan Your Estate*, by Denis Clifford (Nolo), discusses these and other advanced estate tax planning strategies.

Family Limited Partnerships

In the right circumstances, establishing a family limited partnership (FLP) can produce significant tax savings for inheritors. The first requirement here is that you must have a legitimate business, one that the IRS accepts as genuine. You cannot create a tax-valid family limited partnership simply to manage your regular investments, such as your securities or savings accounts.

You, as the original owner of the FLP, transfer, usually by gift, minority interests in the business to your inheritors, normally your children. The value of these minority interests can be "discounted," under IRS rules, from what the value would be if the interests had remained held by the majority owner. The theory is that minority interests, which have no legal control over the business, would be worth proportionally less to a legitimate buyer than a majority interest. The amount of the discount is subjective, and is frequently contested between the IRS and FLP owners.

EXAMPLE: Olivia owns a successful pet food company. She intends to leave the business equally to her three children, who can maintain it or sell it, as they choose. The business is worth $2 million.

Olivia creates an FLP and transfers the business into it. There are 100 shares of the FLP. So it would seem that each share is worth $20,000. But if Olivia gives one share to each child, that share is worth less than $20,000, for gift and estate tax purposes, because, as a minority interest, it has less value to a buyer. So the gift shares may each be worth $17,000, or $15,000, depending only on the discount allowed. Olivia can transfer up to 49% ownership of the FLP to her children, and all those interests will receive minority discounts.

FLPs that save on estate taxes are tricky creatures. The FLP must be operated as a family-owned business, which means that profits must be distributed (roughly) according to legal ownership. If you create a limited partnership but continue to treat the business assets as if they were solely yours, the IRS will include the full value of the business in your estate at your death. In other words, an FLP cannot be run solely as an estate-tax-avoiding shell.

SEE AN EXPERT
You need a lawyer before giving away minority interests. If you want to explore giving interests in a family limited partnership to family members (or anyone else), you must see a lawyer. This is a difficult and rapidly changing area of the law. The IRS is not fond of discounted gifts of an FLP and tries to scrutinize them. You must be sure you do it right, and that requires working with a lawyer knowledgeable in this subject.

State Inheritance and Estate Taxes

There are two types of state taxes to consider when making decisions about how to leave your property—inheritance taxes and estate taxes.

State Inheritance Taxes

At one time, many states imposed inheritance taxes, but now, just a few still do. The states listed below impose inheritance taxes on:
- all real estate owned in the state, no matter where the deceased person lived, and
- the personal property (everything but real estate) of residents of the state.

Inheritance taxes are imposed on the people who receive the property (the beneficiaries), rather than on the estate itself. Typically, beneficiaries are divided into different classes, such as "Class A: Husband or Wife," "Class B: Immediate Family," and "Class C: All Others." Each class receives different tax exemptions and is taxed at a different rate. Generally, the highest exemption and lowest rate goes to spouses, or Class A.

States With Inheritance Taxes		
Iowa	Maryland	New Jersey
Kentucky	Nebraska	Pennsylvania

If you live or own real estate in a state that imposes inheritance taxes, you may want to consider the impact of them. In many instances, the bite taken from an inheritance is annoying, but relatively minor. However, in some states, larger chunks can be taken, especially for property left to nonrelatives.

For example, Nebraska imposes an 18% inheritance tax rate on gifts you leave to your friends (no tax if less than $10,000). But it imposes a 1% tax on gifts you leave to your children or parents (no tax if less than $40,000). And many of the states that impose inheritance tax don't tax property left to a surviving spouse. It's probably rare that someone would change the amount of property left to a beneficiary because of inheritance tax, but you should at least evaluate the issue if it applies.

RESOURCE
Learn more about your state's estate and inheritance taxes in the "Wills, Trusts & Probate" section of Nolo.com.

State Estate Taxes

Even if your state does not impose inheritance taxes, your estate may still face a state estate tax bill. The details of these tax laws vary from state to state, but one important thing to keep in mind is that your estate may owe estate taxes to the state even if it is not large enough to owe federal estate tax.

EXAMPLE: Roy and Ann, unmarried residents of Massachusetts, have a combined estate of $3 million. When Roy died in 2021, his share of the couple's property was $1.5 million. That amount went to Ann. Roy's estate is well under 2021's federal estate tax threshold of $11.7 million, so it owed no federal tax. However, Roy's estate owed tax to Massachusetts, because the state imposes an estate tax on estates worth $1 million or more.

If you and your spouse are worried about state estate taxes, consider making a disclaimer trust which could help reduce state estate taxes when the surviving spouse dies. (See Chapter 4.) If you are single, there may not be much you can do to avoid these taxes, but see "Reducing Estate Tax" earlier in this chapter for some ideas.

States With Estate Taxes

The following states levy estate taxes:

State	Exemption (2020)
Connecticut	$5.1 million
District of Columbia	$5.68 million
Hawaii	$5.49 million
Illinois	$4 million
Maine	$5.8 million
Maryland	$5 million
Massachusetts	$1 million
Minnesota	$3 million
New York	$5.85 million
Oregon	$1 million
Rhode Island	$1.58 million*
Vermont	$4.25 million
Washington	$2.193 million

* Approximately

SEE AN EXPERT

Get more information about state estate taxes. If you live in a state that imposes an estate tax and you want to know details about the impact it might have on your estate, see a good lawyer with up-to-date information about this area of the law.

Your Residence for State Tax Purposes

States that impose estate or inheritance taxes on residents do so on everyone "domiciled in the state." "Domicile" is a legal term. It means the state where you have your permanent residence, where you intend to make your home. Generally, it's clear where your domicile is: It's the state where you live most of the time, work, own a home, and vote.

However, if you divide your residence between two or more states, your domicile may not be clear. If possible, you may want to make an effort to establish your domicile in the state which has fewer taxes. Normally, this means being sure that you maintain all your major personal business contacts and vote in the state you claim as your domicile.

SEE AN EXPERT

Getting your legal residence established. Establishing residence in a no-tax state can be tricky if you also live in a high-tax one, because the high-tax state has a financial incentive to conclude that you really reside there. If you have a large estate and a complicated two-or-more-state living situation, consult a knowledgeable tax lawyer or accountant.

Planning for Incapacity

A living trust can be a big help if you become unable to manage your own financial affairs, because your successor trustee (your spouse, if you make a shared trust) can take over management of trust property. That person, however, has no power over any of your other financial assets or your health care decisions. For that reason, you should prepare a few other documents and coordinate them with your living trust.

Durable Power of Attorney for Finances

The best way to plan for the management of property not covered by your living trust is to use a document called a "durable power of attorney for finances." Every state recognizes this document. It gives a trusted person you choose, called your "attorney-in-fact," the legal authority to manage your finances (except for property owned by your living trust) on your behalf. The document can be worded so that it becomes effective only if you become incapacitated, as certified in writing by a physician.

 RESOURCE

Making a durable power of attorney for finances. You can use *Quicken WillMaker & Trust* software from Nolo to prepare a durable power of attorney for finances that is valid in your state.

Medical Care Documents

If you become unconscious or mentally incapacitated and death seems close, your loved ones may have to decide what sorts of medical intervention, if any, should occur. These decisions are profound, often deeply wrenching and personal.

You can provide binding direction for what you want done regarding life-prolonging medical care. The right to die with dignity and without the agony and expense of artificial life-prolonging procedures has been confirmed by the U.S. Supreme Court, the federal government, and every state legislature. Every state authorizes individuals to create simple documents setting out their wishes concerning end-of-life medical treatment.

There are two basic documents that allow you to do this, both grouped under the broad label "health care directives." You need to prepare both. First, you need a "declaration," also called a "living will." This is a written statement you make directly to medical personnel that spells out the medical care you do or do not wish to receive if you become incapacitated.

Your declaration functions as a contract with the treating doctor, who must either honor your wishes for medical care or transfer you to another doctor or facility that will honor them.

A Health Care Directive by Any Other Name ...

Depending on the state, your health care documents may be called by one of several different names: Advance Health Care Directive, Medical Directive, Directive to Physicians, Declaration Regarding Health Care, Designation of Health Care Surrogate, or Patient Advocate Designation. A health care declaration may also be called a "living will," but it bears no relation to the conventional will or living trust used to leave property at death. Go to www.nolo.com/legal-encyclopedia/living-wills to learn your state's terminology.

POLST Forms

If you are under a doctor's care, you might also consider making a POLST form—if your state allows them. POLST stands for "Physician Orders for Life Sustaining Treatment" and it is a document created by you and your doctor that informs emergency care providers what kinds of treatments you want (and don't want) in a medical emergency. POLST forms are like Do Not Resuscitate (DNR) orders in that they (1) must be signed by a doctor and, (2) instruct emergency medical personnel whether to administer cardiopulmonary resuscitation (CPR). However, POLST forms cover many additional types of medical interventions, such as intubation, antibiotic use, and feeding tubes. POLST forms are available in most states, though they sometimes go by other names—including MOLST, POST, and COLST. You can learn more about POLST forms at www.nolo.com/legal-encyclopedia/physicians-orders-life-sustaining-treatment.

Second, you'll want what's often called a "durable power of attorney for health care." In this document, you appoint someone you trust to be your "attorney-in-fact" (sometimes called your "agent" or "health care proxy") to see that your doctors and other health care providers give you the kind of medical care you wish to receive. You can also give your attorney-in-fact greater authority to make decisions about your medical care, including:

- making decisions about any issues you don't cover in your declaration
- hiring and firing medical personnel
- visiting you in the hospital or other facility, even when other visiting is restricted
- having access to medical records and other personal information, and
- getting court authorization, if it is required, to obtain or withhold medical treatment if, for any reason, a hospital or doctor does not honor your health care directives.

Several states combine the declaration and durable power of attorney for health care into a single document, usually called an "advance health care directive."

RESOURCE

Making health care directives. You can make a health care directive with *Quicken WillMaker & Trust*, software from Nolo. Californians can also use *Living Wills & Powers of Attorney for California*, by Shae Irving (Nolo). Also, in most states, you can obtain forms from the state medical association. You can also get your state's form for free from a nonprofit organization called Caring Connections (800-658-8898; www.caringinfo.org). Finally, caring.com provides information and resources about medical care and other aging-related concerns.

Long-Term Trusts to Control Property

In certain circumstances, you may want to dictate how your property is to be managed and distributed over many years. You may want to leave property to people who, for one reason or another, may not be able to manage it for themselves, even when they are older than age 35. Or you may want to impose strict controls over property left to your spouse for his or her life, to be sure it remains intact to go eventually to your children from a former marriage.

Reminder. For a discussion of how to leave property to a minor or young adult, and have someone manage it until the beneficiary is older, see Chapter 8.

SEE AN EXPERT

Long-term property management is not a do-it-yourself job. See an experienced lawyer if you want to create one of the property management trusts discussed in this section.

AB Trusts Used to Control Property

If you or your spouse have children from a previous marriage, you may want your current spouse to have use of some of your property for the rest of your spouse's life but you may also want that property to go to your children after your spouse's death. One way to do this is to establish a special type of AB trust that limits the surviving spouse's use, and rights, to property in Trust A. Spouses in second or subsequent marriages may want to impose controls over the surviving spouse's rights, to try to ensure that their children will eventually receive the bulk of their property.

EXAMPLE: Ilana and Harvey are both in their 50s. Ilana has a son from her first marriage. Harvey has two daughters from his. Ilana and Harvey purchase, equally, an $800,000 house. If one dies, each wants the other spouse to be able to live in the house for the remainder of the surviving spouse's life. But they both want their shares of the house to go to the children of their first marriages after they have both died. So Ilana and Harvey create an AB trust. Each spouse's Trust A allows the surviving spouse full use of the house, but not the right to sell it and buy another one. Then after both spouses die, half the house goes to Ilana's son, and the other half to Harvey's two daughters.

Many questions need to be resolved in setting up the trust:

- How strict should the controls on the surviving spouse be?
- Can the spouse sell the house to pay for health needs? For any needs?
- Should the spouse be the sole trustee, or is it better to have a child share that job or to have a child be the sole trustee?
- What reports and accountings must be given to the children?

Suppose a wife wants to allow her husband the right to stay in her home while he lives. How specifically does the right need to be pinned down in the trust? Can the husband sell the house and buy another? Can he rent it out? Suppose he needs to go to a nursing home—can the house then be sold? What happens to the profits of the sale? Who gets any income from trust property?

SEE AN EXPERT

An AB trust that is intended to impose controls on the surviving spouse's inherited property must be carefully drafted by a knowledgeable attorney. Inherently, you are dealing with possible conflicts—the basic concern, after all, is that the surviving spouse's desires and interests may be very different from, or directly conflict with, the desires and interests of the deceased spouse's children. To resolve these issues wisely, you need a trust geared to your desires and to the specific realities of your situation.

Spendthrift Trusts

If you want to leave property to an adult who just can't handle money, a "spendthrift trust," where an independent trustee can dole out the money little by little, is a good idea. A spendthrift trust keeps the property from being squandered by the beneficiary or seized by the beneficiary's creditors.

Special Needs Trusts

A person with a serious physical or mental disability may not be able to handle property at any age. Additionally, if that person receives government benefits, that person cannot own substantial amounts of money or property without seriously compromising eligibility for those benefits. In this common situation, loved ones cannot leave gifts directly to persons with disabilities without causing them to lose their benefits. The solution is to leave gifts to the person with a disability through a special needs trust. A well-drafted special needs trust both protects eligibility for government benefits and provides an understanding trustee who carefully manages trust property for the beneficiary.

RESOURCE

Trusts for those with disabilities. *Special Needs Trusts,* by Kevin Urbatsch and Michele Fuller-Urbatsch (Nolo), explains how to create a trust for a disabled loved one. This trust is designed so that the loved one's inheritance will not interfere with eligibility for SSI or Medicaid benefits.

Flexible Trusts

You may want the determination of how your property is spent after your death to be decided in the future by a successor trustee, not by you before you die. The usual way to do this is to create a "sprinkling trust," authorizing the trustee to decide how to spend trust money for several beneficiaries.

Wills

As I urged in Chapters 3 and 14, you'll need to prepare a simple "backup" will, even if you leave most, or all, of your property by your living trust and other probate-avoidance methods. This book provides backup will forms in Appendix B and as forms that you can download from this book's online companion page. (See Appendix A to learn how to download the forms.)

Why Prepare a Backup Will?

It's always sensible to prepare a backup will for one, or probably more, of the following reasons:

- **To name a personal guardian for your minor children.** If you have young children, you need a will to achieve the vital goal of nominating a personal guardian for them. In most states, you can't use your living trust to nominate a personal guardian. Also, in your will you can appoint a property guardian for your children to manage any of their property not otherwise legally supervised by an adult. Younger people with minor children, who don't have much property, may decide that because nominating a personal guardian is the primary thing they're worried about, a simple will is all the estate planning they currently need.

- **To choose a beneficiary for suddenly acquired property.** Anyone may end up acquiring valuable property at or shortly before death, such as a sudden gift, an inheritance, or (even) a lottery prize. Under the will forms in this book, that property will go to the residuary beneficiary of your will. You may well not get around to, or have time to, transfer the property to your trust. Therefore, it cannot be subject to your trust. And if you didn't have a will, the property would, under your state's "intestate succession" laws, go to your closest relatives.

- **To leave property not transferred by a probate-avoidance device.** If you don't get around to planning probate avoidance for all your property (by placing it in your living trust, for example), a will is a valuable backup device. If you have a will, the property will go to whomever you want to have it (the residuary beneficiary of your will) and not pass under the intestate succession laws.

- **To give away property someone left you that is still in probate.** If someone has left you property by will, and that property is still enmeshed in probate when you die, you can't arrange to transfer it by a probate-avoidance device. Since you don't have title to the property, you have no legal right to transfer it. But again, under your will, that property will go to your residuary beneficiary when the probate court releases it.

- **To name your executor.** In your will, you name your executor (and alternate executor), the person with legal authority to supervise distribution of property left by your will and to represent your estate in probate court proceedings. It is a good idea to have an executor even if you have also set up a living trust and named a successor trustee to manage it when you die, because banks and other institutions are often reassured to know an executor exists. Normally, it's best to name the same person as your successor trustee and executor.

- **For married couples, to avoid confusion in case of simultaneous death.** The will for a member of a couple provides that if both members "die simultaneously or under such circumstances as to render it difficult or impossible to determine who predeceased the other," the will writer is conclusively presumed to have outlived the other spouse. This clause works for each spouse, in his or her own will. How can that be, you may ask? Well, the official reason is that each will is interpreted independently from the other. The real reason is that it achieves a desired goal of preventing one spouse's property from going to another's estate if one lives only a few minutes or hours longer than the other.

What You Can Do in a Backup Will

The backup will forms in this book enable you to:

- Make specific gifts—for example, "I leave my piano to Julia Rhodes." You can leave property that you haven't transferred to your living trust—for example, your personal bank account or car—to whomever you choose.

  You can leave a gift to be shared among several beneficiaries (or alternate beneficiaries) in any percentages you choose. Before doing this in your will, be sure to review "Shared Gifts" in Chapter 7.
- Name alternate beneficiaries for these specific gifts in case the primary beneficiary dies before you do.
- Name a residuary beneficiary and alternate residuary beneficiary to inherit any property subject to your will that is not specifically left to other named beneficiaries.
- Nominate a personal guardian and alternate for your minor children.
- Name a property guardian (who can be the same person as the personal guardian) to manage any of your minor children's property that isn't otherwise legally controlled by an adult. It's generally preferable to leave property to your minor children in child's trusts or under the Uniform Transfers to Minors Act rather than relying on a property guardian named in a will that you name only as a backup for property they may acquire from some other source. (See Chapter 8.)
- Appoint your executor.

 CAUTION

Disinheriting a child or spouse. If you want to disinherit a child or your spouse, you must do so in your will. But before you decide to do this, carefully reread "Disinheritance" in Chapter 7. The law may restrict your choices.

 CAUTION

Children born or adopted after you sign your will. If you have a child after preparing your will, prepare a new will that names and leaves a gift for that child. Reread "Disinheritance" in Chapter 7, for a reminder of why this is necessary.

You may decide that you need a more complicated will. For instance, perhaps you want to appoint different personal guardians for different minor children. Or you want to arrange for care of your pets or specifically forgive debts owed you. Some people want to use a "self-proving affidavit" (legal in most states) for their witnesses, which can make it easier to probate a will without a written statement or a court appearance by a witness. If you do want a more complicated will, look into using Nolo's *Quick & Legal Will Book* or *Quicken WillMaker & Trust*.

Pour-Over Wills

A "pour-over will" takes all the property you haven't transferred to your living trust and, at your death, leaves it ("pours it over") to that trust. Some lawyers urge all people who make living trusts to make pour-over wills, arguing that it's always best to send all your property through your living trust. There seems to be something about the name "pour-over will" that impresses people. The term sounds, well, sophisticated, like they're doing something really right. In fact, pour-over wills are not very desirable, in my opinion, for most people with a living trust.

When Not to Use a Pour-Over Will

Pour-over wills do not avoid probate. All property that is left through a will—any kind of will—must go through probate, unless the amount left is small enough to qualify for exemption from normal probate laws. Probate is most definitely not avoided simply because the beneficiary of a will is a living trust.

It's generally better to simply use a standard backup will to take care of your leftover (non-living-trust) property rather than a pour-over will. In the backup will, you can name the people you want to get the will property, and skip the unnecessary extra step of pouring the property through the living trust after your death.

When used as a backup will, a pour-over will actually has a disadvantage that standard wills don't: It forces the living trust to go on for months after your death, because the property left through the pour-over will must normally go through probate before it can be transferred to the trust. Usually, the property left in a living trust can be distributed to the beneficiaries and the trust ended within a few weeks after the person's death.

EXAMPLE: Joy transfers her valuable property to her living trust. She also makes a pour-over will, which states that any property she owns at death goes to the living trust. When Joy dies, the property left through her will goes to the trust and is distributed to the residuary beneficiary of her living trust, her son Louis. The living trust must be kept going until probate of the will is finished, when property left by the will is poured over into the living trust. Normally, keeping the living trust ongoing for several months, or however long probate takes, would not require filing a trust tax return, since there's no income to this trust. Still, it's better to wind up a living trust as quickly as feasible.

If Joy had simply named Louis as sole beneficiary of a simple backup will, the end result would have been the same, but the process would have been simpler. The living trust would have been ended a few weeks after Joy's death. And after probate was finished, Louis would have received whatever property passed through Joy's will.

When You May Want a Pour-Over Will

There are, however, two situations in which you might want to use a pour-over will.

If you set up a child's subtrust for a young beneficiary in your living trust, you may want any property that child inherits through your will to go into the subtrust. Otherwise, you would create two trusts for the beneficiary—one in the will and one in your living trust.

EXAMPLE: Jessica makes a living trust and leaves the bulk of her property to her 12-year-old son. She arranges, in the trust document, for any trust property her son inherits before the age of 30 to be kept in a child's trust, managed by Jessica's sister.

Jessica also makes a backup will, in which she leaves everything to her son and again arranges for a child's trust to be set up if she should die before her son reaches age 30. So if Jessica dies before her son reaches 30, two separate child's trusts will be set up to manage property for him.

If Jessica used a pour-over will, any property her son inherited through the will would go into the trust created by her living trust. With only one trust, only half the paperwork of maintaining the trust is necessary, as compared to maintaining two separate trusts.

Separately, if you decide to create a disclaimer trust, a pour-over will can be desirable. The spouses want the option of placing the maximum amount of property possible in Trust A. So both spouses write pour-over wills that leave their property to the trust. After a spouse dies, the other spouse should amend her or his will or prepare a new one, since there will no longer be a functional trust for the surviving spouse's property to go to.

How to Create a Pour-Over Will

You can use the will forms in this book to create a pour-over will. To do so, you leave property subject to the will to your living trust.

> **EXAMPLE:** Nils, married to Mercedes, wants the property he leaves through his will to go to his living trust. In his will, he lists the beneficiary as "the Nils and Mercedes Janson Living Trust."

Avoiding Conflicts Between Your Will and Your Living Trust

When you make both a living trust and a will, pay attention to how the two work together. If your will and your trust document contain conflicting provisions, at the least you will create confusion among your inheritors, and at the worst, bitter disputes—maybe even a lawsuit—among friends and family. Here are some guidelines to help you avoid problems:

- **Don't leave the same property in your living trust and will, even if it's to the same beneficiary.** If you transfer the property to your living trust and name a beneficiary in the trust document, that's all you need to do. Mentioning the property in your will raises the possibility of probate.

- **Name the same person to be executor of your will and successor trustee of your living trust.** There's one important exception: If you make a shared trust, you'll probably name your spouse as executor of your will, but not as successor trustee—the successor trustee takes over only after both spouses have died. The surviving spouse, however, may want to revise his or her will after the death of the first spouse, to name a successor trustee to be executor.

Your beneficiaries and your trustee/executor don't need a conflict between your living trust and will. If you want to change a beneficiary, change it by amending the document where you named the original beneficiary, not by using your will to override it.

> ⓘ **CAUTION**
> **Watch out in Washington state.** In the state of Washington, a "superwill" statute allows you to leave property held in your living trust, or in other probate-avoidance devices, such as joint tenancy or pay-on-death accounts, through your will. For example, if you write a will after having created a living trust, and in that will name a new beneficiary for property left to someone else in your living trust, your will prevails.

Simultaneous Death Clause

The will form in this book for a coupled person has a simultaneous death clause, which is effective if the couple dies together, or where it cannot be ascertained who died first. This clause is worded somewhat differently than the simultaneous death clause in the shared living trust, because that is a single document covering both spouses, whereas each spouse makes a separate will. But the simultaneous death clause in your will accomplishes the same task as the one in your living trust: Each spouse's property is treated as if that spouse survived the other.

Filling in the Will Form

Here are the steps necessary to prepare your own will from a will form.

Step 1. Select the correct form, depending on whether you are single (Form 9) or a member of a couple (Form 10).

These forms are available to you as downloadable forms and as printed forms in Appendix B. To download the forms, follow the instructions in Appendix A. To use the printed forms in Appendix B, you must retype the entire form on your typewriter or computer. With either form, do not just fill in the blanks by hand (or by typewriter)—*the entire will must be typed as one continuous document.*

As with the living trust forms, the will for a member of a couple is written in terms of a married couple, using the terms "husband" and "wife." If these terms do not apply to you, please make the necessary word changes ("spouse," "partner," each person's name, or whatever you feel works) in the will form, so that it makes sense for your situation.

Step 2. Read through the will form carefully. There are a number of blanks to fill in. The information called for is identified below each blank. While most of this is self-explanatory, here is what you must fill in:

- **Your name.** This should be the form of the name you use to sign such documents as deeds, checks, and loan applications. It needn't necessarily be the way your name appears on your birth or marriage certificate.
- **Your city, county, and state.**
- **The names of all your living children, and names of any children of a deceased child, if any.**
- **The names of the personal guardian, alternate personal guardian, property guardian, and alternate property guardian for your minor children.** You can name only one personal guardian and one property guardian for all your children.
- **Specific gifts.** You do not have to make any specific gifts. You can simply leave all property subject to this will to your residuary beneficiary. If you leave some property to more than one beneficiary, or alternate beneficiaries, follow the instructions in Chapter 9 for the wording of shared gifts. (Remember that in Florida, you cannot leave your house to anyone but your spouse or your children.) The will form provides three specific gift clauses. Repeat or delete these clauses as necessary.
- **The name of your residuary beneficiary and alternate residuary beneficiary.** You can name more than one residuary beneficiary if you want. For example, many people list all their children.
- **The names of your executor and alternate executor.**

You may need to renumber the clauses if you omit items that don't apply to you. Do not sign or date your will yet. You do this when you complete your final will, with your witnesses.

Step 3. Type or print out the final draft of your will. If you used the will forms in the back of the book, use a typewriter or a word processor to type out your final draft. Once your will is typed or printed, do not make any changes by hand. A will with both handwriting and typing risks invalidation.

You do not need to initial each page. Your signature at the end (with the signatures of your witnesses) is all that is needed.

> ⓘ CAUTION
> **Don't fill out your will by hand.** Do not type or handwrite the information required onto a printed form and attempt to use it as your final will. Courts are not used to wills like this. You want your will to look normal and unthreatening to a judge, which means typed, and without the fill-in-the-blank lines and instructions. So you can see how a final draft and a typed will should look, there are samples below of Form 9, a will for a single person.

Type or print out the final draft of your will on standard 8½" x 11" paper. Proofread it carefully and make sure it's letter-perfect. If you find mistakes, fix them and print out the page again. Don't ever make alterations on the face of your will by writing in words or crossing something out and initialing the change. It could make part or all of your will invalid.

Step 4. Date and sign the will in front of witnesses. (Instructions are below.)

Signing and Witnessing Your Will

To be valid, your will must be signed and dated in front of witnesses. You sign the will where the form provides. Then these witnesses must sign the will in your presence, and also in the presence of the other witnesses.

Initial Draft of Will

~~Form 9: Basic Will for One Person~~

Will

of

_____Benjamin Werrin_____
~~your name~~

I, _____Benjamin Werrin_____ , a resident of
~~your name~~

_____Fairmont_____ , _____Dutchess_____ County, _____New York_____ ,
~~city~~   ~~county~~   ~~state~~

declare that this is my will.

1. I revoke all wills and codicils that I have previously made.

2. I am not married.

3. (A) I am the _____father_____ of the _____child_____ whose _____name_____ _____is_____
~~mother/father~~   ~~child/children~~   ~~name/names~~   ~~is/are~~

_____Eric Werrin_____

_____

_____

_____

_____ .

There are _____ living children of my deceased child _____
                                                                        name

_____ , whose name(s) is/are:

_____

_____

_____

_____

_____ .

(B) If I fail to leave, by this will or otherwise, any property to any of the children listed above, my failure to do so

is intentional.

Initial Draft of Will (continued)

(C) If at my death any of my children are minors, and a personal guardian is needed, I nominate _____

_____ to be appointed personal guardian

name of personal guardian

of my minor children. If _____ cannot serve as

name of personal guardian

personal guardian, I nominate _____

name of alternate personal guardian

to be appointed personal guardian.

(D) If at my death any of my children are minors, and a property guardian is needed, I appoint _____

_____ as property guardian for my minor children.

name of property guardian

If _____ cannot serve as property guardian, I appoint

name of property guardian

_____ as property guardian.

name of alternate property guardian

(E) I direct that no bond be required of any guardian.

4. (A) I make the following specific gifts:

I leave _____*all my cameras*_____

property described

to _____*Sid Tropinsky*_____ , or if

beneficiary's name

_____*Sid Tropinsky*_____ fails to survive

beneficiary's name

me, to _____*Nancy Werrin*_____ .

alternate beneficiary's name

I leave _____

property described

to _____ , or if

beneficiary's name

_____ fails to survive

beneficiary's name

me, to _____ .

alternate beneficiary's name

I leave _____

property described

to _____ , or if

beneficiary's name

_____ fails to survive

beneficiary's name

me, to _____ .

alternate beneficiary's name

Initial Draft of Will (continued)

(B) I leave all my other property subject to this will to _____ Eric Werrin _____
residuary beneficiary's name

_____ , or if _____ *he* _____ fails to survive me,
he/she

to _____ Gil Nason _____ .
alternate residuary beneficiary's name

5. (A) I nominate _____ Gil Nason _____
executor's name

to serve as executor of my will. If _____ *he* _____ is unable to serve or continue serving as executor, I nominate
he/she

_____ Nancy Werrin _____ to serve as executor.
alternate executor's name

(B) No bond shall be required of any executor.

I subscribe my name to this will this _____ day of _____ _____ , 20_____ , at

_____ Fairmont _____ , _____ Dutchess County _____ , _____ New York _____ .
city   county   state

_____
your signature

Witnesses

On the date last written above, _____ Benjamin Werrin _____
your name

declared to us, the undersigned, that this was _____ *his* _____ will, and requested us to act as witnesses to it. _____ *He* _____
his/her   He/She

signed this will in our presence, all of us being present at the same time. We now, at _____ *his* _____ request and in
his/her

_____ *his* _____ presence, and in the presence of each other, have signed this will as witnesses.
his/her

We declare under penalty of perjury that the foregoing is true and correct.

_____   _____
witness signature   witness printed name

_____ , _____ , _____
city   county   state

_____   _____
witness signature   witness printed name

_____ , _____ , _____
city   county   state

_____   _____
witness signature   witness printed name

_____ , _____ , _____
city   county   state

Final, Typed Will, Ready to Be Signed and Witnessed

Will

of

Benjamin Werrin

I, Benjamin Werrin, a resident of Fairmont, Dutchess County, New York, declare that this is my will.

1. I revoke all wills and codicils that I have previously made.

2. I am not married.

3. I am the father of the child whose name is Eric Werrin.

4. (A) I make the following specific gifts:

   I leave all my cameras to Sid Tropinsky, or if Sid Tropinsky fails to survive me, to Nancy Werrin.

   (B) I leave all my other property subject to this will to Eric Werrin, or if he fails to survive me, to Gil Nason.

5. (A) I nominate Gil Nason to serve as executor of my will. If he is unable to serve or continue serving as executor, I nominate Nancy Werrin to serve as executor.

   (B) No bond shall be required of any executor.

   I subscribe my name to this will this _____ day of _____, 20_____, at

Fairmont, Dutchess County, New York.

_____

Witnesses

On the date last written above, Benjamin Werrin declared to us, the undersigned, that this was his will, and requested us to act as witnesses to it. He then signed this will in our presence, all of us being present at the same time. We now at his request and in his presence, and in the presence of each other, have signed such will as witnesses.

We declare under penalty of perjury that the foregoing is true and correct.

_____   _____
witness signature   witness printed name

_____ , _____ , _____
            city   county   state

_____   _____
witness signature   witness printed name

_____ , _____ , _____
            city   county   state

_____   _____
witness signature   witness printed name

_____ , _____ , _____
            city   county   state

Although all states require only two witnesses, three is better because it provides one more person to establish that your signature is valid, if that becomes necessary during probate.

Witnesses must also be people who won't inherit under the will. That means anyone who might inherit any gift through your will, including alternate residuary beneficiaries, cannot be a witness. But someone who will receive property from only your living trust can be a valid witness. Some states allow a witness to inherit will property. Still, I strongly recommend against doing that in your will. Having will witnesses who do not inherit eliminates one possible reason for challenging your will.

Witnesses should also be easy to locate in the event of your death. This usually means people who aren't likely to move around a lot and (most of all) who are younger than you are.

Here's how to go about arranging for signing and witnessing your will:

- Have all witnesses assemble in one place.
- Tell them that the paper you hold is your will. They don't need to know what's in it.
- Sign the signature page in the witnesses' presence. Use the exact spelling of your name as you typed in the heading.
- Have each witness sign the last page in the place indicated while the other witnesses are watching. The clause immediately preceding the witnesses' signatures states ("attests") that the events outlined just above have occurred.

The witnesses should also list their city, county, and state of residence (not where the will is signed). Listing the witnesses' addresses is not legally required, but can prove an aid in locating the witnesses later on, when the will becomes operational.

CAUTION

Get the details right. If a will doesn't comply with the technical requirements (say you had only one witness to your will), it cannot be validated by the probate court. It's not hard to do a will correctly. Double-check to be sure you've done so!

TIP

Witnessing challenges during a pandemic. COVID-19 physical distancing requirements may present challenges for witnessing wills in person. If it is not safe or reasonable for you to gather with your witnesses as you would have done before the pandemic, you have to come up with a creative solution. For example, perhaps you could gather your witnesses in your yard, masked, keeping your distance, with the will on a table. Then separately, each person could step up to the table with a pen to sign the will. Or you could meet in a parking lot, with the witnesses parked close together. Then you go up to each car and slip the document through the window for each person to sign. Strange times call for strange measures!

If You Need Expert Help

Many readers, probably the majority, will find the information in this book sufficient to prepare their own living trusts and backup wills. But if you run into a snag of some kind, you may sensibly decide you need a lawyer's help. Throughout this book, I've indicated "red flags" that alert you to the need for professional advice. And, of course, people with estates over the federal estate tax threshold need expert help to review all their estate tax options and prepare the living trusts best geared to their needs.

Hiring a Lawyer to Review Your Living Trust

Hiring a lawyer solely to review a living trust document you've prepared sounds like a good idea. It shouldn't cost much, and seems to offer a comforting security. Sadly, though, it may be difficult or even impossible to find a lawyer who will accept the job.

While this is unfortunate, I'm not willing to excoriate lawyers who won't review a do-it-yourself living trust. From their point of view, they are being asked to accept what can turn into a significant responsibility for what they regard as inadequate compensation, given their usual fees. Any prudent lawyer sees every client as a potential occasion for a malpractice claim, or at least, serious later hassles—a phone call four years down the line that begins, "We talked to you about our living trust, and now…." Many experienced lawyers want to avoid this kind of risk. Also, many lawyers feel that if they're only reviewing someone else's work, they simply don't get deeply enough into a situation to be sure of their opinions. All you can do here is to keep trying to find a sympathetic lawyer—or be prepared to pay more, enough so the lawyer can feel adequately paid to review your living trust.

Working With an Expert

If you have decided you want legal help, the first consideration is what type of expert you should seek out. Questions about estate taxes may be better (and less expensively) answered by an experienced accountant than by a lawyer. Or if you're wondering what type of life insurance to buy, you may be better off talking to a financial planner. But for many sophisticated living trust issues, you'll need to see a lawyer.

What Type of Lawyer Do You Need?

The type of lawyer that is right for you depends on what your problem is. Before you talk to a lawyer, decide what kind of help you really need. Do you want someone to advise you on a complete estate plan or just to go over part of your trust? If you don't clearly tell the lawyer what you want, you may find yourself agreeing to turn over all your estate planning work.

If you've prepared a trust from this book, any good estate practice lawyer should be able to help you. If you want a more sophisticated document—like a QTIP trust or generation-skipping trust—it's important that you see an estate trust specialist, who'll probably cost more than a general practice estate lawyer.

If you hire an "expert," make sure that person really has knowledge or expertise. Many lawyers have discovered the profit-making potential of trusts. Lawyers who know almost nothing about living trusts have found that they can charge substantial fees—$1,500 or more is common—for a simple document. Some use computer programs to churn out trusts and may or may not take into account your specific needs.

It's also important that you feel a personal rapport with your lawyer. You want one who treats you as an equal. (Interestingly, the Latin root of the word "client" translates as "to hear, to obey.") When talking with a lawyer on the phone or at a first conference, ask specific questions that concern you. Let the lawyer know that you've read this book and that you have a good understanding of estate planning. Then, see how the lawyer responds. If the lawyer answers you clearly and concisely—explaining, but not talking down to you— fine. If the lawyer acts wise, but says little except to ask to take care of the problem (with the appropriate fee, of course), watch out. You are either talking with someone who doesn't know the answer and won't admit it (common), or someone who finds it impossible to let go of the "me expert, you peasant" way of looking at the world (even more common).

How to Choose a Lawyer

Finding a competent estate planning lawyer who charges a reasonable fee and respects your efforts to prepare your own living trust may not be easy. Here are some suggestions on how to go about the task.

Ask Friends and Businesspeople

Personal recommendations are generally the best way to find a lawyer you'll like. If you have a close friend who's had a good experience with an estate planning lawyer, there's a good chance you'll work well with that lawyer too.

If friends can't help you, ask any businesspeople you know for referrals. Anyone who owns a small business probably has a relationship with a lawyer. Ask around to find someone you know who is a satisfied client, and get the name of that person's lawyer. Even a lawyer who does not handle estate planning will likely know someone who does. And because of the continuing relationship with your business friend, the lawyer has an incentive to recommend someone who is competent.

Also ask people in any social or other organization in which you are involved. They may well know of a good lawyer whose attitudes are similar to yours. Senior citizens' centers and other groups that advise and assist older people may have a list of local lawyers who specialize in wills and estate planning, and are well regarded.

Look Into a Group Legal Plan

Some unions, employers, and consumer groups offer group legal plans to their members or employees, who can obtain comprehensive legal assistance free or at low rates. If you are a member of such a plan, check with it first. Your problem may be covered free of charge. If it is, and you are satisfied that the lawyer you are referred to is knowledgeable in estate planning, this route is probably a good choice.

Some plans give you only a slight reduction in a lawyer's fee. In that case, you may be referred to a lawyer whose main virtue is the willingness to reduce fees in exchange for a high volume of referrals.

Call an Attorney Referral Service

A lawyer referral service will give you the name of an attorney who practices in your area. Usually, you can get a referral to an attorney who claims to specialize in estate planning and will give you an initial consultation for a low fee.

Most county bar associations have referral services. In some states, independent referral services, run by or for groups of lawyers, also operate.

Unfortunately, few referral services screen the attorneys they list, which means those who participate may not be the most experienced or competent. Often, the lawyers who sign up with referral services are just starting out and need clients. It may be possible to find a skilled estate planning specialist through a referral service, but be sure to take the time to check out the credentials and experience of the person to whom you're referred.

Use a Lawyer Directory

You can also search for a lawyer using an online lawyer directory. These are databases of lawyers that pay to have their profiles appear on a directory's site. You can usually search attorney profiles by practice area and location. A lawyer's profile should give you additional information about that person's practice, like areas of specialization, fees, and standing with the state bar. Because lawyers pay to be on the site, their presence in the directory has no bearing on their quality. However, if you get in touch with a few that meet your criteria, you should be able to tease out which may be a good fit.

RESOURCE

Let Nolo take the guesswork out of finding a lawyer. Two sites that are part of the Nolo family, Lawyers.com and Avvo.com, provide comprehensive and free lawyer directories. These directories allow you to search by location and area of law, and list detailed information about and reviews of lawyers. Whether you're just starting your lawyer search or researching particular attorneys, visit www.lawyers.com/find-a-lawyer and www.avvo.com/find-a-lawyer.

Living Trust Seminars

As discussed in Chapter 3, newspapers, radio, and TV can have ads for free seminars on living trusts. Usually, these events are nothing more than elaborate pitches for paying a business or a lawyer $1,000 to $1,500 to write a living trust. Is it worth it? Probably not. For most estates, the trust forms and instructions in this book are all you need.

Often these seminars are occasions for you to be cajoled by lawyers, financial planners, and insurance agents to pay large sums of money to get your affairs in order before you die.

People are sold on the idea that much of their estate is likely to be gobbled up by estate taxes unless they set up trusts now to avoid some of the tax and buy life insurance to pay the rest. The reality is that most people don't have estates large enough to generate estate tax liability. And the seminar sponsors know it.

The sponsors may try to sell:
- a lot of life insurance, to pay for supposed estate taxes, and
- an AB trust form to reduce estate taxes.

Be sure you need these alleged benefits before paying what will be a substantial amount to acquire them. Is your estate likely to be liable for federal estate taxes? Do you really need an AB trust? If your situation is more complex than what can be handled by using this book, you'll probably be better off paying the money to hire a good lawyer to draft a trust geared to your needs than paying too much for the standard form offered in these seminars.

Lawyer Fees

As you already know, lawyers are expensive. They charge fees usually ranging from $150 to $500 or more per hour. While fancy office trappings, dull suits, and solemn faces are no guarantee (or even a good indication) that a particular lawyer will provide top-notch service in a style you will feel comfortable with, this conventional style almost always ensures that you will be charged at the upper end of the fee range. High fees and quality service don't necessarily go hand in hand. Indeed, the attorneys I think most highly of tend to charge moderate fees (for lawyers, that is), and seem to get along very nicely without stuffy law office trappings.

Depending on the area of the country where you live, generally, fees in the range of $200 to $300 per hour are reasonable in urban areas, given the average lawyer's overhead. In rural counties and small cities, $150 to $250 is more like it.

Be sure you've settled your fee arrangement—preferably in writing—at the start of your relationship. (In California, a written fee agreement is required by law if the bill is expected to be more than $1,000.) In addition to the hourly fee, get a clear, written commitment from the lawyer stating how many hours your problem should take to handle.

Doing Your Own Legal Research

As an alternative to hiring a lawyer, you can explore doing your own legal research. This can work well for relatively simpler living trust questions, such as any specific state law about trust registration or a trustee's duty to manage trust property prudently.

Legal Research in Law Libraries

If you decide you want to do your own research in the library, how do you go about it? First, you need an introduction to how law libraries work. Since you can't hire your own law librarian, the best book explaining how nonlawyers can do their own legal work is *Legal Research: How to Find & Understand the Law,* by Stephen Elias (Nolo). It shows you, step by step, how to find answers in the law library. It is a great legal research book written specifically for nonprofessionals.

Next, locate a law library or a public library with a good law collection. In most counties, there's a law library in the main county courthouse, although quality varies widely. Most county law libraries are supported by tax dollars or by the fees paid to file court papers. The librarians are generally most helpful and courteous to nonlawyers who are venturing to do their own legal research. If the county library is not adequate, your best bet is a law school library. Those in state colleges and universities supported by tax dollars are almost always open to the public.

Many states have estate planning books prepared for practicing lawyers. These books contain specific clauses and forms for wills or trusts, and many other hands-on materials. The best way to locate this type of book for your state is to ask the law librarian or search the library's computerized catalog by looking for the terms "estate planning," "wills," and "trusts."

Unfortunately, I cannot recommend doing your own research for high-end living trust issues, especially regarding estate taxes. Drafting a QTIP or generation-skipping trust that complies with all federal regulations and achieves the goals you want is truly a complicated matter that requires considerable expertise. Remember, you'll consider these types of trusts only if you have substantial assets. The risk that your trust won't be legally correct and therefore won't qualify for the tax breaks you want outweighs any possible savings gained by doing your own legal work.

Legal Information Online

It's possible to find many answers online. If you want information about a recent court decision, a new statute, a current legal issue, or more general information on some aspect of living trusts, you'll probably be able to find it somewhere online. Lots of public libraries now offer online access, if you're not connected at home or at work.

Legal Research: How to Find & Understand the Law, by Stephen Elias (Nolo), provides extensive information on how to do legal research online.

Living Trust Research Books

In most states, you can find books on trusts written for the lawyers of your state.

In California, Continuing Education of the Bar (CEB) publishes several useful estate planning books, including *Drafting California Revocable Trusts.*

Comparable books in New York, including *Blattmachr on Income Taxation of Estates and Trusts,* by F. Ladson Boyle and Jonathan G. Blattmachr, are published by the Practising Law Institute (PLI).

If you want to wade into the murk of estate tax issues, a standard resource is the CCH's (Commerce Clearing House's) *U.S. Master Federal Estate & Gift Tax Guide.*

"Practice guides" like these are useful, but very expensive. You may be able to find copies in your local law library.

 RESOURCE
Go to Nolo.com for free legal information. Nolo provides thousands of free articles on its website. Go to the "Wills, Trusts & Probate" section to learn about estate planning basics, or drill down to the "Living Trusts" section to get into details about how living trusts work. You will also find lots of information about wills, health care directives, powers of attorney, avoiding probate, and do-it-yourself estate planning.

Glossary

AB trust. A trust where one spouse leaves property in what's called "Trust A," allowing the surviving spouse to use the income from that trust and authorizing limited rights to invade the trust principal. After the death of the surviving spouse, the trust property goes to the final beneficiaries. With an AB *disclaimer* trust, the surviving spouse decides how much, if any, of the deceased spouse's property to place in Trust A.

Acknowledgment. A statement in front of a person who is qualified to administer oaths (a notary public) that a document bearing a person's signature was actually signed by that person.

Administration of an estate. The court-supervised distribution of the probate estate of a deceased person. The person who manages the distribution is called the "executor" if there is a will. If there is no will, this person is called the "administrator." In some states, the person is called "personal representative" in either instance.

Adult. A person aged 18 or older.

Affidavit. A written statement signed under oath in front of a notary public.

Augmented estate. The property left by a will plus certain property transferred outside of the will by gifts, joint tenancies, and living trusts. The augmented estate is calculated if a surviving spouse wants to claim the surviving spouse's statutory share of the deceased spouse's property. In the states that use this concept, a surviving spouse is generally considered to be adequately provided for if the surviving spouse receives at least one-third of the augmented estate.

Basis. This is a tax term that has to do with the valuation of property for determining profit or loss on sale. To simplify to the basics, if you buy a house for $200,000, your tax basis is $200,000. If you later sell it for $350,000, your taxable profit is $150,000. *See also* Stepped-up basis.

Beneficiary. A person or an organization that is legally entitled to receive property under a will or trust. A primary beneficiary is a person who directly and certainly will benefit from the will or trust. An alternate beneficiary is a person who inherits property if a primary beneficiary dies before the person who made the will or trust does. *See* Residuary beneficiary and Final beneficiary.

Bond. A document guaranteeing that a certain amount of money will be paid to those injured if a person occupying a position of trust does not carry out the required legal and ethical responsibilities.

Thus, if an executor, trustee, or guardian who is bonded (covered by a bond) wrongfully deprives a beneficiary of property (say, by blowing it during a trip in Las Vegas), the bonding company will replace it, up to the limits of the bond.

Bypass trust. *See* AB trust.

Certification of Trust. (Also called an "Abstract of Trust.") A condensed version of a living trust, which leaves out the key parts of what property is in the trust and who are the beneficiaries. A certificate of trust is used to show financial organizations or other institutions that a valid living trust has been established, without revealing specifics the grantor wants to keep private and confidential.

Child's trust. A trust that is established by the terms of a trust form in this book. It comes into being only if, at the grantor's death, a young beneficiary hasn't yet reached the age the grantor specified in the trust document to receive the gift outright.

If the trust is set up, all trust property the young beneficiary is entitled to automatically goes into it. It will stay in trust until the beneficiary reaches the age specified by the grantor, or, if none is, up to 35. Then the beneficiary will receive the property outright.

Common law marriage. In a minority of states, couples may be considered married if they live together for a certain period of time and intend to be husband and wife.

Community property. Eight states follow a system of marital property ownership called "community property," and Wisconsin has a very similar "marital property" law. Very generally, all property acquired after marriage and before permanent separation is considered to belong equally to both spouses, except for gifts to and inheritances by one spouse and, in some community property states, income from property owned by one spouse prior to marriage. Spouses can, however, enter into an agreement to the contrary.

A surviving spouse automatically owns one-half of all community property. The other spouse has no legal power to affect this.

Conservator. Someone appointed by a court to manage the affairs of a mentally incompetent person. In some states, this person is called a guardian.

Creditor. A person or an institution to whom money is owed. A creditor may be the person who actually lent the money, or a lawyer or bill collector who is trying to collect the money for the original creditor.

Curtesy. *See* Dower and curtesy.

Custodian. A person named to care for property left to a minor under the Uniform Transfers to Minors Act. The custodian manages the property until the minor reaches the age at which state law says the minor must receive it. (In some states, the giver can specify, within limits, at what age the custodianship will end.)

The custodian has essentially the same powers as a child's trust trustee and may use the property for the minor's health, education, and support. The custodian's authority and duties are clearly set out by state law (the Uniform Transfers to Minors Act). No court supervises the custodian.

Debtor. A person who owes money.

Deceased spouse. With a shared living trust or an AB disclaimer trust created by both spouses, the first spouse to die.

Decedent. A person who has died.

Deed. The legal document by which one person (or persons) transfers title (recorded ownership) to real estate.

Disclaimer trust. A trust where a beneficiary has the specific right to disclaim all or any portion of a gift left to that beneficiary, so the gift goes to whomever is next entitled to receive it.

Domicile. The state, or country, where one has a primary home.

Donee. Someone who receives a gift.

Donor. Someone who gives a gift.

Dower and curtesy. The right of a widow or widower to receive or enjoy the use of a set portion of the deceased spouse's property (usually one-third to one-half) if the surviving spouse is not left at least that share. Dower refers to the title that a surviving wife gets, while curtesy refers to what a man receives. Until recently, these amounts differed in a number of states. However, states generally provide the same benefits regardless of sex.

Durable power of attorney. A power of attorney that remains effective even if the person who created it (called the "principal") becomes incapacitated. The person authorized to act (called the "attorney-in-fact" or "agent") can make health care decisions or handle financial affairs of the principal, depending on the authority granted by the document.

Estate. Generally, all the property you own when you die. There are different kinds of estates: the taxable estate (property subject to estate taxation), the probate estate (property that must go through probate), and the net estate (the net value of the property).

Estate planning. Figuring out how to prosper when you're alive, die with the smallest taxable estate and probate estate possible, and pass property to loved ones with a minimum of fuss and expense.

Estate taxes. Taxes imposed on an estate. The federal government exempts a set amount of property, depending on the year of death. Also exempt is all property left to a surviving spouse who is a U.S. citizen. Taxes are imposed only on property actually owned at the time of death. So, techniques designed to reduce taxes usually concentrate on the legal transfer of ownership of property while you are living, to minimize the amount of property owned at death. Some states also impose an estate tax or an inheritance tax.

Executor. The person named in a will to manage the deceased person's estate, deal with the probate court, collect assets, and distribute them as the will specifies. In some states, this person is called the "personal representative." If someone dies without a will, the probate court will appoint such a person, who is called the "administrator" of the estate.

Exemption trust. *See* AB trust.

Final beneficiary. The person(s) or institution(s) who receive the property in a marital life estate trust after the life beneficiary of that trust dies.

Financial guardian. *See* Property guardian.

Funding a trust. Transferring ownership of property to a trust, in the name of the trustee.

Generation-skipping trust. An estate tax-saving trust, where the principal is left in trust for one's grandchildren, with one's children receiving only the trust income.

Gift. Any property given to another person or an organization, either during the giver's lifetime, or by will or living trust after the giver's death.

Gift tax. Tax on gifts made during a person's lifetime. Many gifts are exempt from tax—for example, gifts to tax-exempt charities or the giver's spouse (if the recipient spouse is a U.S. citizen) and, currently, gifts of $15,000 or less to any one recipient in a calendar year.

Grantor. The person or persons who create a trust. Also called the "trustor" or "settlor."

Heirs. Persons who are entitled by state intestate law to inherit a deceased person's property if that person didn't make arrangements for what should happen to the property at death.

Inherit. To receive property from one who dies.

Inheritors. Persons or organizations who inherit property.

Instrument. Legalese for "document"; sometimes used to refer to the document that creates a living trust.

Inter vivos trust. Same as living trust. ("Inter vivos" is Latin for "between the living.")

Intestate. Someone who dies without a will or another valid estate transfer device dies intestate.

Intestate succession. The method by which property is distributed when a person fails to distribute it in a will or another estate transfer device. In such cases, the law of each state provides that the property be distributed in certain shares to the closest surviving relatives. In most states, these are a surviving spouse, children, parents, siblings, nieces and nephews, and next of kin, in that order. The intestate succession laws are also used in the event an heir is found to be pretermitted (not mentioned or otherwise provided for in the will).

Irrevocable trust. Means what it says. Once you create it, that's it; it's unchangeable. A trust that cannot be revoked by the person who created it once it's created. Unlike a revocable, probate-avoidance trust, it can't be amended or changed in any way.

Joint tenancy. A way to jointly own real or personal property. When two or more people own property as joint tenants, and one of the owners dies, the other owners automatically become owners of the deceased owner's share. Thus, if a parent and child own a house as joint tenants, and the parent dies, the child automatically becomes full owner. Because of this "right of survivorship," a joint tenancy interest in property does not go through probate, or, put another way, is not part of the probate estate. Instead, it goes directly to the surviving joint tenant(s).

Liquid assets. Cash or assets that can readily be turned into cash.

Living trust. A trust that is set up while a person is alive and remains under the control of that person until death. Also referred to as "inter vivos trust." Living trusts are an excellent way to minimize the value of property passing through probate. This is because they enable people (called "grantors") to specify that money or other property will pass directly to their beneficiaries after their deaths, free of probate, and yet allow the grantors to continue to control the property during their lifetimes and even end the trust or change the beneficiaries if they wish.

Living trust with marital life estate. *See* AB trust.

Living will. A document, directed to physicians, in which you state that you do not want to have your life artificially prolonged by technological means.

Marital deduction. A deduction allowed by the federal estate tax law for all property passed to a surviving spouse who is a U.S. citizen. This deduction (which really acts like an exemption) allows anyone, even a billionaire, to pass his or her entire estate to a surviving spouse without any tax at all.

Marriage. A specific status conferred on a couple by the state. In most states, it is necessary to file papers with a county clerk and have a marriage ceremony conducted by an authorized individual to be married.

In a few states, however, couples may be considered married without a ceremony in certain circumstances. *See* Common law marriage.

Minor. Person younger than 18 years of age. All minors must be under the care of an adult (parent or guardian) unless they are "emancipated"—in the military, married, or living independently with court permission. Property left to a minor must be handled by an adult until the minor becomes an adult under the laws of the state.

Mortgage. A document that makes a piece of real estate the security (collateral) for the payment of a debt. Most house buyers sign a mortgage when they buy; the bank lends money to buy the house, and the house serves as security for the debt. If the owners don't pay back the loan on time, the bank can seize the house and have it sold to pay off the loan.

Pay-on-death account. An account, often a bank account, where you name a beneficiary to receive the account assets outside of probate when you die. Sometimes referred to as a "Totten trust."

Personal guardian. An adult appointed or selected to care for a minor child in the event no biological or adoptive parent (legal parent) of the child is able to do so. If one legal parent is alive when the other dies, the child will automatically go to the surviving parent, unless the best interests of the child require something else.

Personal property. All property other than land and buildings attached to land. Cars, bank accounts, wages, securities, a small business, furniture, insurance policies, jewelry, pets, and season baseball tickets are all personal property.

Personal representative. *See* Executor.

Pour-over will. A will that "pours over" property into a trust. Property left through the will must go through probate before it goes into the trust.

Power of attorney. A legal document in which you authorize someone else to act for you. *See* Durable power of attorney.

Pretermitted heir. A child (or the child of a deceased child) who is either not named or (in some states) not provided for in a will. Most states presume that persons want their children to inherit. Accordingly, children, or the children of a child who has died, who are not mentioned or provided for in the will are entitled to a share of the estate.

Principal. Property owned by a trust, as distinguished from the income generated by that property.

Probate. The court proceeding in which (1) the authenticity of your will (if any) is established, (2) your executor or administrator is appointed, (3) your debts and taxes are paid, (4) your heirs are identified, and (5) your property in your probate estate is distributed according to your will (if there is a will).

Probate estate. All a decedent's property that passes through probate. Generally, this means all property owned at death less any property that has been placed in joint tenancy, a living trust, a bank account trust, or in life insurance.

Probate fees. Fees paid from a decedent's property to an attorney or court during probate. Typically, fees take 5% or more of the decedent's estate.

Property guardian. The person named in a will to care for property of a minor child not supervised by some other legal method, such as a minor's trust. Also called "the guardian of the minor's estate" or "financial guardian."

QTIP trust. A type of trust that allows a surviving spouse to postpone (until the surviving spouse's death) paying estate taxes that were assessed on the death of the other spouse.

Quasi-community property. A rule that applies to married couples who have moved to California, Idaho, Washington, or Wisconsin. Laws in those states require all property acquired by people during their marriage in other states to be treated as community property at their death.

Real estate. Same as real property.

Real property. All land and items attached to the land, such as buildings, houses, stationary mobile homes, fences, and trees are real property or "real estate." All property that is not real property is personal property.

Recording. The process of filing a copy of a deed with the county land records office. Recording creates a public record of all changes in ownership of property in the state.

Residuary beneficiary. The residuary beneficiary of a trust for one person, or a shared trust created from this book, is that beneficiary who receives any trust property not otherwise given away by the trust document. The residuary beneficiary of a will is the beneficiary who receives any property the will writer owned that was not left to beneficiaries by the will or other methods.

Residuary estate. Property that goes to the residuary beneficiary of a will or trust after all specific gifts of property have been made.

Right of survivorship. The right of a surviving joint tenant (or tenant by the entirety) to take ownership of a deceased co-owner's share of the property.

Separate property. In states that have community property, all property that is not community property. *See* Community property.

Special needs trust. A trust designed to provide for a person with a disability without interfering with that person's eligibility to receive government benefits.

Sprinkling trust. A trust that authorizes the trustee to decide how to distribute trust income or principal among different beneficiaries.

Stepped-up basis. Under current federal law, the tax basis of inherited property is "stepped up" to the market value of the property at the date of the deceased's death.

Successor trustee. The person (or institution) who takes over as trustee of a trust when the original trustee(s) have died or become incapacitated.

Surviving spouse. With a shared or AB living trust created by both spouses, the living spouse after the other spouse dies.

Surviving spouse's trust. The revocable living trust of the surviving spouse, after the other spouse has died.

Taking against the will. State law gives a surviving spouse the right to demand a certain share (in most states, one-third to one-half) of the deceased spouse's property. The surviving spouse can take that share instead of accepting whatever the surviving spouse inherited through the deceased spouse's will. If the surviving spouse decides to take the statutory share, it's called "taking against the will." *See* Dower and curtesy.

Tax basis. *See* Basis.

Taxable estate. The portion of an estate that is subject to federal or state taxes.

Tenancy by the entirety. A form of property ownership available in many states. It is similar to joint tenancy, but is allowed only for property owned by a married couple (or, in some states, same-sex couples who have registered with the state).

Tenancy in common. A way for co-owners to hold title to property that allows them maximum freedom to dispose of their interests by sale, gift, or will. At a co-owner's death, that person's share goes to beneficiaries named in a will or trust or to the legal heirs, not to the other co-owners. *Compare* Joint tenancy.

Testamentary trust. A trust created by a will.

Testate. Someone who dies leaving a valid will or other valid property transfer devices dies testate.

Testator. A person who makes a will.

Title. A document that proves ownership of property.

Totten trust. *See* Pay-on-death account.

Transfer-on-death account. An account, usually a financial or investment account, where the owner has named one or more beneficiaries to receive the funds or assets in the account when the owner dies. Similar to a pay-on-death bank account.

Trust. A legal arrangement under which one person or institution (called a "trustee") controls property given by another person (called a "grantor," "settlor," or "trustor") for the benefit of a third person (called a "beneficiary").

Trust corpus or res. Latin for the property transferred to a trust.

Trustee. A person or an institution that manages trust property under the terms of the trust document. With a revocable living trust created from the forms in this book, the creators of the trust (grantors) are the original trustees.

Trustee powers. The provisions in a trust document defining what the trustee may and may not do.

Uniform Transfers to Minors Act (UTMA). A statute, adopted by most states, that provides a method for transferring property to minors and arranging for an adult to manage it until the child is older. *See* Custodian.

Will. A legal document in which a person directs what is to be done with the property covered by that person's will after the will writer's death.

How to Use the Downloadable Forms on the Nolo Website

You can access this book's fillable forms at **www.nolo.com/back-of-book/LITR.html** These downloadable forms are in Rich Text Format (RTF). You can open, edit, save, and print these RTFs using most word processing programs, such as Microsoft *Word*, Windows *WordPad*, and recent versions of *WordPerfect*.

Editing RTFs

Every word processing program uses different commands to open, format, save, and print documents, so refer to your software's help documents for help using your program. Nolo cannot provide technical support for questions about how to use your computer or your software.

> **CAUTION**
>
> **In accordance with U.S. copyright laws, the forms provided by this book are for your personal use only.**

List of Forms Available on the Nolo Website

To download any of the files listed on the following pages, go to:

www.nolo.com/back-of-book/LITR.html

Form Title	File Name
Form 1: Living Trust for One Person	Form01.rtf
Form 2: Shared Living Trust	Form02.rtf
Form 3: Witness Statement for a Florida Living Trust	Form03.rtf
Form 4: Assignment of Property to a Trust for One Person	Form04.rtf
Form 5: Assignment of Shared Property to a Trust for a Couple	Form05.rtf
Form 6: Amendment to Living Trust for One Person	Form06.rtf
Form 7: Amendment to Shared Living Trust	Form07.rtf
Form 8: Revocation of Living Trust	Form08.rtf
Form 9: Basic Will for One Person	Form09.rtf
Form 10: Basic Will for a Member of a Couple	Form10.rtf
Property Worksheet	Property.rtf
Beneficiary Worksheet 1: Individual Living Trust	Beneficiary1.rtf
Beneficiary Worksheet 2: Shared Living Trust	Beneficiary2.rtf

Forms

Form 1: Living Trust for One Person

Form 2: Shared Living Trust

Form 3: Witness Statement for a Florida Living Trust

Form 4: Assignment of Property to a Trust for One Person

Form 5: Assignment of Shared Property to a Trust for a Couple

Form 6: Amendment to Living Trust for One Person

Form 7: Amendment to Shared Living Trust

Form 8: Revocation of Living Trust

Form 9. Basic Will for One Person

Form 10: Basic Will for a Member of a Couple

Property Worksheet

Beneficiary Worksheet 1: Individual Living Trust

Beneficiary Worksheet 2: Shared Living Trust

Reminder

The circled numbers on the trust forms (**1** , **4** , **7** , etc.) refer to the specific steps described in Chapter 9. These steps explain what information you need to write on the blank lines. Thus the circled **2** refers you to Step 2, "Decide How Many Property Schedules Your Trust Needs." Each step also explains how you can make appropriate revisions for that trust section. If you have any trouble completing a trust form or are puzzled by these numbers, please reread the "Step-by-Step Instructions" in Chapter 9.

Form 1: Living Trust for One Person

The ① _____ Living Trust

your name (or name of trust, if different)

Declaration of Trust

I.   Trust Name

This trust shall be known as The ① _____ Living Trust.

your name (or name of trust, if different)

II.   Trust Property

(A) Property Placed in Trust

① _____ , called the grantor or trustee, declares

your name

that _____ has set aside and holds in The ① _____

he/she   your name (or name of trust, if different)

Living Trust all _____ interest in that property described in the attached Schedule A. ②

his/her

The trust property shall be used for the benefit of the trust beneficiaries and shall be administered

and distributed by the trustee in accordance with this Declaration of Trust.

(B) Additional or After-Acquired Property

The grantor may add property to the trust at any time.

III.   Reserved Powers of Grantor

(A) Amendment or Revocation

The grantor reserves the power to amend or revoke this trust at any time during _____ lifetime, without

his/her

notifying any beneficiary.

(B) Rights to Trust Property

Until the death of the grantor, all rights to all income, profits, and control of the trust property shall be retained by

the grantor.

(C) Homestead Rights

If the grantor's principal residence is held in this trust, grantor has the right to possess and occupy it for life, rent-free

and without charge, except for taxes, insurance, maintenance, and related costs and expenses. This right is intended to give grantor a beneficial interest in the property and to ensure that grantor does not lose eligibility for a state homestead tax exemption for which grantor otherwise qualifies.

(D) Incapacity of Grantor

If the grantor becomes physically or mentally incapacitated and is no longer able to manage this trust, the person or persons named as successor trustee shall serve as trustee. The determination of the grantor's capacity to manage this trust shall be made by those of the persons listed below who are reasonably available when the successor trustee (or any of them, if two or more are named to serve together) requests their opinion. If a majority of these persons state, in writing, that in their opinion the grantor is no longer reasonably capable of serving as trustee, the successor trustee shall serve as trustee.

5
_____
(names(s) of person(s) to determine incapacity)

The successor trustee shall pay trust income at least annually to, or for the benefit of, the grantor and may also spend any amount of trust principal necessary in the trustee's discretion for the needs of the grantor, until the grantor is no longer incapacitated or until the grantor's death.

(E) Grantor's Death

After the death of the grantor, this trust becomes irrevocable. It may not be altered or amended in any respect, and may not be terminated except through distributions permitted by this Declaration of Trust.

IV. Trustees

(A) Original Trustee

The trustee of The **1** _____
                              your name (or name of trust, if different)

Living Trust and all children's trusts created under this Declaration of Trust shall be **1** _____
                                                                                             your name (or name of trust, if different)

_____ .

(B) Successor Trustee

Upon the death of the trustee, or _____ incapacity, the successor trustee shall be
                                              his/her

6
_____ . If _____
                       name(s) of successor trustee(s)   he/she/all of them

_____ unable to serve or continue serving as successor trustee, the successor trustee shall be
         is/are

6
_____ .
                  name(s) of alternate successor trustee(s)

[If you named more than one successor trustee, include ONE of the following two paragraphs here:]

Any of the successor trustees has full and independent authority to act for and represent the trust.

[or]

All of the successor trustees must consent, in writing, to any transaction involving the trust or trust property.

(C) Trustee's Responsibility

The trustee in office shall serve as trustee of all trusts created under this Declaration of Trust, including any child's trust.

(D) Resignation of Trustee

Any trustee in office may resign at any time by signing a notice of resignation. The resignation must be delivered to the person or institution who is either named in this Declaration of Trust or appointed by the trustee under Section IV, Paragraph (E), to next serve as trustee.

(E) Power to Appoint Successor Trustee

If all the successor trustees named in this Declaration of Trust cease to, or are unable to, serve as trustee, any trustee may appoint an additional successor trustee or trustees to serve in the order nominated. The appointment must be made in writing, signed by the trustee, and notarized.

(F) Terminology

In this Declaration of Trust, the term "trustee" includes any successor trustee or successor trustees.

(G) Bond Waived

No bond shall be required of any trustee.

(H) Compensation

No trustee shall receive any compensation for serving as trustee, except that a trustee shall be entitled to reasonable compensation, as determined by the trustee, for serving as a trustee of a child's trust created by this Declaration of Trust, or for serving as trustee because the grantor has become incapacitated.

(I) Liability of Trustee

With respect to the exercise or nonexercise of discretionary powers granted by this Declaration of Trust, the trustee shall not be liable for actions taken in good faith.

V. Beneficiaries

Upon the death of the grantor, the property listed on Schedule A shall be distributed to the beneficiaries named in this section.

(A) Primary and Alternate Beneficiaries

1. **7** _____ shall be given
beneficiary

_____ .
property identified

If _____ does not survive the grantor,
beneficiary

that property shall be given to _____ .
alternate beneficiary

2. **7** _____ shall be given
beneficiary

_____ .
property identified

If _____ does not survive the grantor,
beneficiary

that property shall be given to _____ .
alternate beneficiary

3. **7** _____ shall be given
beneficiary

_____ .
property identified

If _____ does not survive the grantor,
beneficiary

that property shall be given to _____ .
alternate beneficiary

4. **7** _____ shall be given
beneficiary

_____ .
property identified

If _____ does not survive the grantor,
beneficiary

that property shall be given to _____
alternate beneficiary

5. **7** _____ shall be given
beneficiary

_____ .
property identified

If _____ does not survive the grantor,
beneficiary

that property shall be given to _____.

alternate beneficiary

(B) Residuary Beneficiary

The residuary beneficiary of the trust shall be **8** _____,

residuary beneficiary

who shall be given all trust property not specifically and validly disposed of by Section V, Paragraph (A).

If _____ does not survive the grantor,

residuary beneficiary

that property shall be given to **8** _____.

alternate residuary beneficiary

VI. Distribution of Trust Property Upon Death of Grantor

Upon the death of the grantor, the trustee shall distribute the trust property outright to the beneficiaries named in

Section V, Paragraphs (A) and (B), subject to any provision in this Declaration of Trust that creates child's trusts or creates

custodianships under the Uniform Transfers to Minors Act.

VII. Trustee's Powers and Duties

(A) Powers Under State Law

To carry out the provisions of The **1** _____ _____

your name (or name of trust, if different)

_____ Living Trust, and any children's trusts created under this Declaration of Trust, the trustee shall

have all authority and powers allowed or conferred on a trustee under _____

your state

law, subject to the trustee's fiduciary duty to the grantor and the beneficiaries.

(B) Specified Powers

The trustee's powers include, but are not limited to:

1. The power to sell trust property, and to borrow money and to encumber that property, specifically including trust

real estate, by mortgage, deed of trust, or other method.

2. The power to manage trust real estate as if the trustee were the absolute owner of it, including the power to lease

(even if the lease term may extend beyond the period of any trust) or grant options to lease the property, to make repairs

or alterations, and to insure against loss.

3. The power to sell or grant options for the sale or exchange of any trust property, including stocks, bonds,

debentures, and any other form of security or security account, at public or private sale for cash or on credit.

4. The power to invest trust property in property of any kind, including but not limited to bonds, debentures, notes, mortgages, stocks, stock options, stock futures, and buying on margin.

5. The power to receive additional property from any source and add to any trust created by this Declaration of Trust.

6. The power to employ and pay reasonable fees to accountants, lawyers, or investment experts for information or advice relating to the trust.

7. The power to deposit and hold trust funds in both interest-bearing and non-interest-bearing accounts.

8. The power to deposit funds in financial accounts insured or uninsured by the FDIC.

9. The power to enter into electronic fund transfer or safe deposit arrangements with financial institutions.

10. The power to continue any business of the grantor.

11. The power to institute or defend legal actions concerning the trust or grantor's affairs.

12. The power to execute any document necessary to administer any child's trust created in this Declaration of Trust.

13. The power to diversify investments, including authority to decide that some or all of the trust property need not produce income.

(C) Payment by Trustee of the Grantor's Debts and Taxes

The grantor's debts and death taxes shall be paid by the trustee. The trustee shall pay these from

the following trust property: **9** _____

_____

_____ .

If the property specified above is insufficient to pay all the grantor's debts and death taxes, the trustee shall determine how such debts and death taxes shall be paid from trust property.

VIII. General Administrative Provisions

(A) Controlling Law

The validity of The **1** _____

your name (or name of trust, if different)

Living Trust shall be governed by the laws of _____ .

your state

(B) Severability

If any provision of this Declaration of Trust is ruled unenforceable, the remaining provisions shall nevertheless remain in effect.

(C) Amendments

The term "Declaration of Trust" includes any provisions added by amendments.

(D) Accountings

No accountings or reports shall be required of the trustee.

IX. Child(ren)'s Trust(s)

All trust property left to any of the minor or young adult beneficiaries listed below in Section IX, Paragraph (A), shall

be retained in trust for each such beneficiary in a separate trust of this

1

_____ Living Trust.

your name (or name of trust, if different)

Each trust may be identified and referred to by adding the name of that trust's beneficiary to the name of

this trust. The following terms apply to each child's trust:

(A) Trust Beneficiaries and Age Limits

A child's trust shall end when the beneficiary of that trust, listed below, becomes 35, except as otherwise specified in

this section:

10A Trust for   Shall end at age

_____   _____

_____   _____

_____   _____

_____   _____

_____   _____

(B) Powers and Duties of a Child's Trust Trustee

1. Until a child's trust ends, the trustee may distribute to or use for the benefit of the beneficiary as much of the net

income or principal of the child's trust as the trustee deems necessary for the beneficiary's health, support, maintenance, or

education. Education includes, but is not limited to, college, graduate, professional, and vocational studies, and reasonably

related living expenses.

2. In deciding whether to make a distribution to the beneficiary, the trustee may take into account the beneficiary's

other income, resources, and sources of support.

3. Any child's trust income that is not distributed to a beneficiary by the trustee shall be accumulated and added to the principal of the trust for that beneficiary.

4. The trustee of a child's trust is not required to make any accounting or report to the trust beneficiary.

(C) Assignment of Interest of Beneficiary Prohibited

The interests of the beneficiary of a child's trust shall not be transferable by voluntary or involuntary assignment or by operation of law before actual receipt by the beneficiary. These interests shall be free from the claims of creditors and from attachments, execution, bankruptcy, or other legal process to the fullest extent permitted by law.

(D) Compensation of Trustee

Any trustee of a child's trust created under this Declaration of Trust shall be entitled to reasonable compensation out of the trust assets for ordinary and extraordinary services, and for all services in connection with the termination of any trust.

(E) Termination of a Child's Trust

A child's trust shall end when any of the following events occur:

1. The beneficiary reaches the age specified in Section IX, Paragraph (A). If the trust ends for this reason, the remaining principal and accumulated income of the trust shall be given outright to the beneficiary.

2. The beneficiary dies. If the trust ends for this reason, the trust property shall pass to the beneficiary's heirs.

3. The trustee distributes all trust property under the provisions of this Declaration of Trust.

X. Custodianships Under the Uniform Transfers to Minors Act

1. All property **10B** _____ becomes entitled to

beneficiary

under this trust document shall be given to _____

custodian's name

as custodian for _____

beneficiary

under the _____ Uniform Transfers to Minors Act, until

state

_____

beneficiary

reaches age _____ .

2. All property **10B** _____ becomes entitled to
beneficiary

under this trust document shall be given to _____
custodian's name

as custodian for _____
beneficiary

under the _____ Uniform Transfers to Minors Act, until
state

_____
beneficiary

reaches age _____ .
beneficiary

3. All property **10B** _____ becomes entitled to
beneficiary

under this trust document shall be given to _____
custodian's name

as custodian for _____
beneficiary

under the _____ Uniform Transfers to Minors Act, until
state

_____
beneficiary

reaches age _____ .

Certification by Grantor

I certify that I have read this Declaration of Trust and that it correctly states the terms and conditions under which the

trust property is to be held, managed, and disposed of by the trustee, and I approve the Declaration of Trust.

Dated: _____

_____

Grantor and Trustee

[Attached: Notary's Acknowledgment]

All the grantor's interest in the following property:

Form 2: Shared Living Trust

The **1** _____ Living Trust

your names (or name of trust, if different)

Declaration of Trust

I.   Trust Name

This trust shall be known as The **1** _____ Living Trust.

your names (or name of trust, if different)

II.   Trust Property

(A) Property Placed in Trust

1 _____ , called the grantors

your names

or trustees, declare that they have set aside and hold in The **1** _____

your names (or name of trust, if different)

_____ Living Trust all their interest in the property

described in the attached Schedules A, B, and C. **2**

The trust property shall be used for the benefit of the trust beneficiaries, and shall be administered and distributed by

the trustees in accordance with this Declaration of Trust.

(B) Rights Retained by Grantors

As long as both grantors are alive, both grantors retain all rights to all income, profits, and control of the trust property

listed on Schedule A of The **1** _____

your names (or name of trust, if different)

_____ Living Trust.

(1) As long as _____ is alive, she shall retain all

wife's name

rights to all income, profits, and control of her separate property listed on Schedule B of The _____

1 _____ Living Trust.

your names (or name of trust, if different)

(2) As long as _____ is alive, he shall retain all

husband's name

rights to all income, profits, and control of his separate property listed on Schedule C of The _____

1 _____ Living Trust.

your names (or name of trust, if different)

(C) Additional or After-Acquired Property

Either grantor, or both, may add property to the trust at any time.

(D) Character of Property Placed in Trust

While both grantors are alive, property transferred to this trust shall retain its original character. If the trust is revoked, the trustee shall distribute the trust property to the grantors based on the same ownership rights they had before the property was transferred to the trust, as specified below.

1. Shared Property

All trust property listed on Schedule A was shared property:

4 _____

identify the character of shared property listed in Schedule A

_____

_____

_____ .

2. Separate Property

The trust property listed on Schedule B shall retain its character as the separate property of _____

_____ . The trust property listed on Schedule C

wife's name

shall retain its character as the separate property of _____ .

husband's name

[Make appropriate deletions if wife and/or husband has no separate property.]

(E) Revocation

As long as both grantors live, either grantor may revoke The **1** _____

your names (or name of trust, if different)

_____ Living Trust at any time by writing given to the

other grantor. No beneficiary need be given any notice of revocation. After the death of a grantor, the surviving grantor can

revoke his or her continuing revocable living trust, Trust 2, as defined in Section V, Paragraph (B).

(F) Amendment

As long as both grantors live, The **1** _____

your names (or name of trust, if different)

Living Trust may be altered, amended, or modified only by a writing signed by both grantors. After the death of a grantor, the surviving grantor can amend his or her continuing living trust, Trust 2, as defined in Section V, Paragraph (B).

(G) Homestead Rights

If the grantors' principal residence is held in this trust, grantors have the right to possess and occupy it for life, rent-free and without charge, except for taxes, insurance, maintenance, and related costs and expenses. This right is intended to give grantors a beneficial interest in the property and to ensure that the grantors, or either of them, do not lose eligibility for a state homestead tax exemption for which either grantor otherwise qualifies.

III. Trustees

(A) Original Trustees

The trustees of The **1** _____
your names (or name of trust, if different)

Living Trust and any other trust or child's trusts created under this Declaration of Trust shall be _____

1 _____ .
your names

Either trustee may act for, and represent, the trust in any transaction.

(B) Trustee on Death or Incapacity of Original Trustee

Upon the death or incapacity of _____ or
wife's name

_____ , the other grantor shall
husband's name

serve as sole trustee of this trust and any child's trust created under this Declaration of Trust.

(C) Trustee's Responsibility

The trustee in office shall serve as trustee of all trusts created under this Declaration of Trust, including any child's trust.

(D) Terminology

In this Declaration of Trust, the term "trustee" includes any successor trustee or trustees. The singular "trustee" also includes the plural.

(E) Successor Trustee

Upon the death or incapacity of the surviving grantor, or the incapacity of both grantors, the successor trustee shall be

6 _____ . If _____
name(s) of successor trustee(s) he/she/all of them

_____ unable to serve or to continue serving as successor trustee, the next successor trustee shall be
is/are

6 _____ .
name(s) of alternate successor trustee(s)

[If you named more than one successor trustee, include ONE of the following two paragraphs here:]

Any of the successor trustees has full and independent authority to act for and represent the trust.

[or]

All of the successor trustees must consent, in writing, to any transaction involving the trust or trust property.

(F) Resignation of Trustee

Any trustee in office may resign at any time by signing a notice of resignation. The resignation must be delivered to the person or institution who is either named in this Declaration of Trust, or appointed by the trustee under Section III, Paragraph (G), to next serve as trustee.

(G) Power to Appoint Successor Trustee

If all the successor trustees named in this Declaration of Trust cease to, or are unable to, serve as trustee, any trustee may appoint an additional successor trustee or trustees to serve in the order nominated. The appointment must be made in writing, signed by the trustee, and notarized.

(H) Bond Waived

No bond shall be required of any trustee.

(I) Compensation

No trustee shall receive any compensation for serving as trustee, except that a trustee shall be entitled to reasonable compensation, as determined by the trustee, for serving as a trustee of a child's trust created by this Declaration of Trust, or for serving as trustee because the grantors or a grantor becomes incapacitated.

(J) Liability of Trustee

With respect to the exercise or nonexercise of discretionary powers granted by this Declaration of Trust, the trustee shall not be liable for actions taken in good faith.

IV. Beneficiaries

(A) Husband's Primary and Alternate Beneficiaries

Upon the death of _____
                                                    husband's name

trust property owned by _____
                                                    husband's name

as his share of the trust property listed on Schedule A and any separate property listed on Schedule C shall be distributed as specified to the beneficiaries named in this section.

1. Husband's Specific Beneficiaries

a. **7** _____ shall be given

beneficiary

_____ .

property identified

If _____

beneficiary

does not survive _____ ,

husband's name

that property shall be given to _____ .

alternate beneficiary

b. **7** _____ shall be given

beneficiary

_____ .

property identified

If _____

beneficiary

does not survive _____ ,

husband's name

that property shall be given to _____ .

alternate beneficiary

c. **7** _____ shall be given

beneficiary

_____ .

property identified

If _____

beneficiary

does not survive _____ ,

husband's name

that property shall be given to _____ .

alternate beneficiary

d. **7** _____ shall be given

beneficiary

_____ .

property identified

If _____

beneficiary

does not survive _____ ,

husband's name

that property shall be given to _____ .

alternate beneficiary

e. **7** _____ shall be given

beneficiary

_____ .

property identified

If _____
                                    beneficiary

does not survive _____,
                                    husband's name

that property shall be given to _____.
                                                    alternate beneficiary

2. Husband's Residuary Beneficiary

The residuary beneficiary of any trust property owned by _____
                                                                            husband's name

_____ as his share of the trust property listed on Schedule A or any separate property

listed on Schedule C, and not specifically and validly disposed of by Section IV, Paragraph (A)1, shall be

8 _____.
                                    residuary beneficiary

If _____ does not
                                    residuary beneficiary

survive _____
                                    husband's name

that property shall be given to **8** _____.
                                                    alternate residuary beneficiary

(B) Wife's Primary and Alternate Beneficiaries

Upon the death of _____,
                                        wife's name

trust property owned by _____,
                                        wife's name

as her share of the trust property listed on Schedule A and any separate property listed on Schedule B,

shall be distributed as specified to the beneficiaries named in this section.

1. Wife's Specific Beneficiaries

a. **7** _____ shall be given
                                    beneficiary

_____.
                        property identified

If _____
                                    beneficiary

does not survive _____,
                                    wife's name

that property shall be given to _____.
                                                    alternate beneficiary

b. **7** _____ shall be given
                                    beneficiary

_____.
                        property identified

If _____
                                    beneficiary

does not survive _____ ,
                                    wife's name

that property shall be given to _____ .
                                    alternate beneficiary

   c. **7** _____ shall be given
                                    beneficiary

_____ .
                                    property identified

If _____
                                    beneficiary

does not survive _____ ,
                                    wife's name

that property shall be given to _____ .
                                    alternate beneficiary

   d. **7** _____ shall be given
                                    beneficiary

_____ .
                                    property identified

If _____
                                    beneficiary

does not survive _____ ,
                                    wife's name

that property shall be given to _____ .
                                    alternate beneficiary

   e. **7** _____ shall be given
                                    beneficiary

_____ .
                                    property identified

If _____
                                    beneficiary

does not survive _____ ,
                                    wife's name

that property shall be given to _____ .
                                    alternate beneficiary

2. Wife's Residuary Beneficiary

The residuary beneficiary of any trust property owned by _____
                                                            wife's name

_____ as her share of the trust property listed on Schedule A or any separate property

listed on Schedule B, and not specifically and validly disposed of by Section IV, Paragraph (B)1, shall be

8 _____ .
                                    residuary beneficiary

If _____ does not
　　　　　　　　residuary beneficiary

survive _____
　　　　　　　　　　wife's name

that property shall be given to **8** _____ .
　　　　　　　　　　　alternate residuary beneficiary

V. Administration of Trust Property

(A) Terminology

The first grantor to die shall be called the "deceased grantor." The living grantor shall be called the "surviving grantor."

(B) Division and Distribution of Trust Property on Death of Grantor

1. Upon the death of the deceased grantor, the trustee shall divide the property of The **1** _____

_____ Living Trust listed on Schedules A, B, and C
　　　　　　　your names (or name of trust, if different)

into two separate trusts, Trust 1 and Trust 2. The trustee shall serve as trustee of Trust 1 and Trust 2.

2. Trust 1 shall contain all the property of The **1** _____
　　　　　　　　　　　　　　　　　　　　　　your names (or name of trust, if different)

_____ Living Trust owned by the deceased grantor at the time it was transferred to the trustee of this living trust,

plus shared ownership property with a total value equal to one-half of the total value at the time of the deceased grantor's

death of shared ownership property, plus accumulated income, appreciation in value, and the like, attributable to the

ownership interest of the deceased grantor, and his or her share of all property acquired in the trust's name or the trustees'

names. Trust 1 becomes irrevocable at the death of the deceased grantor. The trustee shall distribute the property in Trust

1 to the beneficiaries named by the deceased grantor in Section IV of this Declaration of Trust, subject to any provision of this

Declaration of Trust that creates children's trusts or creates custodianships under the Uniform Transfers to Minors Act.

3. Trust 2 shall contain all the property of The **1** _____
　　　　　　　　　　　　　　　　　　　　　　your names (or name of trust, if different)

_____ Living Trust owned by the surviving grantor at the time it was transferred to the

trustee of this living trust, plus shared ownership property with a total value equal to one-half of the total value at the time

of the deceased grantor's death of shared ownership property, plus accumulated income, appreciation in value, and the

like, attributable to the ownership interest of the surviving grantor, his or her share of all property acquired in the trust's

name or the trustee's names, and any trust property left by the deceased grantor to the surviving grantor.

4. The trustee shall have exclusive authority to determine the paperwork and record keeping necessary to establish

Trust 1 and Trust 2.

(C) Property Left to the Surviving Grantor

Any trust property left by the deceased grantor to the surviving grantor shall remain in the surviving grantor's revocable trust, Trust 2, without necessity of a formal transfer to that trust.

(D) Administration of Trust 2

1. Rights Retained by Surviving Grantor

Until the death of the surviving grantor, all rights to all income, profits, and control of property in Trust 2 shall be retained by or distributed to the surviving grantor.

2. Revocation

The surviving grantor may amend or revoke Trust 2 at any time during his or her lifetime, without notifying any beneficiary.

3. Distribution of Property in Trust 2

Upon the death of the surviving grantor, Trust 2 becomes irrevocable, and the property in Trust 2 shall be distributed to the beneficiaries listed in Section IV, subject to any provision of this Declaration of Trust that creates child's trusts or creates custodianships under the Uniform Transfers to Minors Act.

VI. Incapacity

(A) Incapacity of Both Grantors

If both grantors become physically or mentally incapacitated and are no longer able to manage this trust, the person or persons named as successor trustee shall serve as trustee. The determination of the grantors' capacity to manage this trust shall be made by those of the persons listed below who are reasonably available when the successor trustee (or any of them, if two or more are named to serve together) requests their opinion. If a majority of these persons state, in writing, that in their opinion the grantors are no longer reasonably capable of serving as trustee, the successor trustee shall serve as trustee.

_____

name(s) of person(s) to determine incapacity

The successor trustee shall pay trust income at least annually to, or for the benefit of, the grantors and may also spend any amount of trust income or trust principal necessary, in the successor trustee's discretion, for the needs of the grantors, until the grantors, or either of them, are again able to manage their own affairs, or until their deaths.

5 **(B) Incapacity of Surviving Grantor**

If, after the death of the deceased grantor, the surviving grantor becomes physically or mentally incapacitated and is no longer able to manage Trust 2, the person or persons named as successor trustee shall serve as trustee. The determination of the grantor's capacity to manage the trust shall be made by those of the persons listed below who are reasonably available when the successor trustee (or any of them, if two or more are named to serve together) requests their opinion. If a majority of these persons state, in writing, that in their opinion the grantor is no longer reasonably capable of serving as trustee, the successor trustee shall serve as trustee.

_____
name(s) of person(s) to determine incapacity

The successor trustee shall pay trust income at least annually to, or for the benefit of, the surviving grantor and may also spend any amount of the trust principal necessary in the successor trustee's discretion, for the needs of the surviving grantor, until the surviving grantor is again able to manage his or her own affairs, or until his or her death.

VII. Simultaneous Death

If both grantors should die simultaneously, or under such circumstances as to render it difficult or impossible to determine who predeceased the other, for purposes of this living trust, it shall be conclusively presumed that both died at the same moment, and neither shall be presumed to have survived the other. The trustee shall distribute the trust property to the named beneficiaries.

VIII. Trustee's Powers and Duties

(A) Powers Under State Law

To carry out the provisions of this Declaration of Trust, and to manage the trust property of The

1 _____ Living Trust,
your name(s) (or name of trust, if different)

Trust 1, Trust 2, and any child's trust created under this Declaration of Trust, the trustee shall have all authority and power

allowed or conferred under _____ law, subject to the rights
your state

retained by each grantor in Section II (B) and to the trustee's fiduciary duty to the grantors and the beneficiaries.

(B) Specified Powers

The trustee's powers include, but are not limited to:

1. The power to sell trust property, and to borrow money and to encumber property, specifically including trust real estate, by mortgage, deed of trust, or other method.

2. The power to manage trust real estate as if the trustee were the absolute owner of it, including the power to lease (even if the lease term may extend beyond the period of any trust) or grant options to lease the property, to make repairs or alterations, and to insure against loss.

3. The power to sell or grant options for the sale or exchange of any trust property, including stocks, bonds, debentures, and any other form of security or security account, at public or private sale for cash or on credit.

4. The power to invest trust property in property of any kind, including but not limited to bonds, debentures, notes, mortgages, stocks, stock options, stock futures, and buying on margin.

5. The power to receive additional property from any source and add to any trust created by this Declaration of Trust.

6. The power to employ and pay reasonable fees to accountants, lawyers, or investment experts for information or advice relating to the trust.

7. The power to deposit and hold trust funds in both interest-bearing and non-interest-bearing accounts.

8. The power to deposit funds in financial accounts insured or uninsured by the FDIC.

9. The power to enter into electronic fund transfer or safe deposit arrangements with financial institutions.

10. The power to continue any business of either grantor.

11. The power to institute or defend legal actions concerning the trust or grantors' affairs.

12. The power to execute any document necessary to administer any trust created in this Declaration of Trust.

13. The power to diversify investments, including authority to decide that some or all of the trust property need not produce income.

(C) Payment by the Trustee of the Grantors' Debts and Taxes

1. Wife's Debts and Taxes

_____'s debts and
wife's name

death taxes shall be paid by the trustee. The trustee shall pay these from the following trust property:

9 _____ .

2. Husband's Debts and Taxes

_____'s debts and
husband's name

death taxes shall be paid by the trustee. The trustee shall pay these from the following trust property:

9 _____.

3. If Specified Property Insufficient

If the property specified above is insufficient to pay all a grantor's debts and death taxes, the trustee shall determine

how such debts and death taxes shall be paid from that grantor's trust property.

IX. General Administrative Provisions

(A) Controlling Law

The validity of The **1** _____ Living
your names (or name of trust, if different)

Trust and construction of its provisions shall be governed by the laws of _____.
your state

(B) Severability

If any provision of this Declaration of Trust is ruled unenforceable, the remaining provisions shall nevertheless remain

in effect.

(C) Amendments

The term "Declaration of Trust" includes any provisions added by valid amendment.

(D) Accountings

No accountings or reports shall be required of the trustee.

X. Child(ren)'s Trust(s)

All trust property left to any of the minor or young adult beneficiaries listed below in Section X, Paragraph (A), shall be

retained in trust for each such beneficiary in a separate trust of this **1** _____

_____ Living Trust. Each trust may
your names (or name of trust, if different)

be identified and referred to by adding the name of that trust's beneficiary to the name of this trust. The

following terms apply to each child's trust:

(A) Trust Beneficiaries and Age Limits

A trust shall end when the beneficiary of that trust, listed below, becomes 35, except as otherwise specified in this section:

10A

Trust for   Shall end at age

_____   _____

_____   _____

_____   _____

_____   _____

_____   _____

(B) Powers and Duties of a Child's Trust Trustee

1. Until a child's trust ends, the trustee may distribute to or use for the benefit of the beneficiary as much of the net income or principal of the child's trust as the trustee deems necessary for the beneficiary's health, support, maintenance, or education. Education includes, but is not limited to, college, graduate, professional, and vocational studies, and reasonably related living expenses.

2. In deciding whether to make a distribution to the beneficiary, the trustee may take into account the beneficiary's other income, resources, and sources of support.

3. Any child's trust income that is not distributed to a beneficiary by the trustee shall be accumulated and added to the principal of the trust for that beneficiary.

4. The trustee of a child's trust is not required to make any accounting or report to the trust beneficiary.

(C) Assignment of Interest of Beneficiary Prohibited

The interests of the beneficiary of a child's trust shall not be transferable by voluntary or involuntary assignment or by operation of law before actual receipt by the beneficiary. These interests shall be free from the claims of creditors and from attachments, execution, bankruptcy, or other legal process to the fullest extent permitted by law.

(D) Compensation of Trustee

Any trustee of a child's trust created under this Declaration of Trust shall be entitled to reasonable compensation without court approval out of the trust assets for ordinary and extraordinary services, and for all services in connection with the termination of any trust.

(E) Termination of a Child's Trust

A child's trust shall end when any of the following events occurs:

1. The beneficiary reaches the age specified in Section X, Paragraph (A). If the trust ends for this reason, the remaining principal and accumulated income of the trust shall be given outright to the beneficiary.

2. The beneficiary dies. If the trust ends for this reason, the trust property shall pass to the beneficiary's heirs.

3. The trustee distributes all trust property under the provisions of this Declaration of Trust.

XI. Custodianships Under the Uniform Transfers to Minors Act

1. All property **10B** _____
                                                    beneficiary

becomes entitled to under this trust document shall be given to _____
                                                                        custodian's name

_____ as custodian for _____
                                                                beneficiary

under the _____ Uniform Transfers to Minors Act, until
                        state

_____ reaches age _____ .
                        beneficiary

2. All property **10B** _____
                                                    beneficiary

becomes entitled to under this trust document shall be given to _____
                                                                        custodian's name

_____ as custodian for _____
                                                                beneficiary

under the _____ Uniform Transfers to Minors Act, until
                        state

_____ reaches age _____ .
                        beneficiary

3. All property **10B** _____
                                                    beneficiary

becomes entitled to under this trust document shall be given to _____
                                                                        custodian's name

_____ as custodian for _____
                                                                beneficiary

under the _____ Uniform Transfers to Minors Act, until
                        state

_____ reaches age _____ .
                        beneficiary

Certification by Grantors

We certify that we have read this Declaration of Trust and that it correctly states the terms and conditions under which the trust property is to be held, managed, and disposed of by the trustees and we approve the Declaration of Trust.

Dated: _____

_____

Grantor and Trustee

_____

Grantor and Trustee

[Attached: Notary's Acknowledgment]

Schedule A [3]
Shared Property Placed in Trust

Schedule B
Wife's Separate Property Placed in Trust

All Wife's interest in the following property:

Schedule C
Husband's Separate Property Placed in Trust

All Husband's interest in the following property:

Form 3: Witness Statement for a Florida Living Trust

Statement of Witness

On this _____ day of _____, 20____ , _____

your name(s)

_____ declared to me, the undersigned, that

this Declaration of Trust was _____ living trust and requested me to act as witness to it.

his/her/their

_____ then signed this living trust in my presence. I now

your name(s)

at _____ request, in _____ presence, subscribe my name as witness and declare I understand this

his/her/their his/her/their

to be _____ living trust.

his/her/their

I declare under penalty of perjury that the foregoing is true and correct, this _____ day of

_____, 20_____ .

_____

witness's signature

_____

witness's typed name

_____ , _____ , _____

city county state

Form 4: Assignment of Property to a Trust for One Person

Assignment of Property

I, _____ , as grantor,
your name

hereby assign and transfer all my rights, title, and interest in the following property _____

_____

_____

to _____ , as trustee of the
your name

_____ Living Trust,
your name (or name of trust, if different)

dated _____ , 20_____ .

Executed at _____ , _____ , on
city   state

_____ , 20_____ .
date

_____

Grantor and Trustee

Form 5: Assignment of Shared Property to a Trust for a Couple

Assignment of Property

We, _____ ,
your names

as grantors, hereby assign and transfer all our rights, title, and interest in the following property

_____

_____

_____ to

_____ , as trustees of
your names

The _____
your names (or name of trust, if different)

Living Trust, dated _____ , 20 _____ .

Executed at _____ , _____ , on
city   state

_____ , 20 _____ .
date

_____

Grantor and Trustee

_____

Grantor and Trustee

Form 6: Amendment to Living Trust for One Person

Amendment to Living Trust

This Amendment to The **1** _____

your name (or name of trust, if different)

Living Trust dated _____, 20_____ , is made this _____ day of

date Declaration of Trust signed

_____ , 20_____ , by _____ ,

your name

the grantor and trustee of the trust. Under the power of amendment reserved to the grantor by Section III,

Paragraph (A), of the trust, the grantor amends the trust as follows:

1. The following is deleted from the Declaration of Trust:

_____

_____

2. The following is added to the Declaration of Trust:

_____

_____

[Repeat as needed]

In all other respects, the Declaration of Trust as executed on _____ ,

20_____ , by the grantor is affirmed.

Executed at _____ , _____ , on

city _state_

_____ , 20_____ .

date

_____

Grantor and Trustee

[Attached: Notary's Acknowledgment]

Form 7: Amendment to Shared Living Trust

Amendment to Living Trust

This Amendment to The ① _____

your names (or name of trust, if different)

Living Trust dated _____ , 20_____ , is made this _____ day of _____ ,

date Declaration of Trust signed

20_____ , by _____ ,

your names

_____ the grantors and trustees of the trust. Under the power of amendment

reserved to the grantors by Section II, Paragraph (F), of the Declaration of Trust, the grantors amend the trust as follows:

1. The following is deleted from the Declaration of Trust:

    _____

    _____

2. The following is added to the Declaration of Trust:

    _____

    _____

[Repeat as needed]

In all other respects, the Declaration of Trust as executed on _____ , 20_____

date

by the grantors is affirmed.

Executed at _____ , _____ , on

city   state

_____ , 20_____ .

date

_____

Grantor and Trustee

_____

Grantor and Trustee

[Attached: Notary's Acknowledgment]

Form 8: Revocation of Living Trust

Revocation of Living Trust

On _____ , 20_____ , _____
your name(s)

_____ created a revocable living trust, called

"The _____
your name(s) (or name of trust, if different)

Living Trust," with _____
your name(s)

_____ as the grantor(s) and trustee(s).

Under the terms of the trust, the grantor(s) reserved to _____ the full power to revoke the
himself/herself/themselves

trust.

According to the terms of the Declaration of Trust, and the laws of the State of _____
your state

_____ the grantor(s) hereby revoke the Declaration of Trust and state that the trust is

completely revoked. All property of The _____
your name(s) (or name of trust, if different)

_____ Living Trust shall be returned to the grantor(s)

and legally owned by _____ as defined in the Declaration of Trust.
him/her/them

Dated: _____

_____

Grantor and Trustee

_____

Grantor and Trustee

[Attached: Notary's Acknowledgment]

Form 9: Basic Will for One Person

Will

of

_____
your name

I, _____ , a resident of
your name

_____ , _____ County, _____ ,
city   county   state

declare that this is my will.

1. I revoke all wills and codicils that I have previously made.

2. I am not married.

3. (A) I am the _____ of the _____ whose _____ _____
mother/father   child/children   name/names   is/are

_____

_____

_____

_____ .

There are _____ living children of my deceased child _____
name

_____ , whose name(s) is/are:

_____

_____

_____

_____ .

(B) If I fail to leave, by this will or otherwise, any property to any of the children listed above, my failure to do so is

intentional.

(C) If at my death any of my children are minors, and a personal guardian is needed, I nominate _____

_____ to be appointed personal guardian
name of personal guardian

of my minor children. If _____ cannot serve as
name of personal guardian

personal guardian, I nominate _____
name of alternate personal guardian

to be appointed personal guardian.

(D) If at my death any of my children are minors, and a property guardian is needed, I appoint _____

_____ as property guardian for my minor children.
name of property guardian

If _____ cannot serve as property guardian, I appoint
name of property guardian

_____ as property guardian.
name of alternate property guardian

(E) I direct that no bond be required of any guardian.

4. (A) I make the following specific gifts:

I leave _____
property described

to _____ , or if
beneficiary's name

_____ fails to survive
beneficiary's name

me, to _____ .
alternate beneficiary's name

I leave _____
property described

to _____ , or if
beneficiary's name

_____ fails to survive
beneficiary's name

me, to _____ .
alternate beneficiary's name

I leave _____
property described

to _____ , or if
beneficiary's name

_____ fails to survive
beneficiary's name

me, to _____ .
alternate beneficiary's name

(B) I leave all my other property subject to this will to _____
_____ residuary beneficiary's name

_____ , or if _____ fails to survive me,
he/she

to _____ .
alternate residuary beneficiary's name

5. (A) I nominate _____
executor's name

to serve as executor of my will. If _____ is unable to serve or continue serving as executor, I nominate
he/she

_____ to serve as executor.
alternate executor's name

(B) No bond shall be required of any executor.

I subscribe my name to this will this _____ day of _____ , 20_____ , at

_____ , _____ , _____
city   county   state

_____
your signature

Witnesses

On the date last written above, _____
your name

declared to us, the undersigned, that this was _____ will, and requested us to act as witnesses to it. _____
his/her   He/She

signed this will in our presence, all of us being present at the same time. We now, at _____ request and in
his/her

_____ presence, and in the presence of each other, have signed this will as witnesses.
his/her

We declare under penalty of perjury that the foregoing is true and correct.

_____   _____
witness signature   witness printed name

_____ , _____ , _____
city   county   state

_____   _____
witness signature   witness printed name

_____ , _____ , _____
city   county   state

_____   _____
witness signature   witness printed name

_____ , _____ , _____
city   county   state

Form 10: Basic Will for a Member of a Couple

Will

of

_____
your name

I, _____ , a resident of
your name

_____ , _____ County, _____ ,
city   county   state

declare that this is my will.

1. I revoke all wills and codicils that I have previously made.

2. I am married to _____ .
name

3. (A) I am the _____ of the _____ whose _____ _____
mother/father   child/children   name/names   is/are

_____

_____

_____

_____ .
child(ren)'s name

There are _____ living children of my deceased child _____ ,
name

_____ whose name(s) is/are:

_____

_____ .
grandchild(ren)'s name

(B) If I fail to leave, by this will or otherwise, any property to any of the children listed above, my failure to do so is

intentional.

(C) If at my death any of my children are minors, and a personal guardian is needed, I nominate _____

_____ to be appointed personal guardian
name of personal guardian

of my minor children. If _____ cannot serve as
name of personal guardian

personal guardian, I nominate _____
name of alternate personal guardian

to be appointed personal guardian.

(D) If at my death any of my children are minors, and a property guardian is needed, I appoint

_____ as property guardian for my minor children.
name of property guardian

If _____ cannot serve as property guardian, I appoint
name of property guardian

_____ as property guardian.
name of alternate property guardian

(E) I direct that no bond be required of any guardian.

4. (A) I make the following specific gifts:

I leave _____
property described

to _____ , or if
beneficiary's name

_____ fails to survive
beneficiary's name

me, to _____ .
alternate beneficiary's name

I leave _____
property described

to _____ , or if
beneficiary's name

_____ fails to survive
beneficiary's name

me, to _____ .
alternate beneficiary's name

I leave _____
property described

to _____ , or if
beneficiary's name

_____ fails to survive
beneficiary's name

me, to _____ .
alternate beneficiary's name

(B) I leave all my other property subject to this will to _____
residuary beneficiary's name

_____ , or if _____ fails to survive me,
he/she

to _____ .
alternate residuary beneficiary's name

5. (A) I nominate _____
executor's name

to serve as executor of my will. If _____ is unable to serve or continue serving as executor, I nominate
he/she

_____ to serve as executor.
alternate executor's name

(B) No bond shall be required of any executor.

6. If my spouse and I should die simultaneously, or under such circumstances as to render it difficult or impossible to determine who predeceased the other, I shall be conclusively presumed to have survived my spouse for purposes of this will.

I subscribe my name to this will this _____ day of _____, 20_____, at

_____, _____, _____
city   county   state

_____
your signature

Witnesses

On the date last written above, _____
your name

declared to us, the undersigned, that this was _____ will, and requested us to act as witnesses to it. _____
his/her   He/She

then signed this will in our presence, all of us being present at the same time. We now, at _____ request and in
his/her

_____ presence, and in the presence of each other, have signed this will as witnesses.
his/her

We declare under penalty of perjury that the foregoing is true and correct.

_____   _____
witness signature   witness printed name

_____, _____, _____
city   county   state

_____   _____
witness signature   witness printed name

_____, _____, _____
city   county   state

_____   _____
witness signature   witness printed name

_____, _____, _____
city   county   state

Property Worksheet

I. Assets

Description of Your Property	Net Value of Your Ownership	Who Owns It	Transfer to Trust?

A. Liquid Assets

1. cash

_____ _____ _____ _____
_____ _____ _____ _____
_____ _____ _____ _____
_____ _____ _____ _____

2. savings accounts

_____ _____ _____ _____
_____ _____ _____ _____
_____ _____ _____ _____

3. checking accounts

_____ _____ _____ _____
_____ _____ _____ _____
_____ _____ _____ _____

4. money market accounts

_____ _____ _____ _____
_____ _____ _____ _____
_____ _____ _____ _____
_____ _____ _____ _____
_____ _____ _____ _____

B. Marketable Securities

1. certificates of deposit

_____ _____ _____ _____
_____ _____ _____ _____
_____ _____ _____ _____
_____ _____ _____ _____
_____ _____ _____ _____

2. treasury bills or notes

_____ _____ _____ _____
_____ _____ _____ _____
_____ _____ _____ _____

Description of Your Property	Net Value of Your Ownership	Who Owns It	Transfer to Trust?

3. government bonds and securities

_____   _____ _____ _____
_____   _____ _____ _____
_____   _____ _____ _____
_____   _____ _____ _____
_____   _____ _____ _____
_____   _____ _____ _____

4. listed stocks and bonds

_____   _____ _____ _____
_____   _____ _____ _____
_____   _____ _____ _____
_____   _____ _____ _____
_____   _____ _____ _____
_____   _____ _____ _____
_____   _____ _____ _____
_____   _____ _____ _____
_____   _____ _____ _____
_____   _____ _____ _____
_____   _____ _____ _____

C. Other Personal Property (all your property except liquid assets, business interests, and real estate)

1. automobiles and other vehicles, including planes, boats, and recreational vehicles

_____   _____ _____ _____
_____   _____ _____ _____
_____   _____ _____ _____
_____   _____ _____ _____

2. household goods

_____   _____ _____ _____
_____   _____ _____ _____
_____   _____ _____ _____
_____   _____ _____ _____
_____   _____ _____ _____
_____   _____ _____ _____
_____   _____ _____ _____
_____   _____ _____ _____

Description of Your Property	Net Value of Your Ownership	Who Owns It	Transfer to Trust?
3. clothing			
4. jewelry and furs			
5. artworks, collectibles, and antiques			
6. tools and equipment			

7. valuable livestock/animals

_____ _____ _____ _____
_____ _____ _____ _____
_____ _____ _____ _____
_____ _____ _____ _____
_____ _____ _____ _____

8. life insurance (proceeds payable on death)

_____ _____ _____ _____
_____ _____ _____ _____
_____ _____ _____ _____
_____ _____ _____ _____
_____ _____ _____ _____

9. retirement accounts, including IRAs, 401(k)s, and profit-sharing plans

_____ _____ _____ _____
_____ _____ _____ _____
_____ _____ _____ _____
_____ _____ _____ _____

10. unlisted (private) stocks and bonds

_____ _____ _____ _____
_____ _____ _____ _____
_____ _____ _____ _____
_____ _____ _____ _____

11. promissory notes (owed to you)

_____ _____ _____ _____
_____ _____ _____ _____
_____ _____ _____ _____

12. precious metals

_____ _____ _____ _____
_____ _____ _____ _____
_____ _____ _____ _____

13. digital assets

_____ _____ _____ _____
_____ _____ _____ _____
_____ _____ _____ _____

14. other valuable personal property

_____ _____ _____ _____
_____ _____ _____ _____
_____ _____ _____ _____

Description of Your Property	Net Value of Your Ownership	Who Owns It	Transfer to Trust?

D. Miscellaneous Receivables

(mortgages, deeds of trust, or promissory notes held by you; any rents due from income property owned by you; and any payments due for professional or personal services, or property sold by you that are not fully paid by the purchaser)

E. Real Estate

1. address

2. address

3. address

4. address

5. address

Description of Your Property	Net Value of Your Ownership	Who Owns It	Transfer to Trust?

F. Business Interests

1. sole proprietorships

2. partnership interests

3. shares in limited partnerships

4. shares in limited liability companies

5. shares in corporations, including Subchapter S corporations

6. other business interests

G. Total Net Value of Your Assets $ _____

II. Liabilities

To Whom Debt Is Owed   Amount

A. Personal Property Debts

1. personal loans (banks, major credit cards, etc.)

_____   _____

_____   _____

_____   _____

_____   _____

_____   _____

_____   _____

_____   _____

_____   _____

_____   _____

2. other personal debts

_____   _____

_____   _____

_____   _____

_____   _____

_____   _____

_____   _____

_____   _____

B. Taxes (include only taxes past and currently due; do not include taxes due in the future)

_____   _____

_____   _____

_____   _____

_____   _____

_____   _____

_____   _____

C. Any Other Liabilities (legal judgments, accrued child support, etc.)

_____   _____

_____   _____

_____   _____

_____   _____

D. Total Liabilities (excluding those liabilities already deducted in Section I) $ _____

III. Net Worth (Total Net Value of Your Assets, from Section I.G, above, minus Total Liabilities, from Section II.D, above) $ _____

Beneficiary Worksheet 1: Individual Living Trust

1. Specific Gifts

Item of Property

Primary Beneficiary

Alternate Beneficiary

Item of Property

Primary Beneficiary

Alternate Beneficiary

Item of Property

Primary Beneficiary

Alternate Beneficiary

Item of Property

Primary Beneficiary

Alternate Beneficiary

Item of Property

Primary Beneficiary

Alternate Beneficiary

Item of Property

Primary Beneficiary

Alternate Beneficiary

Item of Property

Primary Beneficiary

Alternate Beneficiary

Item of Property

Primary Beneficiary

Alternate Beneficiary

2. Residuary Beneficiary or Beneficiaries

Residuary Beneficiary(ies)

Alternate Residuary Beneficiary(ies)

Beneficiary Worksheet 2: Shared Living Trust

Wife's Beneficiaries

1. Specific Gifts

Item of Property

Primary Beneficiary

Alternate Beneficiary

Item of Property

Primary Beneficiary

Alternate Beneficiary

Item of Property

Primary Beneficiary

Alternate Beneficiary

Item of Property

Primary Beneficiary

Alternate Beneficiary

Item of Property

Primary Beneficiary

Alternate Beneficiary

Item of Property

Primary Beneficiary

Alternate Beneficiary

Item of Property

Primary Beneficiary

Alternate Beneficiary

Item of Property

Primary Beneficiary

Alternate Beneficiary

Item of Property

Primary Beneficiary

Alternate Beneficiary

2. Residuary Beneficiary or Beneficiaries

Residuary Beneficiary(ies)

Alternate Residuary Beneficiary(ies)

Husband's Beneficiaries

1. Specific Gifts

Item of Property

Primary Beneficiary

Alternate Beneficiary

Item of Property

Primary Beneficiary

Alternate Beneficiary

Item of Property

Primary Beneficiary

Alternate Beneficiary

Item of Property

Primary Beneficiary

Alternate Beneficiary

Item of Property

Primary Beneficiary

Alternate Beneficiary

Item of Property

Primary Beneficiary

Alternate Beneficiary

Item of Property

Primary Beneficiary

Alternate Beneficiary

Item of Property

Primary Beneficiary

Alternate Beneficiary

Item of Property

Primary Beneficiary

Alternate Beneficiary

2. Residuary Beneficiary or Beneficiaries

Residuary Beneficiary(ies)

Alternate Residuary Beneficiary(ies)

Index

NOLO

Save 15% *off your next order*

Register your Nolo purchase, and we'll send you a **coupon for 15% off** your next Nolo.com order!

. Nolo.com/customer-support/productregistration

On Nolo.com you'll also find:

Books & Software

Nolo publishes hundreds of great books and software programs for consumers and business owners. Order a copy, or download an ebook version instantly, at Nolo.com.

Online Forms

You can quickly and easily make a will or living trust, form an LLC or corporation, apply for a provisional patent, or make hundreds of other forms—online.

Free Legal Information

Thousands of articles answer common questions about everyday legal issues, including wills, bankruptcy, small business formation, divorce, patents, employment, and much more.

Plain-English Legal Dictionary

Stumped by jargon? Look it up in America's most up-to-date source for definitions of legal terms, free at Nolo.com.

Lawyer Directory

Nolo's consumer-friendly lawyer directory provides in-depth profiles of lawyers all over America. You'll find information you need to choose the right lawyer.

LITR15